M000239119

A Healthy Classroom

Michael Grinder

Founder of the ENVoY Programs

Acknowledgments

The good Lord provided me with certain abilities; but writing wasn't one of them. I sincerely thank the whole village for sharing their talents in critiquing, expanding, revising and producing this work:

Luke Aitken, Susan Albert, Richard and Pam Anderson, Laura Arellano, Rachel Babbs, Diane Bergeron, Carla Bettens, Jodi Buchanan, Ron Burnett, Phil Callero, Laura Cervantes, Regan Chandler-Nelson, Alexander Christiani, Kathy Coffin, Grace Marie Curtin, Theresa David, Denver Class June 2000, Krista Dettloff, Ellen Dietrich, Gabriele Dolke, Tom Dotz, Jeff Dulcich, Pam Dunnick, Pat Duran, Jill Dutchess, Jenny Edwards, Sabine Eichenmeuller, Sabine Emmerz, Joan Engle, Kathleen Epperson, Linda Fitch, Chrissy Free, Lynda Fudold, Kaze Gadway, Emily Garfield, Mary Gibson, Eric Goodman, Amanda Gore, Gail Grinder, Leticia Gutierrez, Linda Haines, Tim Hallbom, Tom Heaney, Paul Henderson, Wayne Hunnicut, Shirley Jallad, Kris Janati, Mark Jordan, Brooke Kerns, Diane Kizler, Dennis Kobelin, Lauren Kuhn, Liana Lafranier, Barbara and Michael Lawson, Ilene Levy, Wolfgang Linker (Focus Marketing and Mehr, Flensburg, Germany), April Luttman, Anita MacLeod, Greg Meyer, Cindy Miesbach, Margie Nelson, Karrie Olson, Joyce Patterson, Jane Peterson, Connie Portele, Jon Potter, Carol Powles, Jeff Reed, Joe Rodriguez, Sharon Sayler, Hans Schneider, Rudolf Schulte-Pelkum, Chuck Sester, Grace Sibley, Curtis Smith, Suzi Smith, Bill Sommers, Eddi Sowa, Sarah Spilman, John Steinberg, Nancy Stout, Kathryn Tochtrop, Vancouver Class August 2000, Elaine Wetherup, Diane Williams, Rick Williams, Gail and Lou Woodford, Mary Yonek, Mary Yenik, Dianne Yonker, Kendall Zoller and Steve Zuieback.

We ask your understanding and assistance in correcting any errors.

Editor: Mary Yenik, Kathleen Epperson, key@planning4u.com

Illustrator: Olga Gutsalova

Cover Design, Layout Assistance and Screen Savers: Sharon Sayler, webmaster@michaelgrinder.com

Desktop Publishing: Stout Graphics, Nancy Stout, nkstout@comcast.net

ISBN: 1-883407-06-0

Copies of **A Healthy Classroom** can be purchased directly from Michael Grinder & Associates, 16303 NE 259th St., Battle Ground, WA 98604 (360) 687-3238; FAX (360) 687-0595; Website: http://www.michaelgrinder.com

Copyright © 2000 Michael Grinder & Associates. In no way can this publication be reproduced, stored in a retrieval system or transmitted in any form by any means, electronic, mechanical, photocopy, recording or otherwise, without the prior permission of the publisher, Michael Grinder & Associates, except as provided by USA copyright law.

Table of Contents

© 2000 by Michael Grinder & Assoc., ARR. AHC03 (360) 687-3238; FAX (360) 687-0595; http://www.michaelgrinder.com

© 2000 by Michael Grinder & Assoc., ARR. AHC03 (360) 687-3238; FAX (360) 687-0595; http://www.michaelgrinder.com

© 2000 by Michael Grinder & Assoc., ARR. AHC03 (360) 687-3238; FAX (360) 687-0595; http://www.michaelgrinder.com

© 2000 by Michael Grinder & Assoc., ARR. AHC03 (360) 687-3238; FAX (360) 687-0595; http://www.michaelgrinder.com

Preface

"If a fish were an anthropologist, the last thing it would ever discover is water."
Margaret Mead

Norway

I was 45 minutes into my first-ever presentation in Norway. My back was to the teachers. As I finished copying a quote onto the flipchart, a third of the room made a gasping sound. As an American, my only interpretation was "emphysema?" Knowing that my initial reaction would be ethnocentric, I was very attentive to subsequent gasps. By the end of the second day I interpreted the gasps to be a cultural response for, "I emphatically agree with what you said!"

You don't have to understand a culture to participate in it.

A culture can be formally defined as a set of beliefs, values, and behaviors shared by a group of people. An informal definition of culture is something that we all do, and hence, we are not aware that we do it. For instance, on the third morning of training in Norway, we were talking about our profession of teaching as a culture. I stated, "Here in Norway when we emphatically agree with something that has been said, we gasp." (And I made the gasping sound.) The whole room in unison made the gasping sound. Then they immediately said, "No, we don't!" Hence, the above quote from Margaret Mead.[1]

If you intuitively understand a cultural trait, you are probably a member but cannot see it.

Obstacles to Understanding Group Dynamics: Educational Cultures

This book is about healthy classrooms which can only occur when group dynamics are the foundation of management. Certain educational cultures are very attentive to group dynamics. Principals learn very quickly to never respond to a request from an individual faculty member without taking into account how the rest of the staff will be affected by their decision. Coaches of athletic teams are acutely aware of how the coach's treatment of one member of the team will have ramifications for the team as a whole.

Generally, the concept of group dynamics is outside the cultural awareness of classroom teachers, like gasping is to the Norwegians. Evidence of this is the teacher of 6th–9th grade students who literally awaits the beginning of a semester and the challenge of establishing ownership of the classroom turf. Often a student, with a reputation that precedes the

If you can see the cultural trait, you probably aren't a member yet.

student does an inappropriate behavior and the teacher immediately puts on the "invisible six-shooter." The classroom is transformed into the OK Corral, and the identity of the "marshal" is established. No consideration of how the rest of the students view the situation is taken into account. By the instructor's behavior, the template for the term is set into place: "THIS IS MY CLASSROOM AND THE RULES ARE..." In such cases, the group may never be fully formed and the possibility of modeling *shared responsibilities* is probably ruined.

> **The hidden "culture of power" prevents many teachers from taking advantage of the sophisticated benefits of group dynamics.**

Power is to the educational culture as water is to a fish.

So, too, like Margaret Mead's fish being unaware of water, as teachers we are similarly oblivious to the fact that power is a major tenet of our culture. The concept of *culture* is critical to understanding the awareness, or lack thereof, of group dynamics. For instance, the teacher that "laid down the law" in the previous scenario might be an outstanding coach who would never act that way in the sports world. This teacher's membership in the one culture (i.e., sports coach), and the awareness that accompanies that culture (i.e., sensitivity to group dynamics), usually doesn't transfer with the person when s/he enters into a different culture (i.e., the classroom). The person switches to the cultural awareness associated with the new context.

The same thing is true for the principal when the principal opens a debrief conference following a classroom observation with, "There were two to three students over by the window who were not engaged." The principal suspends the principal's sensitivity to complexities that may be incumbent with engaging those two to three students.[2] Attempts at engaging them may actually be counterproductive. That teacher may not gain value for the effort expended compared to that same energy spent with students who are seeking assistance.

Let the Fire Burn

There is one more major group dynamics concept. The idea comes from the U.S. Forest Service. In the past, the response to any forest fire was to intervene and *control* the situation. Officially, in 1995, they changed their policy and now evaluate each fire, often letting one burn because it is actually more beneficial in the long run.

A Healthy Classroom[3] contends that the culture of education has traditionally been very control and power oriented. Evidence of this belief is seen in the emphasis that administrators place on "control" of the class-

© 2000 by Michael Grinder & Assoc., ARR. AHC03 (360) 687-3238; FAX (360) 687-0595; http://www.michaelgrinder.com

room. For example, consider how the following three classroom dynamics would be ranked by a visiting administrator.

1. Teacher A calls for the class' attention and gets it.

2. Teacher B calls for the class' attention and does not get it. Then with a loud, booming and angry voice, Teacher B asks a second time and the class frightfully complies.

3. Teacher C calls for the class's attention and does not get it. As the teacher pauses, some of the students turn to those who have yet to comply and say, "Sh!" The class then becomes attentive.

It makes perfect sense for the evaluating administrator to view the first situation as the best of the three scenarios. But, to assess the second situation as better than the third fails to recognize the group dynamics that are in place.

A Healthy Classroom[3] is based on the following quote.

> **We are inadvertently in love with the "influence of power" and we need to be in love with the "power of influence."**

Like the "pistol-wielding" teacher we met earlier, the second situation above is a *power* template. The third scenario is an influence template; the class has a sense of its own identity and responsibility.

What does A Healthy Classroom do?

Traditionally, managing the individual student has been a primary focus of evaluating the classroom setting. *A Healthy Classroom* focuses on the larger picture: How will the teacher's interaction with the individual student impact the classroom as a whole? *A Healthy Classroom* looks not only at how the teacher is when managing the individual student but how the class will view the teacher after the management is done. Will the class see the teacher in an adverse light? For example, will they think, "The teacher is in a bad mood because of the residue from the negative interaction with the managed student?" Or worse, will they think, "The teacher was too harsh when managing that student!"

A Healthy Classroom provides educators with the guidelines for recognizing the patterns of classroom dynamics, for knowing when and if to intervene and, if so, how. These guidelines are tools educators can use to increase their ability to predict what is likely to happen. By predicting what is about to happen, teachers are not caught off guard and can calmly

A Healthy Classroom *provides the teacher the ability to predict.*

© 2000 by Michael Grinder & Assoc., ARR. AHC03 (360) 687-3238; FAX (360) 687-0595; http://www.michaelgrinder.com

manage from a proactive, instead of a reactive, posture. *A Healthy Classroom* helps teachers arrive at such professionalism.

A Healthy Classroom[3] proposes that education needs classrooms that are managed by influence instead of power. This work postulates that teachers resort to inappropriate power when they are surprised. One of the most important benefits of understanding classroom dynamics is the ability to predict. *A Healthy Classroom* helps the teacher to predict both what situations are likely to arise on a given day and what is likely to happen if the teacher responds in predictable patterns.

> *Predicting prevents surprises.*

Recalling the principal's debrief, the "two to three students by the window who were not engaged" is the Forest Service equivalent of "fire." The teacher's knee-jerk reaction is to intervene and control. *A Healthy Classroom* applies the Forest Service's enlightened view to the classroom.

> *Sometimes it is better to stay out than to enter and then try to get out.*

Benefits of A Healthy Classroom

> What do you walk away with?

Perspective

Historically the microscope provided us with an overall image of the cellular level of life. There was a need for a deeper view of the makeup of what we were seeing hence, the Electronic Scanning Microscope was added to graphic imaging. At first what was revealed was a bewildering mess. Seeing the pictures begged for understanding. In time the scientists trained their eyes to see meaningfulness. So too, *ENVoY* and *ENVoY II* provided clarity of management strategies to a generation of teachers. Those trained in the *ENVoY* model also begged for a deeper understanding of the ultimate outcome of effective classroom management. Consequently, *A Healthy Classroom* was created and the blueprint for a healthy classroom was revealed.

Learning Levels and Transcending Culture

The students of *A Healthy Classroom* will be simultaneously learning on four levels:

© 2000 by Michael Grinder & Assoc., ARR. AHC03 (360) 687-3238; FAX (360) 687-0595; http://www.michaelgrinder.com

1. Being reminded of what we already know.

2. Learning a skill that can be implemented immediately.

3. Understanding a skill which will require practice before it can be implemented.

4. Appreciating what is humanly possible.

Neil Diamond, one of the most enduring and endearing singers of all time certainly changed what he was capable of. He went to college on a fencing scholarship.

The last level is designed for those teachers who are "ready" to become outstanding managers. The word "ready" warrants an explanation. When we are student teachers, our view of teaching is very different than is our view of teaching in our first year of actually teaching in our own class-room. Somewhere around our fifth year in the profession, we settle into a view of what our career will be like. *A Healthy Classroom* demands that we reexamine what we are humanly capable of doing as managers. Literally, we need to break with tradition.

> **Literally, we need to break with tradition.**

Vignette: "Tradition, Tradition"
(a line from the play *Fiddler on the Roof*)

The problem with following old habits and traditions is that we usually do not explore other, more attractive alternatives. We get stuck doing it "the old way." We are reminded of the modern-day cook who would buy a ham, cut off the end of it, and stick it in the oven to cook. When asked why, she replied "I don't know—that's how my grandmother always did it." One day while visiting her grandmother she asked why the tradition was in place and the grandmother laughingly replied, "Because in my day I had a very small baking oven. I had to cut off the ends of the ham to make it fit in the oven."[4]

> **We must be willing to get rid of the life we've planned so as to have that life that is waiting for us.**

In this author's opinion, the culture of education doesn't recognize out-standing teachers. Outstanding teachers transcend their culture.[5] The concept of "culture" is critical to comprehending *A Healthy Classroom* concepts. The reference is not made towards the teacher as a person but to the behaviors that are common to teachers when managing (i.e., the vast majority of teachers are the salt of the earth—healthy, giving, caring people; but when the teacher is managing, the teacher's behavior can

© 2000 by Michael Grinder & Assoc., ARR. AHC03 (360) 687-3238; FAX (360) 687-0595; http://www.michaelgrinder.com

seasonally be unhealthy). Two examples of a subgroup having certain cultural characteristics assigned to it are "Don't go postal!" and "TV weather people are more bizarre than other members of a newscast team." (David Letterman started as a weather person.)

"It is important to transcend the places that hold us."[6]

The teacher's transcendence is viewed by colleagues differently based on the grade level the outstanding educator teaches. Outstanding elementary, especially primary teachers, are viewed by their colleagues as normal people who are outstanding teachers. The words "respect" and "admiration" are often associated with these outstanding educators. The profile of the outstanding secondary teacher fits more the image from the movie *Dead Poet's Society*. Such descriptions range from "different" to "odd" to "weird." In my opinion, there is a tendency for outstanding secondary teachers to be kind, tolerant, and accepting of students; they ignore their teaching colleagues (the outstanding teachers avoid visiting the faculty lunch room), and they may be intolerant of the administration whom they see as ancillary to the teacher.

There is never a question of the quality of atmosphere in such classrooms. These teachers have transcended the educational norms.

Vignette: Food Fight[7]

Curt Culinary has taught seventh grade science forever. He knows that the faster he can gel a group together the more accelerated learning will occur. On the first day of school he explains the importance of cooperation, and tells them that the expectations of the classroom are such that safety around the Bunsen burner and other equipment are paramount.

One particular year he knew he was going to have a difficult class. Instead of his traditional lecture on cooperation and expectations for safety, he passed out baggies with six marshmallows in each bag. He then announced that a game was going to be played. The rules were visually outlined on the board. When signaled to do so, the marshmallows are removed one at a time. They have to be thrown at six different people who are at least a meter stick away from the thrower. Then a whistle is blown and the group has 45 seconds to pick up the marshmallows—there must be six marshmallows in each bag. As Curt says, "Go!" the room is in total chaos. Since they have to throw at six different people, they kinesthetically have contact with classmates that would normally take them much longer to meet. As the whistle blows, the amount of cooperation done in a fun way produces the group dynamics in an accelerated manner.

© 2000 by Michael Grinder & Assoc., ARR. AHC03 (360) 687-3238; FAX (360) 687-0595; http://www.michaelgrinder.com

A Healthy Classroom invites the educator to critically view our culture and consider transcending what is normal; it shows how to rise above the "average." *A Healthy Classroom* is an alternative to the inadvertent counterproductive management behaviors that tend to occur seasonally, usually due to fatigue. It isn't the teacher, personally, that *A Healthy Classroom* speaks to but our unconscious cultural tradition of needing to control. Without alternatives the average classroom appears "healthy." By delineating what are the heretofore secret behavioral ingredients of the outstanding teachers' classrooms, we now know what a healthy classroom actually is and that it is within the grasp of the "average teacher."

> **A Healthy Classroom *walks educators to places to which they hoped to go but could not conceive the way. And once there the view broadens even more.*** [8]

The recognition of the educational culture's unconscious use of power and how this overuse of power prevents group dynamics is the foundation for a healthy classroom. Howard Gardner introduced the concept of *interpersonal intelligence*, which is the same as understanding group dynamics.[9] *A Healthy Classroom* provides the how-to.

Curriculum

There are ever-increasing demands to achieve learning objectives (i.e., "Standards"). The purpose of classroom management is to provide the time for curriculum to be taught.[10] But learning only occurs through relationships.[11] It is especially important that the teacher reaches the students who are hard to reach—the independent, self-selective cats of the classroom.[12] *A Healthy Classroom* provides the much needed atmosphere wherein thinking can occur. It is only when the students have a relationship with each other (which is different than the teacher having a relationship with the students individually) that the atmosphere of safety is created within the classroom so that the dialogue needed for thinking can occur.

Currently education is committed to providing students of special needs a "least restricted environment." This noble and healthy goal has never been properly funded. Literally, the teacher often doesn't have time to individualize instruction. The only hope is that students voluntarily assist their fellow classmates. Such ownership is a result of healthy group dynamics. "Osmotic Learning" in Chapter Five will further elaborate on this concept.

© 2000 by Michael Grinder & Assoc., ARR. AHC03 (360) 687-3238; FAX (360) 687-0595; http://www.michaelgrinder.com

Being Proactive because the Teacher can Predict

An unhurried sense of time is the luxury that comes with perception.

Stephen Covey indicates that one of the *Habits of Highly Effective People* is being *proactive*. This is only possible when a teacher can predict what is likely to happen. The key is for the teacher to increase the teacher's recognition of the pattern that lies beneath the surface chaos. As Margaret Wheatley[13] says: "Confusion is chaos seen from a shorter time period. A longer view shows patterns that are predictable....What is seen as chaos is a mislabel which occurs because the perspective on the situation is too close. A longer view shows that there are patterns which are predictable. Confusion is just myopic sight."

Problem Solving and a View of Success

"To be successful in life one must develop strategies for mistake management."[14]

Every profession has problems and dilemmas. Have you honestly considered if the trials and tribulations of teaching are the ones you want to grapple with? As mentioned earlier, the outstanding manager transcends the educational culture and becomes increasingly comfortable with independently deciding what is success and what is not success.

One of the tenets of the teaching culture is the tendency to define ourselves based on how others view us. Gloria Steinem, one of the leaders of the feminist movement, could have been speaking about teachers when she said, "I still have the female psychological disease of knowing what other people are feeling better than knowing what *I'm* feeling. (I only felt real when I was helping other people or was needed in some way...)"[15] The outstanding managers are not dependent on others' approval and are willing to absorb the consequences of such independence. An educator who is committed to lifelong learning may have the urge every six to nine months to send out postcards to former students and say, "I am better now." The outstanding educators must reflect on their quality level of previous management and give themselves "grace."[16]

This book is designed to assist the educator in sorting what the teacher is responsible for. The corporate world has been guided by Stephen Covey's concept of "Circle of Concern" vs. "Circle of Influence."[17] The former is what the educator cares about while the latter is what is within the teacher's range of doing something about. You will save time and energy by not trying to solve those difficulties which are unsolvable. In education, we need to replace the criterion of "success is when the teacher gets results," which is based on power management, with a criterion based on influence. Success needs to be viewed as, "How did I do based on the level of influence I was able to obtain?"[18] With this understanding comes an adaptation of the well-known Serenity Prayer applied to the classroom.

© 2000 by Michael Grinder & Assoc., ARR. AHC03 (360) 687-3238; FAX (360) 687-0595; http://www.michaelgrinder.com

> *"Lord, grant me the serenity to accept the things I can't change,*
> *the courage to change the things I can*
> *and the wisdom to know the difference."*

You will be able to anticipate and minimize problems that occur when classroom dilemmas, or polarities, are not managed well. Your decision making will improve. This is especially true with decisions where you must choose between two sides of a set of apparent opposites. The educator wants to avoid situations where the teacher has to select between what is good for the class and what is good for the individual students. The ability to anticipate allows the teacher to replace "either/or" thinking with "both/and."

Time

The classroom can be viewed with educational binoculars. One tube focuses on the management aspects of the learning environment. The other lens zeroes in on the curriculum. While the educational tubes of curriculum and management are inseparable, *A Healthy Classroom* restricts itself to the management aspects of the classroom. An outstanding teacher is outstanding in both the curriculum and management tubes. Admittedly, being an outstanding instructor (curriculum) is a result of long hours and creative lesson design presented with insightful and often dramatic delivery; in contrast, being an outstanding manager takes less time than operating from ineffective management templates. *A Healthy Classroom* is an extension of *ENVoY* and *ENVoY II*. The earlier works demonstrated that it takes less teacher time to employ effective management techniques than traditional counterproductive efforts. The difference is that the practitioner of *A Healthy Classroom* has to have concentrated effort for three to five years to arrive at a proficiency level where the healthy classroom operates with less teacher effort than the traditional classroom.

"It's not the hours you put in your work that counts, it's the work you put in the hours."[20]

> **It takes less time to be an effective manager**
> **than to be an ineffective one.**

Challenging the Brightest and Creating a Legacy

As an educational consultant, I see education as often unable to keep its brightest members as teachers. There are many possibilities why this is so. May I add to this list one of the partial reasons why teachers leave our profession? They are looking for something worthy of their challenge. *A*

© 2000 by Michael Grinder & Assoc., ARR. AHC03 (360) 687-3238; FAX (360) 687-0595; http://www.michaelgrinder.com

Healthy Classroom provides a long-term, continuous learning curve suited for such a population.

The dropout rate of teachers in their first three years of teaching is higher than the dropout rate of high school students. The sheer time demands of all teachers is daunting. We are willing to give of ourselves and our family time because of the rewards of seeing light bulbs go on in the eyes of students, the thrill of facilitating growth and understanding, and the joy of adding richness to another human's life. I would suggest that while the preparation time needed of new teachers is shocking to them (and even more so for their spouses), there are two things that drive teachers from our profession—a lack of practical management tools and the lack of support. As America's number one motivational speaker[19] suggests, "The biggest thing missing in our society is mentoring." Mentoring is a growing practice in education. *A Healthy Classroom* provides our outstanding teachers a way of understanding the substructure from which they operate and, in so doing, reveals the science of their artistry—the finest examples of classrooms that are managed by influence instead of power. This is a gift to our next generation. "Success doesn't give you satisfaction—progress does."[21]

Success doesn't satisfy the ambitious teacher —progress and improvement do.

The artist of classroom management thinks, perceives, labels and responds differently than the scientist. The ultimate goal of *A Healthy Classroom* is an increase in healthy classrooms and the teacher's unequaled personal satisfaction that comes from operating from a blueprint that allows for continuous professional improvement.

> *"The highest form of learning is when art learns from science and when science learns from art."* Leonardo De Vinci

We tell our students that they need to be lifelong learners. So, too, do our veteran teachers have as much right and need to continually grow as the new members of our profession. I would submit that often a seasoned teacher who is cynical is an idealist who has never found the map to the promised land. As the title of this work indicates, as educators we need a vision of what a healthy classroom is and we need to know how to influence the dynamics for one. Finally, here is a blueprint to fulfill your dreams of why you became a teacher.

August 23, 2000
Michael & Gail Grinder
Battle Ground, WA

© 2000 by Michael Grinder & Assoc., ARR. AHC03 (360) 687-3238; FAX (360) 687-0595; http://www.michaelgrinder.com

Summary of Benefits of A Healthy Classroom

This work provides a blueprint of:

- transcending the educational culture of power to achieve governance via influence because group dynamics are formed and maintained

- moving from a one-on-one view of communication to the group dynamics view

- recognizing the seasons of a school year and knowing how to adjust

- identifying the actual ingredients of a healthy classroom

- increasing time for teaching curriculum

- creating the atmosphere of safety, so needed in order for the dialogue to occur which is the gateway to thinking

- fostering an environment in which students assist classroom mates of special needs

- transitioning from *reactive* to *proactive* management because the teacher can predict what is likely to happen before it happens

- sorting out what the teacher is responsible for and thereby increasing the teacher's inner tranquility

- understanding the components of negotiation

- eventually accomplishing the above with less time than it takes compared to employing the traditional power approach to classroom management

- providing an ongoing challenge that is worthy of our brightest new teachers so that they continue to select teaching as their profession

- providing a conscious understanding to our artisans so they can mentor others.

© 2000 by Michael Grinder & Assoc., ARR. AHC03 (360) 687-3238; FAX (360) 687-0595; http://www.michaelgrinder.com

End Notes

1. Of course it would have been impolite to have pointed out that their gasping non-verbally spoke volumes compared to their verbal level denial of their cultural norm. The reason is, humor is a reaction to hearing how another culture is foolish; a joke about the culture you are speaking to is not funny.

2. The principal already knows how to view the faculty with the lens of group dynamics. *A Healthy Classroom* will help the principal transfer this ability to classroom observation.

3. All three of the ENVoY programs (*A Healthy Classroom, ENVoY* and *ENVoY II*) operate on this basis.

4. Supplied by Debbie Johnson, financial planner.

5. Adapted from Joseph Campbell, *Reader's Digest*, September, 2000.

6. From the movie *The Hurricane* starring Denzel Washington.

7. Inspired by Hank Sauer, teacher in Washington.

8. Adapted from a poem by Mary Anne, Macy Bryce and Lewis Radmacher, 1999.

9. *Multiple Intelligences: The Theory in Practice* by Howard E. Gardner. Paperback, March 1993.

10. ENVoY provides that time.

11. Elaborated in Osmotic Learning, p. 158.

12. *ENVoY II* outlines how.

13. Author of *Leadership and the New Science*.

14. Tim Prior, professional tennis coach.

15. Interview with Gloria Steinem in *Modern Maturity*, May-June, 1999.

16. The Hebrew definition of *grace* is "unmerited favor."

17. *Seven Habits of Highly Successful People.*

18. Sam Ewing, *Reader's Digest*, September, 2000.

19. Anthony Robbins on the Charlie Rose TV show, Spring, 2000.

20. Ibid.

© 2000 by Michael Grinder & Assoc., ARR. AHC03 (360) 687-3238; FAX (360) 687-0595; http://www.michaelgrinder.com

How to Read This Book

As educators we read a book in the summer time as if it were a novel and during the school year we want the same material to be quickly accessible as a diagnostic and prescription reference.[1] The attempt here has been to provide both. Browsers start where their interest lies and then cross-reference to meaningful links. Some starting points:

Tabs—A tab at the beginning of each chapter indicates when that chapter might be employed. For the self-contained teacher who has the same students all year, the first chapter would be the focus for September. For the secondary teacher who teaches by semesters, the first chapter is applicable both in September and January. The first four chapters are identified by the month that the educator is most likely to implement them.

Chapter One, Class Formation	**1st Month** September/January
Chapter Two, Reading A Class	**2nd Month** October/February
Chapter Three, Stages	**3rd Month** November/March
Chapter Four, Seasons	**4th Month** December/April
Chapter Five, Managing A Healthy Classroom	**5-year Plan**
Chapter Six, Managing Special Situations	**Special Situations**

Wide Margins—The space allows you to take notes, capture ideas that come to you while reading and plan a course of action.

Vignettes—Many of us learn best through stories. These are boxed and shown in a different font. Some readers will jump to them and when engaged will then read the text; others will read the text and use the vignettes for reinforcements. The Index lists the vignettes both by title and major characters.

Question bubble—The question bubble asks the reader if this is a question that interests the reader; if so, then the text provides the answer.

Shadow box—The key sayings are in shadow boxes. Some readers surf pages to read the shadow boxes. This influences them to read the text.

Rubrics—The rubrics at the end of every chapter capture the essence of the book: pages 54, 80, 101, 129, 165 and 193. When intrigued by a strand (i.e., row), read that section of the chapter. The Appendix gathers them in a collective manner. The Plan of Action on page 200 is an excellent format for a teacher's professional development.

© 2000 by Michael Grinder & Assoc., ARR. AHC03 (360) 687-3238; FAX (360) 687-0595; http://www.michaelgrinder.com

Marginal Quotes—*Like the shadow box, the reader is often intrigued with a provocative saying that leads the reader to read the text that accompanies the quote.*

Post-its—3M has a product for inkjet and laser printers, PC410. At present these are available online at PCSound.com and also at Best Buy, Office Max, and CompUSA. Office Max uses their number SKU 2003 3116 to identify the PC410. Six Post-its (3" x 4") are positioned on an 8½" x 11" sheet. The software allows the user to position key concepts and sayings which are printed on the six Post-its. At the end of each chapter of *A Healthy Classroom*, summaries from the chapter are already made up. By placing these sheets in a photocopy machine with the 8½" x 11" sheets from 3M, the educator can run off these Post-its and then place them in a planning book, on white board, and/or on a lectern as reminders.

End Notes—References to specific skills in *ENVoY* and *ENVoY II* are found in the end notes so that *A Healthy Classroom* is a stand-alone text. Appendix C, page 210, compares this book to the other books of the *ENVoY* trilogy.

Screen Savers—The accompanying CD contains screen savers for the book's major concepts. The concepts are summarized in thought-provoking quotations and sayings. They are artistically presented with beautiful backgrounds. There is one set for the Mac and the identically set for a PC. The best use of the screen savers is to put them on your computer during the appropriate month. The chapters are organized so that the first four chapters correspond with the first four months of the year/semester. Because the files are quite large, it is recommended that prior to installing a new screen saver file, the previous file be uninstalled (*My Computer, Control Panel, Add/Remove Programs*). As you walk by your computer the quotation will intrigue you. The page number is mentioned for easy follow up reading.

Worksheets and Margin Icons—All of the major concepts of the book are formatted into easy to use worksheets. These forms allow the teacher the opportunity to practice the skills. The self forms are ones that you fill out on yourself. After a self form has been completed the corresponding peer form can be employed for reinforcement. The peer forms are much briefer and only focus on what is externally verifiable during an observation. There may be circumstances that warrant your using a generic worksheet. Two are provided: one for planning and one for reviewing. A worksheet is indicated by a computer icon, chapter number and worksheet number in the margin of the text. The worksheets can be found on our web site (http://www.michaelgrinder.com). Your login and password are the initials of this book: AHC.

Chapter-Page

End Note

1. Dr. Mary Yonek, principal of an ENVoY-trained school, Vancouver, Washington.

© 2000 by Michael Grinder & Assoc., ARR. AHC03 (360) 687-3238; FAX (360) 687-0595; http://www.michaelgrinder.com

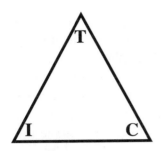

INTRODUCTION

THE TRIANGLE OF THE CLASSROOM

The teacher is invited to switch from managing with power to being empowered to manage with influence.

The Art & Science of Managing

While *teaching* is often described as the *"Art* and *Science* of Teaching," or in the case of ENVoY trilogy[1] the *"Art* and *Science* of *Management,"* in reality they are learned in the reverse sequence. The competencies of the science have to be consistently present before the art is broached. Just like wisdom is not the same as knowledge but is based on knowledge, so too, the art of managing has as its foundation the science of managing— but the art is not the same as the science.

There are four stages to a teacher's professional development. The first two stages are the science and the other two are the art.

} = Art

} = Science

Science

The first stage of an educator's career is focused on knowing the content. This is the *curriculum* tube of the educational binoculars.[2] This stage of the person's development takes two to four years to master. Initially, the teacher is just learning the words to the content, then the teacher increases her repertoire of how to deliver the content. It is only after teaching the same content for this length of time that the teacher recognizes where the students have difficulty and how to present such concepts in a

---

To be respectful of gender equality and yet provide the educator with a fluid reading style, in this chapter the teacher is referred to by the female pronoun and the student by the male pronoun.

© 2000 by Michael Grinder & Assoc., ARR. AHC03 (360) 687-3238; FAX (360) 687-0595; http://www.michaelgrinder.com

meaningful manner. This includes, but is not limited to, packaging the components of concepts in palatable sizes and in a sequence that is comprehensible. This is especially true for the special needs students. Most teachers have to concentrate on how to create the presentation for the class as a whole before addressing how to individualize instruction for these pupils.

It is a terrible hardship on teachers, both novice and veterans alike, that the scope and sequence of each curriculum subject (e.g., math, English) seem constantly in flux. Instructors have tremendous stress because the winds of curriculum are continuously changing. Unless the curriculum can be stabilized, educators can't practice the same content for three years and thus master delivering it.

Curriculum

The second stage of the teacher's development is the process of managing. This level of professional development consists mostly of skills and strategies—commonly referred to as competencies.[3] To successfully operate on *A Healthy Classroom*'s level of classroom dynamics, the teacher must have certain competencies. Veteran teachers who systematically employ non-verbal strategies might have all or some of these competencies.[4]

The question is, "What are the prerequisite competencies for a teacher to be an effective manager while preserving relationships with the students?" By answering this question, we identify the *science* of managing so we can mentor ourselves and others towards the *art* of managing. The answer has four components.

> *R*—the teacher has established *relationships* with the class as a whole[5] and especially the hard-to-reach students.

> *S*—the teacher individualizes instruction so that the students, especially the inclusion students, are academically *successful*.

> *V*—the teacher *visually* communicates.

> *P*—the teacher *pauses*.[6]

The first letter of the italicized words spell out the acronym RSVP. You are invited to A Healthy Classroom, and our four prerequisites competencies are your RSVP. Being group-oriented doesn't necessarily mean that the group takes precedence over the individual student; rather, it means that the needs of the group are held in paramount importance except during seatwork.

© 2000 by Michael Grinder & Assoc., ARR. AHC03 (360) 687-3238; FAX (360) 687-0595; http://www.michaelgrinder.com

Management
Curriculum } = Science

Art

The final two stages of our craft are *Perception-Timing* and *Healthy Classrooms*. The artisan of management has these two stages mastered.

Healthy Classroom
Perception-Timing } = Art (*A Healthy Classroom*)

The *art* of management can't be understood on the strategy/maneuvers/intervention level alone. The *art* of management is the timing of employing these competencies with consideration to group dynamics. The printed word is not the appropriate vehicle for the teaching of perception-timing. Watching an artisan of classroom management on video, especially fast forward and frame-by-frame speed, allows the viewer to recognize the timing of the artisan. Once a teacher is trained in observing reality in "distorted" time, *A Healthy Classroom* provides the framework for viewing the classroom in real time. So while it would be easy to conclude that the benefit of practicing *A Healthy Classroom*'s concepts is the entrance to the *art* of managing, actually, *A Healthy Classroom* presents the cognitive tenets of the *art*. This work provides the framework of managing classroom dynamics.

The four stages to one's professional development are:

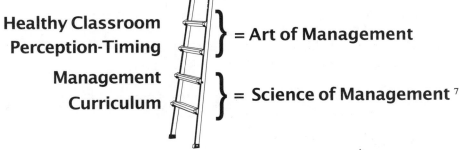

Healthy Classroom
Perception-Timing } = Art of Management

Management
Curriculum } = Science of Management [7]

In *A Healthy Classroom* we define classroom dynamics as the interaction between the teacher, the individual students and the class as a whole. Respectively, they are referred to as the teacher (T), individual (I) and the class (C). The interplay among these parties can be represented by a triangle.

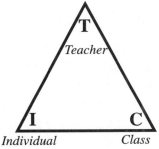

© 2000 by Michael Grinder & Assoc., ARR. AHC03 (360) 687-3238; FAX (360) 687-0595; http://www.michaelgrinder.com

The triangle is the strongest of all geometric shapes because pressure experienced on one side is equally felt by the other two sides. The next time you cross a river via a grid-constructed bridge, notice the omnipresent triangles. The triangle is the ideal icon for understanding classroom dynamics because pressure experienced by one corner equally affects the other two corners.

The first three phases of a lesson are:[8] Getting Their Attention, Teaching and Transition to Seatwork. The fourth phase is what the teacher does with individual students: Seatwork. The four phases of a lesson can be superimposed on the triangle of classroom dynamics in the following manner:

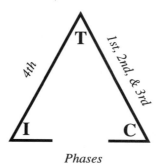

Phases

Note how there is no connection between the individual student corner and the class corner.[9]

A Healthy Classroom broaches the two hardest management situations an instructor encounters. These are situations when all three corners are affected by an interaction. This is the definition of classroom dynamics.

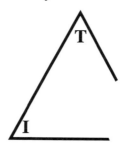

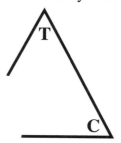

Graphically speaking, ENVoY focuses on either the teacher interacting with the individual corner

or

the teacher interacting with the class corner

© 2000 by Michael Grinder & Assoc., ARR. AHC03 (360) 687-3238; FAX (360) 687-0595; http://www.michaelgrinder.com

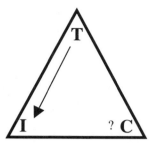

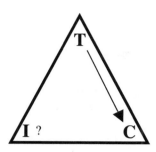

The teacher is dealing with an individual and is concerned because the class isn't appropriately engaged.

The teacher is dealing with the class and is concerned because individual students are not appropriately engaged.

There are two more critical classroom dynamic situations.

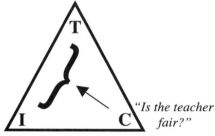

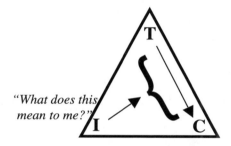

One is when the teacher is managing an individual and is concerned because of how the class might be interpreting it.

Secondly, when the teacher is managing the class and is concerned about how an individual student might be interpreting it.

Summary

While the reader may be anxious to practice the dynamics in this work, the author cautions that it takes two to four years to master the competencies of RSVP.

> **R**—the teacher has established *relationships* with the class as a whole and especially the hard-to-reach students.

> **S**—the teacher individualizes instruction so that the students, especially the inclusion students, are academically *successful*.

> **V**—the teacher *visually* communicates.

> **P**—the teacher *pauses*.

The mastering of these competencies insures that the teacher is a *scientist* of classroom management. The teacher is consistent thus creating a safe atmosphere for learning. These are the prerequisites to *A Healthy Classroom*. It is the author's estimation that five years of constantly employing the concepts from *A Healthy Classroom* are needed to move

An educator shifts from a template of power to a paradigm of influence before the focus of group dynamics is addressed.

© 2000 by Michael Grinder & Assoc., ARR. AHC03 (360) 687-3238; FAX (360) 687-0595; http://www.michaelgrinder.com

from the *scientist* to the *artisan* level of sophistication. The rubrics at the end of the chapters provide the progression during those five years.

A Healthy Classroom equips the educator with management strategies that simultaneously take into account both the effects of the management on the individual student and the effects on the class as a whole.

The *Introduction* presents a model of professional development that separates the *science* of managing from the *art* of managing. The *science* includes techniques, interventions, and maneuvers. The teacher is consistent thus creating a safe atmosphere for learning. It is the "how" of managing. The artisan has a range of behaviors and systematically employs them. It is essential that the teacher's perception affords her the ability to predict what is likely to occur before it does. Research finds that the effective teacher does something just before the class is about to do something; whereas the less effective teacher does it afterwards.[10] The *art* refers to the perception needed to *time* the employment of the techniques. It is the "when" of managing. The artist's ultimate goal is to achieve receptivity with the class so that they are responsive to the teacher's influence. The more influence the teacher has the less power the teacher needs to employ. The ultimate artistic form of managing is to manage by influence because the potential for the classroom being healthy increases.

The concept of "culture" mentioned in the *Preface* is essential to understanding the framework that this book is based on. Throughout *A Healthy Classroom* references are made to the "culture of education." At times the reference is other than positive; e.g., that as a profession we seek control and are power-oriented. At no time does the author mean to imply that the reader, as a human being, personally seeks control or is power oriented, and yet the reader will statistically behave that way when donning the mantle of teaching. It is the author's bias that the outstanding teacher transcends our culture of being power and control-oriented.

> **The outstanding teacher transcends our culture of being power and control oriented.**

Rubrics for A Healthy Classroom

What is a healthy classroom?

The question of "What is a healthy classroom?" is a complex one and deserves more than a simple answer. At the end of every chapter is a rubric that contains behavioral descriptors of a healthy classroom. The Appendix has all of the rubrics gathered in one location. The teacher/

© 2000 by Michael Grinder & Assoc., ARR. AHC03 (360) 687-3238; FAX (360) 687-0595; http://www.michaelgrinder.com

coach/principal can use these rubrics as an assessment of where the teacher is and what the teacher's next professional development phase might be.[11]

> *The rubrics' right columns are the composite definition of a healthy classroom.*

© 2000 by Michael Grinder & Assoc., ARR. AHC03 (360) 687-3238; FAX (360) 687-0595; http://www.michaelgrinder.com

Introduction Rubric

Transcends the Educational Culture

	Struggling Novice	Apprentice	Scientist	Artisan of Healthy Classroom
R.S.V.P., p. 17	The teacher is missing most of the R.S.V.P. competencies, especially relationships.	The teacher has most of the competencies. Usually the R or the S is the last to be mastered.	The teacher has all four competencies.	The teacher knows how to employ the R.S.V.P. competencies towards a healthy classroom.
Group Dynamics, p. 17	The teacher operates on a blind philosophy of power and does not take into account the feelings of the individual students or the dynamics of the class as a group. Classroom is dysfunctional.	While caring about people, the teacher operates the classroom from the premise that it is the teacher's class.	The teacher has a sense of the interplay between the individuals who make up the class and the class as a whole; isn't able to articulate fully such understanding.	The teacher takes into account the class dynamics when assessing and making decisions. The students are held accountable for their behaviors, and yet they are accepted as individual people.
Teacher's Range of Behaviors and Behaviors Systematically Employed, p. 21	The teacher doesn't have a range of behaviors and is inconsistent with the behaviors exhibited.	The teacher is not *systematic*; the teacher is either too accepting (the "individual student" is always more important than the class) or the teacher is too strong on accountability (the productivity of the class is all-important).	The teacher employs patterns of influence.	The teacher has a *range* of behaviors and *systematically* applies the appropriate behaviors. The teacher is comfortable employing both Patterns of Power and Patterns of Influence.
Teacher's Consistency, p. 21	The teacher is inconsistent most of the time.	The teacher's inconsistency leaves the class unsafe a good portion of the time.	The teacher follows the Golden Rule: she treats students the way she wants to be treated. Students are held accountable for their behaviors and there are high expectations for productivity.	The teacher follows the Platinum Rule: teacher operates the way the class and individual students need the teacher to operate.
Teacher's Ability to Predict, p. 21	The teacher is constantly surprised.	The teacher is frequently surprised.	The teacher's perception is of what is occurring at the moment and not long-term.	The teacher can predict what is likely to happen over time if the individual student(s) or class continue to operate the way they are. The teacher knows whether it is actually appropriate to intervene and how to intervene.
Classroom Safety, p. 21	The class is unsafe most of the time.	The class is unsafe a good portion of the time.	The teacher provides the safety, and safety is present as long as the teacher is present.	Safety is provided by the class and is very present as evidenced by the students breathing low/abdominally.

© 2000 by Michael Grinder & Assoc., ARR. AHC03 (360) 687-3238; FAX (360) 687-0595; http://www.michaelgrinder.com

Norms and Standards [12]

When the reader views the rubrics' four categories, several explanations are warranted.

1. The far right column of each rubric lists the descriptors of an outstanding teacher who fosters a fully functioning classroom.[13] The natural tendency is to describe the opposite terminal of the continuum as the opposite of *functional*–dysfunctional. While it may be an accurate term for a very small percentage of veteran teachers who aren't developing into adequate teachers and, consequently, function in the first column, the pejorative connotations of the word "dysfunctional" might be offensive to the reader. *A Healthy Classroom* proposes the acronym **f.a.l.o.w.** = **f**ollow **a**nother **l**ine **o**f **w**ork (a description of veterans who have never developed into adequate teachers).[14] Since the *A Healthy Classroom* rubrics are templates to chart the development of a new teacher's professional development, references to f.a.l.o.w. will be held to a minimum.

2. In no way is the rubric format intended to imply a new teacher would necessarily begin at the far left end of each rubric. Even if a new teacher does start her career in the far left column, in time she can *cultivate* herself into a solid teacher.

3. A given teacher could employ the rubric to chart or compare to where she is in her development. What is the connection between rubrics (criteria reference or standards) and the more traditional bell shaped curve (normative reference) in which teachers are compared to each other? The extremities of f.a.l.o.w. and artisans are apparent.

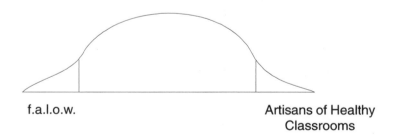

f.a.l.o.w.   Artisans of Healthy
                                                     Classrooms

What is interesting is the connection between the middle section of the bell shape and the two middle categories of the apprentice and the scientist. If common parlance is applied, namely, that these categories comprise 80% of teachers, so translation between the reference systems is very important.

© 2000 by Michael Grinder & Assoc., ARR. AHC03 (360) 687-3238; FAX (360) 687-0595; http://www.michaelgrinder.com

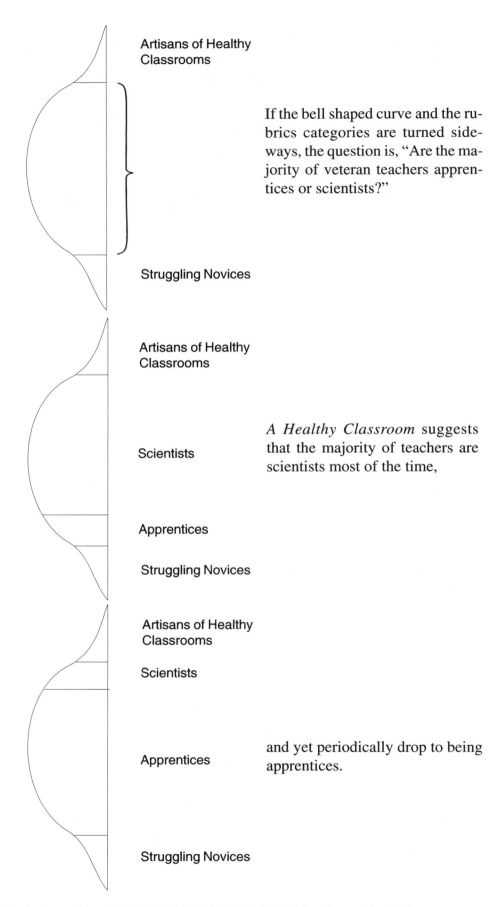

Artisans of Healthy
Classrooms

If the bell shaped curve and the rubrics categories are turned side-
ways, the question is, "Are the majority of veteran teachers apprentices or scientists?"

Struggling Novices

Artisans of Healthy
Classrooms

Scientists

A Healthy Classroom suggests
that the majority of teachers are
scientists most of the time,

Apprentices

Struggling Novices

Artisans of Healthy
Classrooms

Scientists

Apprentices

and yet periodically drop to being
apprentices.

Struggling Novices

© 2000 by Michael Grinder & Assoc., ARR. AHC03 (360) 687-3238; FAX (360) 687-0595; http://www.michaelgrinder.com

Why is this so? To answer that question and to prevent such a drop from occurring so frequently, *A Healthy Classroom* borrows a term from environmental studies: SAD (Seasonal Affected Disorders). This work is about group dynamics because group dynamics is the foundation of a healthy classroom. Group dynamics, both the fostering of group dynamics and the utilization of group dynamics by the teacher, is what leads to a healthy classroom. The educational equivalent of SAD is *SAG* (*S*easonal *A*ffected *G*roup Dynamics). The majority of teachers are seasonally affected and *sag* from being scientists to being apprentices.

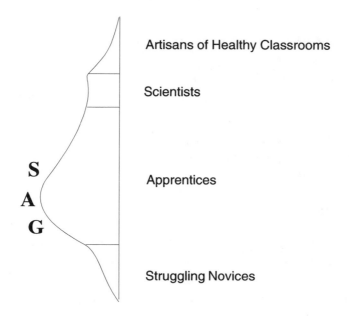

Consistency is a major ingredient that separates the scientist from the apprentice. It would seem that the more a teacher is consistent throughout the year, the more competent/scientist the teacher would be. However, since seasonal fatigue will affect the classroom dynamics, both the pupils with each other and their relationship with the teacher, what is deemed consistent in one season will be seen as rigid and inflexible during another season.

It is only natural that the teacher becomes fatigued at the same time the class does. Examples abound! Video footage would show the teacher standing and sitting straighter in September than mid November.

Colin Powell[15] said this about seasonal fatigue:

"Moments of stress, confusion and fatigue are exactly when mistakes happen. And when everyone else's mind is filled or distracted, the leader must be doubly vigilant. Avoid having your ego so close to your position that when your position falls your ego goes with it."

© 2000 by Michael Grinder & Assoc., ARR. AHC03 (360) 687-3238; FAX (360) 687-0595; http://www.michaelgrinder.com

In September	Later
In September the teacher says a student's name then employs her hands to gesture management directives.	By Thanksgiving, the teacher is using her hands to prop up her body (e.g., leaning on desks). This is exactly why when the teacher needs to be non-verbal, the teacher is verbal because the hands are occupied.
Early in the year the teacher works hard to form cohesiveness in the room. The teacher is at the door greeting students. By mid-October, the class operates by established routines. The teacher doesn't have to spend much time or energy on cohesiveness and safety.	By early November, the teacher is seasonally shocked because the pupils are not responding like they normally have been.
Academically, the teacher is clear on expectations. The teacher devotes much preparation, visually demonstrating concepts and writing out directions to assignments (Exit Directions). In time the class follows the routines of "always..." and "never..." so well the teacher switches to being more oral: "Remember class, we always put our heading on the paper and when finished put math in the blue tray." Sometimes the teacher can even drop the verbiage and the class operates very successfully.	The teacher is lulled into the quiet before the seasonal storm. Just when life is getting easier, it becomes harder. What worked no longer does. Instead of adjusting, the room is filled with teacher retorts such as, "Where have you been?" "Since September we always put math papers in the blue tray!"

Fatigue causes the teacher's brain to lock up and, with it, the teacher's flexibility decreases. One of the purposes of a school-wide wellness/fitness program is for the teacher to have a different season than the students. The teachers and school weather the season. The more knowledgeable the teachers are about group dynamics, the more the teachers adjust their management approach. By being sensitive to and compensating for seasonal fatigue, the teachers avoid *SAG*. Instead of *sag*ging, exercise will provide teachers with a firmness.

© 2000 by Michael Grinder & Assoc., ARR. AHC03 (360) 687-3238; FAX (360) 687-0595; http://www.michaelgrinder.com

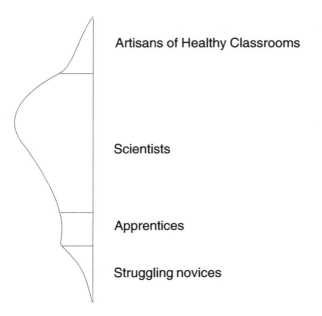

If the sole purpose of *A Healthy Classroom* were to assist the majority of teachers in transitioning from *apprentices* to *scientists* of classroom management, the project would be noble.[16] *A Healthy Classroom* is much more ambitious. It offers the scientist of classroom management a template of how to become an artisan of a healthy classroom. Placing student teachers with artisans certainly helps. However, the artisans' explanation of what they do isn't sufficient because their daily strategies are behaviorally employed, often at an unconscious level. *A Healthy Classroom* contends that the outstanding teacher's philosophy doesn't explain why the classroom is so healthy. This work suggests that a healthy classroom is the direct result of the teacher's utilization of group dynamics. The purpose of this book is to reveal those strategies so that many scientists have a blueprint for becoming outstanding teachers. And secondly, as artisans become conscious of what they do, the next generations of teachers can evolve into the professionals they dream of being.

A Healthy Classroom Reshapes the Bell Curve

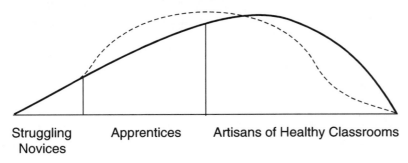

© 2000 by Michael Grinder & Assoc., ARR. AHC03 (360) 687-3238; FAX (360) 687-0595; http://www.michaelgrinder.com

Introduction Post-its

RSVP

Which of the four prerequisites do I perform well and which might I want to improve even more?

Introduction, p.17.

Teacher's Consistency

Have I moved beyond the Golden Rule of treating students the way I would want to be treated? Am I following the Platinum Rule of operating the way the class and individual students need me to operate?

Introduction, p. 20.

Group Dynamics

Do I have tendencies towards being group oriented or individually centered? Do I want to balance myself more with holding students more accountable for their behaviors or accepting students more as individual people? And when do I want to do which?

Introduction, p. 17.

Teacher's Ability to Predict

What are the situations in which I can recognize what is likely to happen before it actually occurs? Which circumstances still surprise me? How can I better see the early indicators of what is likely to happen? Am I intervening based on what students need instead of how I feel?

Introduction, p. 20.

Teacher's Range of Behaviors and Systematically Employed

Do I tend to have a wide range of behaviors and want to emphasize being more systematic? Or am I pretty systematic and want to increase my range of behaviors?

Introduction, p. 20.

Classroom Safety

Can I distinguish between when the class needs me to provide the safety for learning and when they are able to furnish their own safety? How competent am I at transferring the source of the safety from myself to the class.

Introduction, p. 20.

© 2000 by Michael Grinder & Assoc., ARR. AHC03 (360) 687-3238; FAX (360) 687-0595; http://www.michaelgrinder.com

End Notes

1. *ENVoY, ENVoY II*, and *A Healthy Classroom.* The purpose of ENVoY management books is: *ENVoY*–preserving relationships; *ENVoY II*–establishing and preserving relationships; *A Healthy Classroom*–accelerating classroom dynamics and creating healthy classrooms.

2. "The classroom can be viewed with educational binolculars. *ENVoY* focuses on the management aspects of the learning environment. Equally important is the other educational tube—curriculum." p. 155 of *ENVoY*.

3. The purpose of *ENVoY* and *ENVoY II*, being the science level of management, is to provide these competencies.

4. Appendix C.

5. In general, during the *Seatwork* portion of the lesson the instructor is more individual student-oriented. This concept of "the class, as a group, comes before the individual student" is the major shift in classroom management in the last decade. Students are not just more demanding than previously, but more impatient than ever. If we respond to the person who is making the most noise, then the tail wags the dog. Because of the change in the classroom demographics, as educators we have to retrofit ourselves. When push comes to shove, the group comes first.

6. See *Science of Non Verbal Communication*.

7. *ENVoY* and *ENVoY II*.

8. As outlined in *ENVoY*, p. 12.

9. *ENVoY* and *ENVoY II* intentionally do not address classroom dynamics. A case could be made that some of the *ENVoY* skills could be extrapolated into group dynamics; in particular *Opposite Side of Room* (in the pre-2000 edition, this skill was called *Body Close and Eyes Far*) and the section of *OFF/Neutral/ON Refinement*—"Audience-addicted Student" that is taught during training.

10. Kounin (1970) analyzed thousands of hours of videotapes of classroom interactions and discovered significant differences between the behavior of effective and ineffective classroom managers just prior to students' misbehavior.

11. See Appendix B for suggested details.

12. Norms, or normative references, illustrate how teachers are compared to each other. Standards, or criteria reference, compare where a specific teacher is on his developmental scale.

© 2000 by Michael Grinder & Assoc., ARR. AHC03 (360) 687-3238; FAX (360) 687-0595; http://www.michaelgrinder.com

13. Functioning is defined as capable of serving the purpose for which it was designed: in this case a classroom where learning occurs in a safe atmosphere. All definitions are from The Random House Dictionary, 1966 edition.

14. The acronym has an added advantage of being one letter ("l") short of the real word *fallow*. Fallow is a description of land that is plowed and left unseeded for one season or more, uncultivated. *Cultivation* is defined as "a culture; refinement." *Cultivate* is listed as "to produce by culture; to develop or improve by education or training; to refine; to promote the growth or development of an art... to devote oneself to an ...art."

15. *My American Journey* by Colin Powell and Joseph E. Persico, 1995, Random House, NY

16. The purpose of *ENVoY* and *ENVoY II* is to accomplish this outcome.

© 2000 by Michael Grinder & Assoc., ARR. AHC03 (360) 687-3238; FAX (360) 687-0595; http://www.michaelgrinder.com

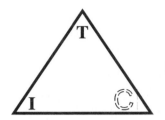

CHAPTER 1

Class Formation

The teacher has just made a statement that the one student, with his hand up, loves. The student in the far back corner represents the pupils who are fine with the first student's joy. But the rest of the class, represented by the cats, are not happy. To form a cohesive class, the teacher can employ four techniques which will be introduced on page 42.

To be respectful of gender equality and yet provide the educator with a fluid reading style, in this chapter the teacher is referred to by the male pronoun and the student by the female pronoun.

Introduction

When the semester starts the students in the classroom are referred to as a "class." In classrooms where successful group dynamics occur, the "class" eventually becomes a unified group. This chapter explores the stages of the class formation, the indicators of those stages, the advantages of pupils operating as a class, how to accelerate its formation and the adjustments of the teacher to the formation. The disadvantages of a class lacking class identity are also examined. The hardest class to manage is one that is not unified. A class without commonality often tempts the teacher to attempt individual rapport with each and every student–an improbable task, and an approach that inevitably leads to power management.

If the class is "new" in that the members don't know each other, then initially, there really isn't a group as much as there is a gathering of individuals. This is represented by the dashes that make up the title of this chapter. The number one task of the teacher is to provide *safety*.

On the surface it seems a teacher only works with Class Formation concepts at the beginning of the semester. There is a very real metaphor that farmers understand that explains the frequency of Class Formation. Every time a new cow is introduced into the herd, from a status perspective, the new member has to find its place in the group. Every time a group has a new member introduced, head butting occurs. This is especially true when the new member threatens to take the position held by a member already present. Be sensitive to which subgroup the new member might have membership in (e.g., "humorous," "smart," "good looking").

The concepts of Class Formation and their effect on a class are greatly influenced by whether the program is self contained or on a rotating schedule. Often primary teachers and instructors of special needs groups (English Language Development, Gifted & Talented, Special Education) find that their students are not socially developed enough for some group dynamics concepts to be present.

The caterpillar does all the work and the butterfly gets all the glory.[1]

Initial vs. Eventual Formation

Following the precepts of classroom dynamics, the teacher's behavior is based on how the class is doing. The class' group identity goes through a chrysalis stage. By knowing the stages, the teacher can anticipate which behaviors are appropriate. There are six indicators that reflect the stages of group formation. The indicators are in a question format.

© 2000 by Michael Grinder & Assoc., ARR. AHC03 (360) 687-3238; FAX (360) 687-0595; http://www.michaelgrinder.com

1-1

1. Where is the class looking?

At teacher

Initially: On the first day of school the students are likely to be looking toward the front of the classroom. This indicates their dependence on the teacher. The students anticipate they will take their direction from the instructor. The representation of this dependency is age-specific and culture-specific. For example, in the primary grades the students are often greeted at the door and funneled into an activity immediately. In suburbia, as the bell rings the fourth graders are more likely to be in their seats with store-bought supplies—awaiting the teacher's official greeting. Likewise, the surface impression of inner city seventh graders is, "What bell rang?!" And finally, a tenth grade honors class finds the students quietly talking and yet capable of settling down quickly when the call for attention is given. Taking into account the specifics of the age and culture of the pupils, the more the students are looking at the front of the room when the lesson begins, the more the group has not been formed.

At each other

Eventually: Eventually the students get to know each other and are talking and looking at each other at the start of the day. The primary students' behaviors range from coloring and talking to whomever their neighbors happen to be, to being distracted and off task. In fourth grade, the students are sharing with each other but ready to redirect their attention to the teacher. The seventh graders come to school for the social gathering and cluster in subgroups. They are slow to respond and reluctant to give heed to the teacher's call to commence. The tenth grade classroom finds students either finishing up homework or quietly socializing. They are ready to respond to the call for attention.

2. What is the speed of the transition into an activity?

Initially they turn heads toward each other while still looking at teacher.

Initially: During the lesson when the teacher announces a cooperative learning activity, how fast do the students switch from being focused on the teacher to looking and interacting with their table mates? When the class is not yet formed as a unit, the students often will start to turn their heads toward their partners, but their eyes are still looking at the teacher.

Eventually: In time the students are familiar with their table mates and will readily turn both their heads and eyes to their designated learning partners.

They turn eyes and heads toward each other.

© 2000 by Michael Grinder & Assoc., ARR. AHC03 (360) 687-3238; FAX (360) 687-0595; http://www.michaelgrinder.com

3. What is the speed of the transition from an activity back to the teacher?

Very quick

Initially: The speed of the transition from an activity to the teacher indicates the level of the students' bonding as a group. When the teacher requests attention from a cooperative learning activity back to himself and the students quickly turn their heads toward the instructor, the group isn't formed yet. Students' quickness to respond to the teacher's call for attention indicates that the teacher is still more important to the students than they are to each other.

Eventually: Over time the students form bonds with each other. When the teacher indicates a transition back to the teacher, the students have the urge to finish their last sentence or, in some cases, paragraph before returning to the teacher's instruction.

Slower

4. How well are the individual students known?

Initially: At the beginning of the year the students often don't know each other. No one knows who are the smarter students, troublemakers, questioners or class clowns. When the class isn't formed yet, how the teacher treats each student is how the rest of the class believes they will be treated. Initially, they see themselves as all alike. That is why the teacher's management of an individual student must be gentle[2]. If the teacher perceives student X as being different from the rest of the class and "deserving" of a consequence, the teacher wants to determine if the class sees student X as different. If the pupils don't distinguish student X as different from the rest of the class, which is the case initially, then they perceive that what the teacher does to student X will happen to all of them. For example, if student X is held in from recess, every student is afraid she will be held in. The veteran teacher's ability to quickly assess in the first day or two those students who need clearly-set boundaries doesn't mean the class, as a whole, has the same speed of detection. From a group dynamics standpoint, the teacher wants to make sure the class can see what the teacher perceives.

Initially, how the teacher treats each student is how the rest of the class believes they will be treated.

Eventually: Being in the microcosm of the classroom increases the students' familiarity with each other. The students come to know who is likely to act in certain ways. Very quickly the students learn, "How student X is treated by the teacher doesn't apply to me." In Chapter Five *Managing a Healthy Classroom* and Chapter Six, it will be recommended that the function of the

© 2000 by Michael Grinder & Assoc., ARR. AHC03 (360) 687-3238; FAX (360) 687-0595; http://www.michaelgrinder.com

teacher's crystal-ball-perception of who the teacher will eventually manage is to form relationships with these students. Then when the teacher does manage a student, the class thinks, "Gee, the teacher likes student X, so it must be student X's behavior that is inappropriate."

At first, the students with unique physical characteristics are noticed, such as those who are tall or short, thin or heavy, pretty, handsome or least attractive. In time, the different unique mental characteristics become apparent. The class almost has a high school yearbook sense of "most likely to...." In Chapter Five, there is a focus on the teacher attempting to prevent stereotyping. The absence of stereotyping allows the student to blossom into a fuller person.

> *A healthy classroom is one where every student,*
> *as a person, is accepted and, at the same time,*
> *the student is behaviorally held accountable.*

Satisfy, Satisfy, Delay

1-2

This strategy is an expansion of the concept "Individuals Seen as Unique." When a class hasn't been formed yet, how the teacher responds to one pupil is interpreted as how the teacher could respond to any pupil. That is why the teacher wants to answer (satisfy) the first and second questions a student asks. This is because the class doesn't see anyone as different from anyone else. Perception is in the eyes of the beholder (class). However, after the same student has asked several questions, the teacher has the class' permission to delay answering the questions. Examples include, "Let me talk to you after the class is engaged," and "Please hold your questions." Techniques, in and of themselves, do not determine if "power" or "influence" management is being employed by the teacher. It is the teacher's timing when employing the techniques that determines if power or influence is present.

© 2000 by Michael Grinder & Assoc., ARR. AHC03 (360) 687-3238; FAX (360) 687-0595; http://www.michaelgrinder.com

Recommended:

Satisfy

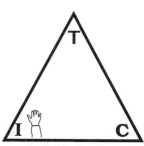

Individual asks a question.

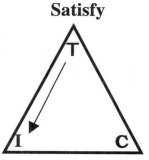

Teacher answers respectfully

Class notices the individual is satisfied and senses they would be treated the same way if they had a question.

Satisfy

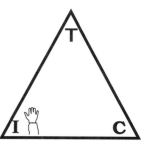

Same individual asks a second question.

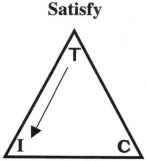

Teacher answers respectfully

The class notices the individual is satisfied and senses she might be unique in asking a lot of questions.

Delay

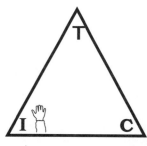

Same individual raises a hand to ask a question.

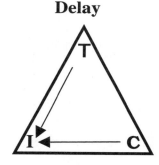

The teacher and the class notice the same individual is about to ask a question.

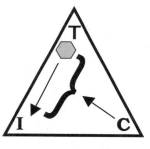

Teacher nonverbally (or verbally) signals questions will be entertained in a little while.

The class is fine with the teacher doing the *Delay* on two counts:

1. The individual has distinguished herself as different from the rest of the class. Because of this, the teacher may *Delay* with her but *Satisfy* anyone else who has a question.

2. The teacher's priority is the needs of the class over the needs of the individual.

© 2000 by Michael Grinder & Assoc., ARR. AHC03 (360) 687-3238; FAX (360) 687-0595; http://www.michaelgrinder.com

Least Recommended:

An example of an individual not being distinguished as different from the rest of the class is:

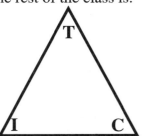

On the first day of school a person comes in late and loud.

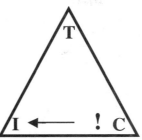

Class stunned by individual.

Teacher openly reprimands individual. As stunned as the class is by the individual's inappropriate entrance, they are even more shocked by the teacher's response.

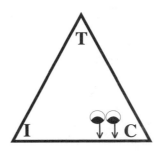

They look down because they are unsafe. They could be the next victim of the teacher's wrath.

5. Who is providing the safety?

Teacher provides

Initially: At the beginning of the semester the teacher is the single most important person in the classroom. Surprisingly, this is even true for the sixth through ninth grades. The teacher conveys, especially non-verbally, his reactions and the students unconsciously respond to such reactions. The classroom atmosphere is influenced more by the teacher than by any other single variable. An extreme example of this influence was discovered while coaching a second grade teacher who was wearing a Hawaiian shirt in the middle of winter. When asked about it, he said, "We are on the north side of the building and the engineering is such that we are colder than the other rooms, so I do a unit on Hawaii and emphasize how hot it sometimes gets. They are second graders—they feel warmer."

Eventually: As the class becomes a group, the students provide their own safety. One unusual example is found in the Steiner school system where the teacher stays with the same class for eight years.[3] One year, the fifth grade class' teacher was on maternity leave for a whole school year. The staff decided to collectively cover the class for that year. While the group was perfunctorily polite to every instructor, the faculty was concerned that no

Class provides

© 2000 by Michael Grinder & Assoc., ARR. AHC03 (360) 687-3238; FAX (360) 687-0595; http://www.michaelgrinder.com

teachers were making emotional progress with the class. They decided to hire a long-term substitute teacher—same results. The class had become a fully functioning emotional unit; they had no need for an adult.

6. Is there a unisance of response?

No

Initially: When the class is asked to do something, the response is staggered. If they are to turn to page 25, students begin to open their books at different times, frequently in waves. When the class comes in from lunch, how many waves are there? Sometimes the lack of unisance of response stems from good intentions. For example, it is common in the classes below fifth grade for the smarter students to want to answer quickly–thus creating a division in the group during oral recitation. A class that is not formed as a unit is more likely to not respond in unisance.

The unisance of response is the single clearest indicator that a class is a group.

Eventually: The unisance of response is the single clearest indicator that a class is a group. This includes laughing, moving into small group activities, quieting, coming back from breaks on time. From a group dynamic standpoint, it is more important that the group does what they do in unison as compared to doing what the teacher desires. For example, if the class comes back from lunch two minutes late, that is more important than having half of the pupils on time and the other half two minutes late. The unisance of response will vary based on the specific age and culture of the students. Teachers in the primary grades often have high auditory and kinesthetic techniques to create the unisance, such as clapping and singing with gestures. (I have a friend that claims that the adult equivalent is group aerobics at a gym; even joggers find the time passes quickly when they are occupied either by a companion or Walkman. We unconsciously jog to the beat of the music.)[4]

Yes

> *In the preceding section on* **Indicators,** *the two essential questions that need addressing to understand class dynamics were:* **Where is the class looking? and, Is there a unisance of response?**

Breathing

As pupils become more comfortable with themselves, they breathe better, as evidenced by an increase in fluidity of movement, finding words and stillness. While difficult to detect, very formed classes actually breathe in unison.

© 2000 by Michael Grinder & Assoc., ARR. AHC03 (360) 687-3238; FAX (360) 687-0595; http://www.michaelgrinder.com

---

Vignette: How Not to Get Shot

Art Full has been a teacher for over a decade. He knows if he announces, "Let's do a small group activity now..." and the class holds their breath, he is in trouble. If Art begins the activity, the class won't learn very well, and yet not to start violates the linear logical side of the class who heard the activity was to begin immediately. If Art is less specific as to when the simulation will commence (e.g., "In a little while we will do an activity..."), and if Art sees that the class holds their breath, there are several techniques that he can use to shift the class. Of course, if the class is receptive to doing the activity, then Art has the option of saying, "... in fact, let's start now." The techniques include:

1. Explain the "why" of the "what" and "how" of the activity they are doing.

2. Demonstrate the activity.

3. Visually explain the steps involved.

4. Acknowledge the resistance behind the class not wanting to do it.

Art claims it is important to notice the time of day, situation-content, and evidence of the class holding their breath because as the teacher's permission changes, Art adjusts his degree of specificity.

Breathing: Humor

There are many ways to shift our own and others' breathing to a deeper level: exercise, meditation, yawning, singing and laughing. The most acceptable method in a class setting is humor.

The Changing Role of the Teacher

1-3

As the class becomes formed as a group, the role of the teacher is affected. Below the following paragraphs are two lists. The first describes the teacher's behaviors associated with times when the pupils are initially with each other and the second lists the behaviors exhibited when the class is a unit.

© 2000 by Michael Grinder & Assoc., ARR. AHC03 (360) 687-3238; FAX (360) 687-0595; http://www.michaelgrinder.com

Pilot vs. Flight Attendant

The difference between how the teacher operates *initially* compared to how the teacher will *eventually* manage is analogous to airline personnel. The students are the equivalent of the passengers. They expect the pilot to employ a credible voice pattern (i.e., a flat voice that curls down at the end) which communicates one-way messages (e.g., "This is your captain speaking. Our flight today will be three hours and fifteen minutes."). Such a voice pattern reassures the passengers that they are in good hands because the captain is competent and in charge. The flight attendants, on the other hand, are expected to employ an approachable voice pattern (i.e., rhythmic voice that curls up at the end) and seek input from the passengers (e.g., "Would you like a beverage?"). If the airplane personnel switched roles, the passengers would not be secure. For example, if the pilot, in an approachable voice pattern said, "Howdy, this is your captain. Listen, we have a lot of fuel and it is a cloudless day, so we are going to vote on what route to take. Press your call button if you are in favor of going over...." Likewise, if the flight attendants make a non-negotiable announcement in a credible voice pattern, the passengers would feel insulted. For instance, "Hey, keep your elbows and feet out of the aisles because we are going to be moving our carts up and down...."

Pupils are comfortable with the teacher *initially* being like the pilot and, as the group is formed, *eventually* switching more to the flight attendant's style. When the class' unity decreases seasonally, the teacher is back to being the pilot.

© 2000 by Michael Grinder & Assoc., ARR. AHC03 (360) 687-3238; FAX (360) 687-0595; http://www.michaelgrinder.com

Initially A Credible Teacher

credible

- Relies on his own strength

- Gets the control
- Knows answers
- Is in charge of
- Is factually oriented
- Is structured
- Sends information

- Dispenses as students listen

- Is jazzy and dramatic

- Doesn't have to walk his talk

- Has to fix all problems and squabbles

Synonyms of Credible
hierarchical
determined
convincing
authoritarian
reliable

approachable

Eventually An Approachable Teacher

- Relies on the strength of the class

- Gets the influence
- Knows questions
- Is in service to
- Is process oriented
- Is flexible
- Fosters thinking about information

- Facilitates as students interact with content

- Is more low key and in the background

- Is perceived as genuine and sincere

- Allows the class to own and solve the problems and squabbles

Synonyms of Approachable
easy to talk to
friendly
amicable
sociable

The teacher often exhibits the following physical behaviors:

Physical Behaviors	Initially	Eventually
posture	stand	sit
palms	down	up
extension of gestures	great	small
voice volume	↑	↓
head	still	bob
undulation	flat	rhythmic
pause with frozen hand gesture	longer	shorter

© 2000 by Michael Grinder & Assoc., ARR. AHC03 (360) 687-3238; FAX (360) 687-0595; http://www.michaelgrinder.com

When migrating, geese form a group.

Vignette: Sense of a Goose[5]

In the fall when you see geese heading south for the winter flying along in a "V" formation, you might be interested in knowing what science has discovered about why they fly that way.

Scientists have learned that, as each bird flaps its wings, it creates an uplift for any bird flying just behind. By flying in a "V" formation, the whole flock adds at least 71% greater flying range than if each bird flew on its own.

Whenever a goose falls out of formation, it suddenly feels the drag and resistance of trying to go it alone and quickly gets back into formation to take advantage of the lifting power of the bird immediately in front.

(If we have as much sense as a goose, we will work together in a supportive formation which allows us to move more easily in the same direction.)

When the lead goose gets tired, it rotates back to become part of a wing of the "V" and another goose flies as leader or point.

Geese honk from behind to encourage those up front to keep up their speed and spirit.

Finally, scientists have found that when a goose gets sick or is hurt and falls out, two geese fall out of formation and follow him down to help and protect him. They stay with him until he is able to fly, and then they launch out on their own or with another formation to catch up with the group.

(Clearly, there is much to learn from the "sense of the goose" about how to help and stand by each other.)

Blending a Class is EASY

The last *indicator* listed was unisance of response. It is the unified reaction that determines the degree to which a class becomes a group and identifies with each other. Examples of unified reactions include students arriving and leaving at the same time, making transitions into and out of their cooperative learning groups, and their collective volume in the room staying at a certain maximum volume level.

This indicator is a most interesting excuse to address our culture of power. If a teacher is given a choice between two classes, one where some stu-

© 2000 by Michael Grinder & Assoc., ARR. AHC03 (360) 687-3238; FAX (360) 687-0595; http://www.michaelgrinder.com

dents "like" the teacher and some students do not, and a second class where the students are unified against whoever the teacher is, the teacher would pick the first class. The teacher thinks the first group is easier to manage, whereas the second class is actually easier to manage. In the first class, the group is not formed, whereas in the second one, the group is formed. It is common in the military to have the initial training (i.e., boot camp) be an experience where the soldiers from all over the country are bonded together. How do people from such diverse cultures become cohesive? Often by hating a common enemy–their drill sergeant.

 A split class is the hardest to manage. It creates several new corners of the classroom triangle that the teacher must take into account. It is as if the teacher has to interact with each student separately to form a bond.[6]

Without a formed class, the dependency on the teacher is burdensome and not healthy.

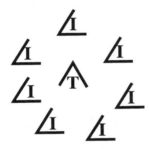

$\triangle I$ vs. $\triangle I$ There are many advantages for a teacher to have a formed class.[7] One situation that graphically illustrates the advantage of a formed class occurs when individual students disagree with each other.

> *If the class is a unit then the members who are at odds with each other are more likely to assign "good intention" to their opponents.*

It therefore behooves the teacher to unify the students into a group. There are four methods that blend a class together; the acronym **EASY** spells them out.

Echo

Ready

When a class responds in unison, it is an indication that the class has gelled. The teacher can speed

"Hello, Hello"

1-4

© 2000 by Michael Grinder & Assoc., ARR. AHC03 (360) 687-3238; FAX (360) 687-0595; http://www.michaelgrinder.com

up this natural process by structuring such a response. For example, the teacher wants the class to repeat an axiom, "Always put your name and date in the top right-hand corner." The teacher can drag his voice out as he says, "Let's say it together: r e a d y." This is especially helpful when the teacher uses hand gestures to guide the verbal response—much like that of an orchestra leader.

For some classes the above example may not work. We have to have an academic pretense for the students to tolerate *echoing*, (e.g., "By repeating this our memory doubles. We have longer memories by storing the information in more than one channel. When we repeat what we hear, we cross reference the information. When we hear the information, it enters the memory through auditory input. When we say it aloud, we add auditory output."). Usually the students will have varying degrees of enthusiasm. Two or three repetitions help blend the class.

Auditory Transfer

Auditory Transfer is a form of Echo. It is used when new words or full sentences are being learned. The technique increases the participants' long-term memory. Steps:

- Teacher says the new word/sentences.

- The teacher and class say it together. Using the r e a d y technique, the class is cued to repeat in unison the new word/sentences.

- The teacher silently mouths the new word/sentences while the class says it aloud.

Often sixth graders and above won't tolerate all three steps. The first and last steps are normally done.

Acknowledge

When a teacher acknowledges possible resistance, "the class knows that the teacher knows." There are varying degrees of acknowledging this possible resistance based on the level of sophistication the situation needs. The whole purpose of acknowledging is to influence the amount of oxygen the resistant students are getting to their brains. When we are successful, the students indicate they are breathing better by:

"Hear Ye, Hear Ye"

© 2000 by Michael Grinder & Assoc., ARR. AHC03 (360) 687-3238; FAX (360) 687-0595; http://www.michaelgrinder.com

Low/Abdominal Breathing Indicators	
If they are	*they would*
moving	move with fluidity
talking	find words with fluidity
reposing	be more still than stiff

It is suggested that the teacher do the acknowledgment away from the lecturing location. At the end of the acknowledgment, the teacher breaks his body posture while breathing and returns to the lecturing location. This maneuver results in *amnesia* occurring[8].

Break & Breathe = Amnesia[9]

One of the easiest ways to understand why acknowledging works is to realize it is a *proactive* maneuver.

Simple Acknowledgment

Sometimes it is as simple as a teacher saying, "Some of you/us may not like to do cooperative learning, and yet we all know the Chinese saying, 'If you/we hear it, you/we forget; if you/we hear it and see it, you/we understand; and if you/we hear it, see it and do it, you/we can duplicate it.'" Another example, "Some of you may not be finished copying the overhead yet... and by putting down y/our pens and looking up here we can see what else we are going to be doing. You will have time to finish copying." When we can, we want to use *humor* because laughing is the fastest way to shift a class' breathing to a deeper level.

1-5

The teacher can't get past resistance until he acknowledges that it exists.

© 2000 by Michael Grinder & Assoc., ARR. AHC03 (360) 687-3238; FAX (360) 687-0595; http://www.michaelgrinder.com

1-6

Sophisticated Acknowledgment

Surface Resistance

Acknowledge the content/issue/behavior the class might find objectionable. There are different levels of acknowledging.

1. If the entire class objects, then say, "You really...."

   If the class is split, then saying the above will offend those who weren't resisting and they might resent being misrepresented by the statement, "You really...." Therefore, we might select one of the next two statements.

2. "Some of you really...."

3. "Some of you might really...."

"Some" and "might" are called *softeners* and are helpful when we want to appear as though we are suggesting rather than imposing.[10]

Acknowledgment of Intention Behind Surface

If the teacher has a solid relationship with the class, then he wants to align himself with the minority group in the room.

Behind the students' surface resistance is the motivation/intention/concern that is generating the surface resistance. While the class' resistance often isn't appropriate, the intention is always positive.[11] By changing the focus of our acknowledgment from the surface to the intention level, we can honestly say they are "right" on the motivation level. The easiest way of getting to the intention level is to finish this sentence, "And there is a good reason why (describe the surface resistance)." Then say the reason. It is essential that we progress from acknowledging their surface resistance to the positive reasons behind the surface resistance. If we skip the acknowledgment of the surface resistance, we often lack their permission to mention the positive reasons.

Preface to Reframing[12]

We want to offer a different interpretation of the situation or reframe. A metaphor helps explain how this interpretation works. We have all had the experience of taking a print to have framed. As we look at the possible colors of the matting, we realize that each color highlights the different hues of the actual picture. So while the students still might object on one level, they are being offered the option of a new perspective. This process is called *reframing*. One of the ways to increase the likelihood that the class will let us offer the reframe is to progress from acknowledging surface resistance to mentioning the positive reasons for resistance, and then saying one of the next two lines:

"Part of you...."

"Part of us...."

© 2000 by Michael Grinder & Assoc., ARR. AHC03 (360) 687-3238; FAX (360) 687-0595; http://www.michaelgrinder.com

The substitution of the word "part" for the word "some" serves several purposes. The latter connotes that the class is **split** with some individual students in resistance and some who are not. "Part" is accurate enough to be a synonym for "some" and yet ambivalent enough to also indicate that each individual person is **split** between being in resistance and not being in resistance.

Reframing

By saying the *Preface to Reframing*, we have acknowledged the resistance portion of each student. We now can access the opposite side of the ambivalence—the part that isn't in resistance—and we can offer a new perspective.

The *Acknowledgment and Reframing* can be done metaphorically through a vignette.

Vignette: Ron Respectful

Last July, Ron Respectful begrudgingly attended the workshop. He knew that the two credits would put him into the final column of the pay scale, and he also wanted to be a better elementary teacher as well as a smart consumer. He cautiously participated, not convinced that he would find a gem of practical wisdom that he could use in the classroom. Now it is November and one of the gems he has incorporated into his daily habits is acknowledging the diverse levels of abilities in his classroom. When some students are finished and others are still working, Ron gets their attention by saying, "I know some of you are still working but, by looking up here, we can see what we will be doing next." The technique was simple but the effect was complex. The students who worked quickly would have something to do and those who were not ready would visually be able to see what they will start to do next. But it was more than just a technique; his classroom is more peaceful than other years and the students get along better. He described the mood to his wife as a "more caring" atmosphere.

© 2000 by Michael Grinder & Assoc., ARR. AHC03 (360) 687-3238; FAX (360) 687-0595; http://www.michaelgrinder.com

1-7

Choreography of Acknowledgment

"Class, look up here!"

1. The teacher is at the board and gets their attention.

"Today we start our research unit."

2. The teacher announces something that the pupils may not be receptive to.

3. The teacher, having announced the irritating subject, moves to a new location with a frozen hand gesture[13].

"Now, before we begin..."

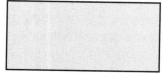

4. From the new location, the teacher acknowledges possible resistance. Teacher's voice and other nonverbals are different from voice and nonverbals employed in Steps 1 and 2.

"Some of us might be concerned because we have too much work in our other subjects. Some of us might be concerned because of the current heavy school athletic schedule, and that's why a part of us might be concerned because we haven't done a research paper before."

© 2000 by Michael Grinder & Assoc., ARR. AHC03 (360) 687-3238; FAX (360) 687-0595; http://www.michaelgrinder.com

5. When the teacher has finished the acknowledgments, he pauses and then starts to walk back to the board.[14] The teacher pauses half way back to offer a reframe. Again, change voice and other nonverbals.

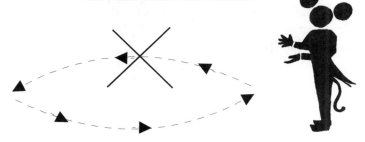

"When you think about it, while there is a part of us that may resist this research unit, many of us are going on to college both for academic as well as athletic reasons. Getting used to a heavy homework load now will serve us well later. We will walk you through every step of the research project so that you can be successful."

6. The teacher pauses again then returns to the board to begin the lecture. Teacher employs exact same voice and nonverbals as in Steps 1 and 2.

Silence

Carl Rogers[15] was the fountainhead of many ideas. One of them was a way to read the progression of class formation. When the class was comfortable in silence, (i.e., the silence didn't have to be filled) group safety had been achieved.

"Sh..."

The teacher now can artificially accelerate the progress by creating a silence and breathing deeply because when the teacher breathes deeply, the modeling influences the class. The content that is used is often, "Any questions?" An even more important occasion is at the end of the morning or afternoon session when the teacher asks, "Who would like to share what they are learning?" This technique works when there is a modicum of permission from the class.

Your Hands

The fourth technique of blending a group together involves either having them raise their hands, as in "Raise your hand if you traveled

1-8

Silence is sometimes the answer.
Estonian proverb

1-9

© 2000 by Michael Grinder & Assoc., ARR. AHC03 (360) 687-3238; FAX (360) 687-0595; http://www.michaelgrinder.com

more than 50 miles over the holidays," or "Raise your hand if your family stayed home over the vacation," or it could involve the teacher using his own hands. He could say, "Some of us (teacher has hand extended towards the class) have attended other schools, and some of us (teacher extends the other hand) have always gone to school in (say town)." With each hand representing the different parts of the class, the teacher can now say, "What we are here (and put the hands together) for is...," thus symbolically bringing the two diverse groups together.

Vignette: Micro UN

Donna Diplomat feels honored to be the teacher of the high school leadership course. She knows that she not only has the leaders of the school but, likely, the future voices of the community. Today Donna has a challenge. The administration has summarily canceled a previously-approved town hall meeting on preventing violence by looking at prejudice in school. The Associated Student Body President and Vice President are especially livid. The anger in the room is so blatant that Donna wisely pulls a map down over the agenda for today's lesson and then walks to the side board where she silently becomes an impartial scribe, writing the salient points on the board. Once the members start to repeat themselves, Donna knows she has permission to offer a perspective. Once she has their attention with a frozen hand gesture she moves from the side board to the corner where the side board and the back wall meet. Holding her right hand parallel to the ground Donna acknowledges their frustrations in a loud voice, "Some of you are angry (as she turns and points to the side board) because the principal reneged on his promise. You feel like doing something equally forceful. There is a good reason why you want to allow your impulsiveness out." Amid sounds of agreement, she drops to a whispery voice and continues, "You value integrity–a promise made is a promise kept." Stepping halfway back towards the side board, Donna pauses, looks and points to the side board where their frustrations are listed. "What you are grappling with..." The lack of sentence completion causes a slight level of confusion.

After a pregnant pause, she slowly walks to the back of the room, with her left hand extended and in a different voice says, "And yet there are some of you who, while greatly disturbed by the inconsistency of the administrators, want to 'do what is right.'"

---

continued on next page

© 2000 by Michael Grinder & Assoc., ARR. AHC03 (360) 687-3238; FAX (360) 687-0595; http://www.michaelgrinder.com

Stepping into an aisle, Donna sits in a student desk as though she were a student. She looks at the spot where she had stood, both hands extended, the right hand representing the students who impulsively want to take action and the left hand representing the students who are more conservative, and says, "The larger question is how can we all look back on this situation when we are in college and be proud of how we collectively operated." Donna slowly draws her hands together and rests them on her lap.

After a long moment of silence the group begins to process aloud. Their voices are calmer and they are listening to each other better. Donna Diplomat attentively is present while inside smiling because she knows it is not realistic to expect Camelot—where there is peace and no conflicts. She works for peaceful ways of handling conflicts.

Summary

This chapter has explored the difference between a teacher managing a unified classroom and a class when the students haven't gelled yet. It is always easier to manage the former. The six indicators that reflect the degree of class formation are shown on the next page.

These six indicators let the teacher know what style of management is warranted. The more the class is not formed into a unit, the more the teacher has a directive/credible role. The more the class is unified, the more the teacher is facilitative/approachable. Curriculum-wise the movement for years has been to switch the teacher from a dispenser of content to a facilitator of thinking and processing. *A Healthy Classroom* is proposing that the teacher's ability to focus on the academic arena is directly tied to the teacher's ability to effectively and efficiently manage. Perhaps a teacher could academically begin a semester as a curriculum facilitator while being a directive/credible manager. But it might make even more sense for the management and curriculum tubes of the educational binoculars to be coordinated. This would mean the semester would start with the teacher employing the directive approach in both tubes. Then, as the class becomes formed, the teacher switches his teaching from the directive/credible style to the facilitative/approachable mode while gradually beginning to manage by influence instead of power.

Three essential questions that aid one's understanding of group dynamics are: Where is the class looking? Is the pupils' breathing relaxed or stressed? Is there a unisance of response?

It behooves a teacher to bond a class together as quickly as possible. The fluctuation of not being unified and then becoming unified happens throughout the year. The chapters on Stages and Seasons directly address these issues. The four techniques that accelerate class formation are:

© 2000 by Michael Grinder & Assoc., ARR. AHC03 (360) 687-3238; FAX (360) 687-0595; http://www.michaelgrinder.com

Indicators of Class Formation

Initially   *Eventually*

1. Where is the class looking?

At teacher   *At each other*

2. How fast do the students make the transition from the teacher into a group activity?

Initially they turn heads towards each other while still looking at teacher.

They turn eyes and heads towards each other.

3. How fast do the students make the transition from a group activity back to being attentive to the teacher?

Very quick   *Slower*

4. How well do the students know each other?

5. Who is providing the safety?

Teacher provides   *Class provides*

6. How is the unisance of response? (This is the most important indicator.)

© 2000 by Michael Grinder & Assoc., ARR. AHC03 (360) 687-3238; FAX (360) 687-0595; http://www.michaelgrinder.com

E—Teacher has the students echo information aloud to achieve a unisance of response.

A—Teacher verbally acknowledges any diversity in the room, thus increasing the safety provided by the teacher; and since the teacher is OK with the diversity it must be OK to have diversity.

S—Teacher is comfortably silent when asking for input. This results in students operating in a sophisticated level of familiarity.

Y—When the teacher is doing the verbal acknowledgment, the teacher can represent the diverse groups via "your hands." By bringing his/her hands together, the diverse groups are symbolically blended together.

The concepts of Class Formation and their effect on a class are greatly influenced by whether the program is self-contained or on a rotating schedule. Often primary teachers and Special Education teachers find that their students are not socially developed enough for some of group dynamics concepts to be present.

The concept of *dogs & cats*[16] is essential to understanding class formation. Dogs are students who accommodate and operate from a win-win template. Cats are pupils who expect others to accommodate them. It is not that cat students would intentionally impose, presume or insult. They are just being themselves—oblivious to operating win-lose. On the surface, a classroom of dogs will seem more formed and cooperative than a classroom of cats. We need to examine this more closely because a teacher can herd dogs but not cats.

> *A healthy classroom only occurs when the pupils have formed into a unit, because it is only with a formed group that a teacher can fully operate and manage with influence instead of power.*

© 2000 by Michael Grinder & Assoc., ARR. AHC03 (360) 687-3238; FAX (360) 687-0595; http://www.michaelgrinder.com

Rubric for Chapter One: Class Formation

	Struggling Novice	Apprentice	Scientist	Artisan of Healthy Classroom
Initial Class Formation p. 32	The teacher is inconsistent and oblivious to his effect on the class.	The teacher operates from a style and philosophy that isn't based on dynamics (e.g., does either "Satisfy" or "Delay").	The teacher knows that it is natural for the group to evolve and can articulate and foster some of the indicators of the formation.	The teacher knows, recognizes and accelerates the six indicators of class formation.
Eventual Class Formation, p. 32	For the teacher, "eventually" doesn't exist as a concept.	The teacher doesn't change when formation could be fostered with such a change.	The teacher knows the class formation is changing and implements some of the EASY strategies.	The teacher's perception allows him to be patient. Employs EASY strategies to accelerate the formation.
Changing Role of the Teacher, p. 39	The teacher is inconsistent.	The teacher operates only from power. Or, the teacher sometimes operates from power and sometimes is inappropriately kind.	The teacher is appropriately credible initially and gradually becomes approachable.	The teacher is appropriately credible initially and gradually becomes more approachable. Can select degrees of credible-approachable based on the degree of formation.

Transcends the Educational Culture

© 2000 by Michael Grinder & Assoc., ARR. AHC03 (360) 687-3238; FAX (360) 687-0595; http://www.michaelgrinder.com

Chapter One Post-its

Class Formation

Based on the six indicators, are we more in the initial or eventual stage?

Chapter One: Class Formation, pp. 32-38.

Unisance=Formed Group

What affects the unisance of response?

Chapter One: Class Formation, p. 38

EASY—Degree of Familiarity

Which EASY techniques am I proficient in and which do I want to master?

Chapter One: Class Formation, pp. 42-50.

EASY—Application

When do I employ the EASY techniques?

Chapter One: Class Formation, pp. 42-50.

Changing Role of the Teacher

When am I the credible pilot and when am I the approachable flight attendant?

Chapter One: Class Formation, p. 39.

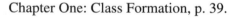

Changing Role and Seasons

What seasonal changes affect initial vs. eventual stage warranting changes in the teacher's role?

Chapter One: Class Formation.
Chapter Four: Seasons.

© 2000 by Michael Grinder & Assoc., ARR. AHC03 (360) 687-3238; FAX (360) 687-0595; http://www.michaelgrinder.com

End Notes

1. Donald Walker, *Never Try to Teach a Pig to Sing*.

2. See *Satisfy, Satisfy, Delay*, p. 35, and *Stages* in Chapter Three.

3. While founded in Germany, it is somewhat common in the larger USA cities to find such private, prestigious schools. In the city of Portland, Oregon, it is called the Waldorf School.

4. Using the concept from *ENVoY II* of "dogs and cats," the unison with "dog-oriented" students will be more uniform than with "cat-oriented" students. As Dr. Bill Sommers says, "Dogs can behave like a pack, but it is an oxymoron to say one can 'herd cats.'" Bill is an ENVoY trainer and coach. He is Director of Minneapolis Public School Staff Development.

5. Credited to Stromberg in Roland Barth's *Improving Schools from Within*.

6. Chapter Five, p. 158, *Osmotic Learning*, explores how the academic dependency on the teacher is burdensome.

7. See *Levels of Teachership*, p. 117, and *Pushing a Class*, p. 124.

8. These maneuvers are called *Decontamination* (*ENVoY*, p. 58) and *Break and Breathe* (*ENVoY* p. 62).

9. See Michael Grinder's *Science of Non Verbal Communication*, Break & Breathe.

10. From Neuro Linguistic Programming Course.

11. From Neuro Linguistic Programming Course.

12. J. Grinder and R. Bandler, *Reframing*.

13. See *ENVoY II*, "Frozen Hand Gesture."

14. These maneuvers are called *Decontamination* (*ENVoY*, p. 58) and *Break and Breathe* (*ENVoY* p. 62).

15. One of the leading humanists of the 1960s and 70s; author of *Becoming a Person*.

16. Dogs & Cats is the central theme of *ENVoY II*.

© 2000 by Michael Grinder & Assoc., ARR. AHC03 (360) 687-3238; FAX (360) 687-0595; http://www.michaelgrinder.com

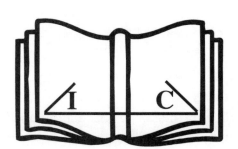

Most of the information about *Reading the Class* is based on visual cues. There are also a number of auditory patterns that assist the teacher in identifying the leaders, barometers and liaisons in the class.

When the class is engaged in cooperative learning, there are different collective voice patterns which can be accurately interpreted by the teacher. By listening, the teacher can auditorally detect when the small groups have wandered from being productive to socializing. This awareness lets the teacher know when to draw the class' attention back to the her.

To be respectful of gender equality and yet provide the educator with a fluid reading style, in this chapter the teacher is referred to by the female pronoun and the student by the male pronoun.

*To understand class dynamics, the teacher suspends her perception
and is attentive to how the class sees the situation.*

Introduction

The term "reading a group" or "reading the class" has been around for
decades. However, the term is an outgrowth from the one-on-one communication model. At one of our local community colleges the new students are given an entrance questionnaire that identifies their learning
preference. The professors receive their class rosters with the student's
learning style coded next to the student's name. At the bottom is a composite of the entire class. That is as logical as the scientist who studies
and knows the properties of the elements "hydrogen" and "oxygen" and
concludes that since hydrogen is explosive and oxygen is the fuel for
fire, then combining the hydrogen and oxygen will be very explosive.
Instead, the result is water (H_2O). *A Healthy Classroom* is both suggesting that the group cannot be understood by studying the individuals that
will make up a group and that the individual can only be understood in
the context of the group. Only after the dynamics of a group are understood in a predictable manner can one predict how individuals will inter-
actively behave in the group.

This chapter will explore how to identify the leaders of a group and determine if they are positive or negative leaders; how to utilize the leadership of the class; how to understand the subgroups within the class and
recognize who are the barometers of such groups; and, most importantly,
to notice how a barometer's response indicates how the rest of the members of that subgroup will eventually react. Then, by acknowledging the
subgroup's reaction before they actually react, the class perceives the
teacher as an insightful mind reader. Lastly, the chapter will give ways to
assess what the values of the class are and foster any values that are
desired but absent.

2-1

Leaders

(How does a teacher identify a leader?)

Chapter One focuses on formation of a class. One of the characteristics
that a class is forming as a unit is the emergence of students as unique
people. One of the first students to emerge as unique is the leader. When
a student is given attention from the class, the student is a leader. There
are several avenues by which the class bestows the distinction:

• Reputation from outside the room.

© 2000 by Michael Grinder & Assoc., ARR. AHC03 (360) 687-3238; FAX (360) 687-0595; http://www.michaelgrinder.com

- The first student to ask a content question; e.g., "How does this apply to...?"

- When all pupils who have the same concern see their classmate as their leader, that student is the subgroup's representative.

- The first student to represent a style; e.g., "visual-oriented learner" or "skeptical."

- Stress—if the class is empathetically-oriented[1] then someone who is a high/shallow breather will be a leader.[2]

- Pausing—someone who has the ability to pause when speaking will be the leader. This is especially effective if the pause is done near the beginning of the initial sentence and a frozen hand gesture is maintained during the pause.[3]

- Credibility—a leader usually employs a voice pattern that is flat and has an intonation at the end that curls down.

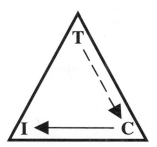

A leader is someone who gets the class' attention. How?
- *Before the semester starts: reputation accomplishments*
- *During class: content process*

It is important to note that normally a class looks when giving a leader attention. Yet, when the student is a negative leader[4] the class might look down at their desks. It is more accurate to describe a leader as someone who influences a class to *shift*. Sometimes the leader doesn't have to talk; walking quickly in the classroom will produce a *shift*.

Admittedly, there are many more avenues by which a student is noticed and therefore is a leader. Of the ones listed, the first five are what the person did to become a leader whereas the last two are based on the person's style.

Practice

Practice identifying how pupils become or are leaders. The teacher wants to simultaneously notice what the particular student does and how the rest of the class responds. This is especially important because not all leadership is obtained verbally. Some leaders are totally silent; e.g., some leaders walk in such a way that they are noticed. For instance, if a pupil leaves or enters the room during lecture in a hurry, the class is aware of the person; hence, attention is gained. *A Healthy Classroom* equates leadership with attention. This is apart from whether the student is a "positive" or "negative" leader.

© 2000 by Michael Grinder & Assoc., ARR. AHC03 (360) 687-3238; FAX (360) 687-0595; http://www.michaelgrinder.com

> **Vignettes: Opening Day of Junior High**
>
> The following are snippets from an all-too-typical seventh grade classroom.
>
> It is the first day of junior high. The night before most of the students have phoned their closest friends to compare schedules. The students are filing into their homerooms. Since there are several elementary schools that funnel into this school, each subgroup clusters together to inspect those who enter the door.
>
> ### Athletic
>
> The cool "in-group" of course will enter last. As Samantha Swift appears, there is a quick glance towards her from her classmates at her former school, then just as quickly the observers' eyes fall to their desks. "Sam" was the athlete of her elementary school, the top scorer in soccer and basketball. She is excited to start sports. Try-outs are next week.
>
> ### Looks
>
> Ravenous Roger must have fed his face with fries all summer. He has gone from over weight to nearly obese. He will be picked on in some classes and feared by some in others. After the attendance is finished, a new girl enters the room. As Jane Buxom comes in, all eyes are focused on someone who is precociously developed.
>
> ### Brains
>
> There are two students who are seated in the front row and off to the side. They won't be noticed until the first test results are announced.
>
> Each age group will have its own standards that determine which students will initially be the class leaders.

Leader's Voice and Timing

So far the kinds of class leaders explored have been "leadership by doing." This includes athletic, looks, and brains. Attention can also be gained by the student communicating in a certain manner–sometimes referred to as "leadership by style." These class leaders have a certain way of being—usually it is their "timing" when communicating. The most common timing used by leaders basically employs the following components:[5]

- Getting the class' attention.

© 2000 by Michael Grinder & Assoc., ARR. AHC03 (360) 687-3238; FAX (360) 687-0595; http://www.michaelgrinder.com

- Pause, especially with a frozen hand gesture. The leader's ability to freeze a hand gesture during his/her pause greatly adds to maintaining the group's attentiveness.

- Deliver the actual message.

Practice

It is recommended that as a reader you personally experience what is meant by *pausing and timing*. Work in teams of two to practice getting a group's attention, e.g., at a faculty or committee meeting. When you are about to practice getting one or more persons' attention, signal your partner to watch the targeted audience's response to you. Afterwards, have your partner discreetly debrief with specific feedback as to what you did and how the group responded. Make sure the feedback is very specific by including what was actually seen or heard; avoid interpretation/evaluation—stay with specific descriptions.

In Chapter Three there will be an additional example of timing as the base of a student's leadership. When a class is grappling with a decision-making process and the frustration level is approaching annoyance, if a member of the class times his suggestion and it is a decent suggestion, the whole class discovers its hero.

More Vignettes: Opening Day of Junior High

Voice Patterns

Frank Baritone

Frank Baritone is a taller, socially shy student seated in the back row. The teacher is calling out each student's name and they answer with a "here." When it is Frank's turn to indicate his presence, his guttural response is so much lower than the other males that the girls turn to see who it is.

Thelma Thespian

Thelma Thespian is only in third grade but she has the ability to hold her classmates' attention when she speaks. During a class discussion about manners, Thelma sits with her hand raised. As the teacher calls on her, she initially speaks in a louder than normal voice, "I was thinking." This is followed by a pause. Over half the room turns and looks at Thelma. Then she continues with a voice that is barely audible, "If we were …." The softness of her voice intrigues the segments of the room who weren't looking in her direction. They not only turn towards her, but lean as if to hear better.

A Leader's Timing

A balance between speaking and pausing

- Get the class' attention

- Pause

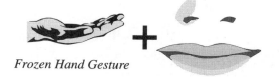

Frozen Hand Gesture   *Breathing*

- Message

Speed of delivery and breathing are other
variables that assist in TIMING.

*The pause is the single most powerful
non-verbal signal that can be used.*

© 2000 by Michael Grinder & Assoc., ARR. AHC03 (360) 687-3238; FAX (360) 687-0595; http://www.michaelgrinder.com

Leaders: Positive or Negative

2-2

Knowing who the leaders are in a classroom is a different skill than the ability to determine if the student is a positive or negative leader. There are two vantage points from which to view whether a student is a positive or negative leader. One perspective is whether the class sees the student as a positive or negative leader. The evidence that the pupils view a particular student as positive or negative is *simple but not easy*. If the class breathes low/abdominal when attention is given, the student is a positive leader in the eyes of the class. Likewise, if the class breathes high/shallow when giving the student attention, the student is seen as negative.

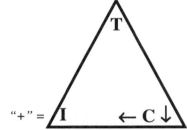

When the class gives the student attention, if they breathe low/abdominal, the student is a positive leader.

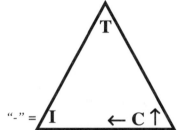

When the class gives the student attention, if the class breathes high/ shallow, the student is a negative leader.

The axiom that observing pupils' breathing levels indicates their evaluative reaction to a leader applies both to the class as a whole as well as to subgroups. Notice the members of a subgroup. When a member is representing the values of the subgroup, the members breathe low.

If a class sees a student as positive, the pupils will tend to look at the student when giving the student attention; however, if the class sees a student as negative, the class might not look in the student's direction. If the class sees the student as inappropriate and beneath them, they will look at the student. This example is further explained in Chapter Three, Stages. When the class is annoyed with the inappropriate student, they often look at the student in disgust. However, if the pupils don't see the inappropriate student as beneath them, the class may not look at the student while holding their breath. This is the case of the *Bully* which is explained in Chapter Three. The pupils are afraid to look at the student for fear of reprisal.

The second perspective to determine if a student is a negative or positive leader is the teacher's vantage point. It is fascinating that a class can see the student as a positive leader and the teacher clearly sees the student as inappropriate. This can be a daily occurrence for teachers of adolescents. The more a sixth through ninth grade student exhibits bizarre behavior, the more

© 2000 by Michael Grinder & Assoc., ARR. AHC03 (360) 687-3238; FAX (360) 687-0595; http://www.michaelgrinder.com

likely the rest of the pupils will assign even higher status. Bravado is highly valued among early adolescents for this peer pressure age group.

What is a teacher to do when the student is inappropriate in the teacher's mind? There are two major strategies that can be employed: *Indirect Acknowledgment* and *Decreasing the Status* of the student. The latter is covered in Chapter Three. Indirect acknowledgment follows. Please keep in mind that a given strategy can be activated for several reasons. This is said as a caution to indirect acknowledgment. The technique can be employed both when the student is inappropriate and appropriate.

Responding to a Leader

2-3

There are basically two ways of acknowledging an individual:

- Direct: Teacher looks and gestures as the teacher says a reference to the person's status; e.g., "You would know best...."

- Indirect: Teacher gestures, without looking at the person, as the teacher says a generic reference to expertise; e.g., "Experts know that...."

When the teacher does direct acknowledgment, both the student and the class as a whole recognize the deference. When an indirect acknowledgment is done, the class doesn't recognize the deference and very likely the student isn't conscious that he is being acknowledged. Why? The students follow the teacher's eyes. Indirect acknowledgment is when the teacher looks away from the student and at the class while the teacher's hand is directed towards the student. The gesture communicates to the student's unconscious mind while the conscious mind is focused on where the teacher is looking.

Why doesn't the teacher want to do direct acknowledgment with a negative leader? In some cases the class interprets that the teacher has just "given the store over to a new owner;" the student is in charge instead of the teacher. The indirect acknowledgment satisfies the student as an expert/leader and yet on the surface it seems like it is the teacher's class.

© 2000 by Michael Grinder & Assoc., ARR. AHC03 (360) 687-3238; FAX (360) 687-0595; http://www.michaelgrinder.com

Leaders Over Time

External auditory-oriented leader

Not all students who are leaders at the beginning of the class formation will remain as leaders. The primary example of this dynamic is the external auditory-oriented learner. The majority of auditory-oriented people are not external auditory-oriented. Some auditory-oriented people can talk to themselves silently. The reference is only to someone who, in order to think, has to speak. Some classes have a value for members who think before speaking. These students are called visual-oriented people. The external auditory-oriented student will initially be a leader because he speaks up; but in time the class decreases the amount of attention given to the person. Why? When anyone becomes very auditory-oriented:

- He becomes focused on his own internal cassette and wants to say the whole tape. The time given to this student by the class is disproportionate to other members. In time, the student is seen as hogging the microphone.

- His voice pattern tends not to have a pause and, therefore, the listeners drift off.

- His voice is rhythmic and the intonation curls up at the end of the sentence, which is the opposite of the voice pattern associated with being credible.

- His timing is off. It is especially important to notice when the class' attentiveness fades.

In a healthy classroom, leadership varies and is shared.

Tracking an external auditory-oriented person over a period of time will reveal how the class gives less and less attention to such a student. This is true both in the classroom and in faculties—the pattern is especially noticeable when a district-wide committee is formed.

There are other circumstances when the leadership of a classroom is altered over time. In Chapter Five the concept of *Stereotyping* is broached. In a healthy classroom the leadership varies based on what kinds of tasks warrant what kinds of leadership. The leadership is shared so that it is sometimes difficult to tell who the leader is because it is done by a sub-group or the group as a whole.

© 2000 by Michael Grinder & Assoc., ARR. AHC03 (360) 687-3238; FAX (360) 687-0595; http://www.michaelgrinder.com

Vignette: the Fading Leader

Perceptive Priscilla has taught middle school forever. She likes opening the semester with a class dialogue about the "rules of the room." The students have a sense of ownership. Besides creating an atmosphere of democracy regarding norms and consequences, the activity provides Priscilla an opportunity to get an early look at the leadership of the group. It has taken her years to learn that often the student who initially shines as a leader sometimes is ephemeral. The concept of an auditory-oriented student helps clarify this understanding as to why some people don't retain the attention they initially have. Priscilla calls these students "Audrey Auditory" in honor of a student named Audrey who was a classic example of such a phenomenon. When the class meeting started, there was the typical silence and shyness followed with the clever snide remarks. This lasted a very short amount of time. Once Audrey Auditory started to talk, with all eyes on her, there were no silent gaps. All voids in conversation were filled with Audrey either restating what was said or making tangential remarks. Now Priscilla can recognize the pattern of someone speaking early and often. Within two to three school days, more than half the students didn't look at Audrey Auditory when she talked. By the start of the second week other students literally would talk over her. If the setting were in a theater, it would be called "stepping on one's lines."

Perceptive Priscilla has had many student teachers as interns and everyone has been schooled in recognizing an Audrey Auditory. Because of the pattern of auditory people fading as leaders, all student teachers under Priscilla's tutelage are trained to pause more when talking to the class, especially when getting their attention. Priscilla studied her student teachers with auditory tendencies—they were incessant talkers partially from fear of losing the attention of the listeners. It was obvious that the intention of wanting students to hear them was noble, but in fact the opposite was occurring—the more the student teacher talked the less the students were listening. It almost seems that the more one speaks the less importance is given to what is said. Only recently has Priscilla discovered the necessity of holding the *Frozen Hand Gesture*[6] during the pause to maintain attention. This mesmerizing technique is now a Perceptive Priscilla signature that is imprinted on every intern's behavioral style.

© 2000 by Michael Grinder & Assoc., ARR. AHC03 (360) 687-3238; FAX (360) 687-0595; http://www.michaelgrinder.com

Barometers [7]

2-4

(What is a *barometer* and how does the concept mesh with classroom dynamics?)

In any class dynamic setting, there are pupils who are barometers of the health of the class. These individuals signal, like a pebble dropped in a pond, that larger ramifications will follow the initial smaller circles of reactions.

Examples in Nature

Miners take canaries into mines with them because the birds' breathing is more vulnerable than that of humans. If the birds stop singing, it is the signal for the miners to run to *safety*.

Likewise, vineyards have roses planted at the end of the rows of grapes. The roses are more susceptible to diseases than the grapes. If the roses look healthy then the grapes are *safe*. The birds and flowers are barometers for the miners and vitners.

Characteristics

A student is a barometer if he has the following three qualities:

1. The student is a member of a subgroup.

2. The student tends to react sooner/ quicker/before the rest of the subgroup. And the student's reaction is a representation of how the subgroup will react in time.

3. The teacher can easily read the student's reaction.

    It would be wonderful if there were barometers for the entire class. As the class formation occurs, subgroups emerge. Each subgroup's common denominator varies. The common bond is usually a specific value, style or content. In newly formed groups, there are usually four to six students who are the barometers. Watching these people allows the teacher to read the class. The categories that the subgroups are clustered around are varied: humor, speaking out, curiosity, higher level thinking, fairness,

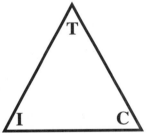

Individual   Subgroup

barometer of --------- *humor*	*membership*
barometer of -------- *critical*	*membership*
barometer of ------ *kindness*	*membership*
barometer of ---------- *detail*	*membership*

© 2000 by Michael Grinder & Assoc., ARR. AHC03 (360) 687-3238; FAX (360) 687-0595; http://www.michaelgrinder.com

neatness/orderliness, questioning/skeptical, productivity, morale, style of thinking/processing.

The numbers of subgroups are endless and very age-group specific. Students belong to more than one subgroup. Generically speaking, look for the following barometers:[8]

- Clarity—if this particular student understands the concept and what to do, the teacher can presume that the rest of the class also understands.

- Left-brain oriented—if this student is following, the teacher is most likely being logical, linear and sequential enough for all the pupils who think similarly.

- Entertainment—if this future HBO couch potato is chuckling frequently enough, the teacher is maintaining a sense of humor.

- Kinesthetic-oriented student—if this student is learning, the unit has enough hands-on content and is personalized enough for everyone.

- Difficult-time-grasping—this is frequently a special-needs student who warrants additional assistance. Often this student can only be accommodated during the *Seatwork* portion of the lesson.[9]

Vignettes of Barometers

Mrs. Melodie Pitch is about to start the music appreciation unit of *Peter and the Wolf*. Knowing that some of the children still have difficulty distinguishing between fantasy and reality, she sets a picture of each character, including the animals, on the chalk tray. Explaining that this is a story and everything turns out fine at the end, the teacher places a Post-it of a smile over each of the pictures. Melodie's barometer is Bailey. To say that Bailey Bawl is a sensitive third grader is an understatement. In the scene where the bird starts to dive down at the wolf and the wolf lunges at Sasha, Bailey Bawl's eyes are watering up. The teacher stops the video and, standing next to the pictures, she reminds the class that this is pretend and that everything is going to turn out fine. Mrs. Pitch knows that if her timing is off and she reminds the class after they are too afraid for the animals, she will have a hard time with them emotionally recovering. By watching Bailey Bawl, the barometer of sensitivity and kindness, the teacher can proactively intervene.

---

continued on next page

© 2000 by Michael Grinder & Assoc., ARR. AHC03 (360) 687-3238; FAX (360) 687-0595; http://www.michaelgrinder.com

Leonard Linear is a solid A student. His mind is logical and he processes information sequentially. If he is confused about one detail, his mind stops hearing the next information that is delivered by the instructor. Rebecca Random is a fine 9th grade history teacher. She is self-aware and knows her presentation is sometimes global and intuitive. By peripherally watching Leonard Linear, Rebecca Random is cued when her style does not match with the more left-brain oriented pupils. She has also discovered that the more she visually writes on the board, the more she can show where different information, especially tangential stories, fits in the larger timeline.

Using Barometers Proactively

2-5

(How does a teacher use *barometers proactively* to "read a class?")

What are the benefits of being able to recognize barometers? Since one of the most important components of classroom dynamics is to be proactive, barometers will indicate early how the rest of the barometer's subgroup members will soon be. If the teacher doesn't want the subgroup to react as the barometer is reacting, the teacher changes. (E.g., she steps to the side while breathing.[10] This influences the listeners to have amnesia about what happened or who did it.) Literally, the teacher is reactive with barometers to be proactive with the subgroup. The example used is of a teacher who presents a complex concept.

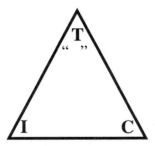

Teacher starts to explain a complex concept.

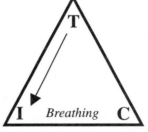

Teacher notices barometer of hard-time grasping subgroup starts to breathe high.

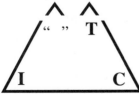

Teacher steps to a new location before the hard-time grasping subgroup is aware that they are going to initially struggle.

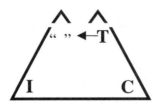

Teacher (looking and pointing to the concept on the board) says, "Some of us may find this concept difficult to understand. Be patient and we will do fine."

© 2000 by Michael Grinder & Assoc., ARR. AHC03 (360) 687-3238; FAX (360) 687-0595; http://www.michaelgrinder.com

Disclaimer

What does a teacher do when she "steps in it?"

Disclaimer gives new meaning to being beside oneself.

In the previous section, the teacher read the barometer and in so doing appeared proactive to the subgroup. The teacher read the subgroup's resistance through that subgroup's barometer and acknowledged the resistance. But what can a teacher do if the subgroup has already negatively reacted to something the teacher did? For instance, when the subgroup has reacted adversely to the joke, the teacher steps to the side while breathing. This is the same maneuver mentioned in *Using Barometers Proactively*.[11] Instead of acknowledging resistance, the teacher is dissociating herself from the joke; e.g., "We are not here to tell jokes, especially one that is so insensitive. [The teacher gestures back to the spot where she had told the joke.] Our focus today is a very serious subject."

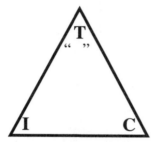

Teacher tells a joke.

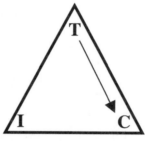

Teacher notices subgroup of fairness shocked and holds breath.

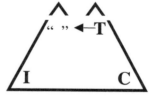

Teacher steps to a new location.

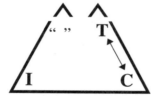

"We (gesturing between the class and teacher) are not here to tell jokes."

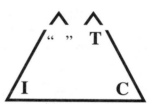

Teacher (looking and pointing to the joke location) says, "Some of us may be offended by that joke, and for good reasons...." Then the teacher continues with amnesia to the faux pas.

© 2000 by Michael Grinder & Assoc., ARR. AHC03 (360) 687-3238; FAX (360) 687-0595; http://www.michaelgrinder.com

2-6

Interpretation of Class Voice Patterns

(How does a teacher interpret the class' voice undulation?)

Most of the information about *Reading the Class* is based on visual cues. There are also a number of audio patterns that indicate where a class is.

When the pupils are doing small group work the teacher often wonders what the clues are that determine when to bring them back to the next lecture portion of the presentation. Listening to the collective voice patterns can provide the teacher with invaluable information.

When the collective sounds are flat, the members are still learning, processing or concentrating = credible (⟍). If the collective voices are more rolling/rhythmic and of varying pitches, the class is socializing = approachable (∧∧↗).

This auditory method of *hearing a class* allows the teacher to make more effective decisions. The decisions are based on the outcomes the teacher has. For instance, if the pupils are in new cooperative learning groups and the teacher hears the collective voice pattern in the room switch from flat to rhythmic, the teacher may choose to let the individual groups continue to socialize because their safety as a unit is partially based on their comfort with each other. If the teacher's outcome is productivity, the teacher asks for attention as the class changes from a flat to rhythmic voice pattern.

© 2000 by Michael Grinder & Assoc., ARR. AHC03 (360) 687-3238; FAX (360) 687-0595; http://www.michaelgrinder.com

2-7

Class' Values

How does a teacher determine the culture of a class?

In Chapter One the idea of understanding the class by understanding the individuals who make up the class was exposed as faulty thinking. Instead, the culture of a class is understood by viewing the collective composite of the group. One of the ways of accomplishing this is to recognize that the leaders reflect the values of the class as a whole. The following includes three different approaches to recognizing the values of the class.

Credible vs. Approachable Leaders

The suggestion is that students can be categorized by their voice patterns. One pole of the voice pattern continuum will be labeled "credible" and the other "approachable." The description of the two types is:

Category	Credibility	Approachability
Head	Still	Bobs
Voice undulation	Flat ——	Rhythmic ⌇⌇
Intonation	Curls down ↘	Curls Up ⌇➤
Results in	"Sends information"	"Seeks information"
Gender association	Male	Female
Position	Superior	Subordinate

The teacher is interested in voice patterns because the patterns can provide the teacher with information on the personality of the class. The ultimate purpose is to understand whether the class' personality encourages health. *A Healthy Classroom* proposes that the more students have credible voice patterns, the more they value accountability. And, conversely, the more the students have approachable voice patterns the more they value acceptability.

A healthy classroom holds students accountable for their behavior while simultaneously accepts the students as people.

This work suggests that a healthy classroom is one in which the students are both being held accountable for their behavior and simultaneously accepted as people. Teachers want to foster both voice patterns since the goal is a healthy classroom. Educators want to have those students who have the most credible voice patterns display high acceptance of other members, while those students who have the most approachable voices

© 2000 by Michael Grinder & Assoc., ARR. AHC03 (360) 687-3238; FAX (360) 687-0595; http://www.michaelgrinder.com

display high accountability toward members. When this condition is present, the class dynamics is healthy. The previous chart can be expanded to:

Seeks	High Productivity	High Morale

Analyzing Group Dynamics as Seen by Students

The following applies to group situations both inside and outside a classroom.

Ask a class that has been formed to look at a list of everyone's name and select the five people they personally "look up to" (or other equivalent wording which would indicate the leadership of the class—apart from titular positions).

> Who do you "look up to"?
> Put a check next to five names.
> Larry
> Abby
> Lisa
> Albert
> Chris
> Carol
> _____
> _____

Analysis One:

Tally all the votes. Then respectfully listen to the "leaders'" voice patterns. If the collective votes indicate that the selected leaders are more at one end of the voice pattern continuum than the other, the teacher knows what the class' composite values are.

Analysis Two:

In Analysis One, the focus was on the class' composite values. Analysis Two focuses on each member's values. Look at each individual's list of five leaders. If an individual selected all or most of her leaders from one end of the voice pattern continuum, then the teacher knows that student's values. If an individual's selected leaders are from both ends of the voice pattern continuum, the individual is balanced, and an excellent person to assist in the formation of a healthy classroom.[12] For the sake of simplicity, the examples only show some names and pretend the names beginning with the letter "A" (i.e., Abby and Albert) have approachable voice patterns; the names beginning with the letter "C" (i.e., Chris and Carol) have credible voice patterns.

© 2000 by Michael Grinder & Assoc., ARR. AHC03 (360) 687-3238; FAX (360) 687-0595; http://www.michaelgrinder.com

Who do you "look up to"? Put a check next to five names. Larry Abby ✓ Lisa Albert ✓ Chris Carol _____ _____	Who do you "look up to"? Put a check next to five names. Larry Abby Lisa Albert Chris ✓ Carol ✓ _____ _____	Who do you "look up to"? Put a check next to five names. Larry Abby ✓ Lisa Albert Chris ✓ Carol ✓ _____ _____
Person X selected people with approachable voice pattern.	Person Y selected people with credible voice pattern.	Person Z selected people who had a variety of voice patterns.

Analysis Three:

Look at Analysis One and Analysis Two preceding. In Analysis One, the tabulation was collective. In Analysis Two, the analysis was done individually. Sometimes the overview from Analysis One would indicate a balanced class, but after further viewing, Analysis Two might indicate that the individual members either picked leaders from just one end or the other of the voice pattern continuum. Person X is drawn to people who are approachable whereas person Y likes leaders who are credible. This means that the class is very split. Usually this results in a class operating in a very divided way. What is needed are students who are *liaisons*.

Analysis Four:

Ask a class to follow the same directions as above, and, in addition, place their selected leaders on a scale of "wants high productivity" to "wants high morale."

If some individuals have a selected leader at the "wants high productivity" end and that same selected leader appears on someone else's list as "wanting high morale," then the selected leader is a collective liaison for a healthy class.

Person X's Sheet

Who do you "look up to"?
Put a check next to five names, then indicate if you see the person representing which of the two commitments.

	High Productivity	High Morale
Larry	✓	
Abby		
Lisa	✓	
Albert		
Chris		
Carol		
_____		
_____		

Person Y's Sheet

Who do you "look up to"?
Put a check next to five names, then indicate if you see the person representing which of the two commitments.

	High Productivity	High Morale
Larry		✓
Abby		
Lisa		✓
Albert		
Chris		
Carol		
_____		
_____		

© 2000 by Michael Grinder & Assoc., ARR. AHC03 (360) 687-3238; FAX (360) 687-0595; http://www.michaelgrinder.com

For the sake of simplicity, the names with the letter "L" (i.e., Larry and Lisa) are seen by some members as representing one commitment (high productivity) and by others as representing the other commitment (high morale). ("L" = liaison.) If a class doesn't have liaisons, then attempt to foster them.

Analysis Five:

If the selected leaders who are placed at the "wants high productivity" end have approachable voices and those selected leaders who are placed at the "wants high morale" end have credible voices, then the class is already operating in a healthy atmosphere. The ramifications of using the above are endless. They range from understanding faculties to families to corporations and to the training room.

Analyzing Group Dynamics from the Teacher/Observer's Perspective

The preceding was an analysis by the teacher based on input from the members. An alternative is to have the teacher watch the members and, by observation, make the same analysis as above.

Analysis One:

If the teacher's observations indicates that the selected leaders are more at one end of the voice pattern continuum, then the teacher knows what the composite values of the class are.

Analysis Two:

Observe which pupils each student admires. If a class member selects leaders from one end of the voice pattern continuum, then the teacher knows the values of that class member. If the class member selects leaders from both ends of the voice pattern continuum, then the individual is balanced and an excellent person to assist in fostering a healthy classroom.

Analysis Three:

In Analysis Two, the analysis was done individually. A close view of Analysis Two might indicate that some members individually admire leaders from just one end of the voice pattern continuum while other members admire leaders from the opposite end of the voice pattern continuum. This means that the class is very split. Usually this results in a class operating in a very divided way. What is needed are students who are *liaisons*, that is, students who are seen by some pupils as committed to high productivity and perceived by other classmates as committed to high morale.

© 2000 by Michael Grinder & Assoc., ARR. AHC03 (360) 687-3238; FAX (360) 687-0595; http://www.michaelgrinder.com

If possible, the teacher would profit from having another educator observe the teacher's class and offer an analysis.

> **Vignette: Sensitivity Training**
>
> Any of us who have experienced "sensitivity training" will recall the awkwardness of the initial phase of the group formation as new members resist and the group, as a whole, flounders because there is no "lead" person. In that culture anyone who does "lead" is either immediately or later chastised for assuming such a posture. From a group dynamic standpoint, we need to remember that the *length* of time the sensitivity group would be together is long—that's why they are often called *marathon sessions*.

2-8

The Value of a Liaison

(Why is a *liaison* so valuable?)

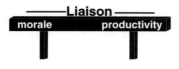

Class' Values[13] indicates that the most valuable student in any classroom is a liaison. A "liaison" is seen by some colleagues as being committed to, and motivated by, productivity and by other colleagues as committed to, and motivated by, morale. Literally, a liaison has membership in multiple subgroups. This means that the liaison has a range of behaviors. The liaison's colleagues see him as a leader, which is interpreted as evidence that the liaison is systematic when exhibiting various behaviors.

As a teacher, there is a direct correlation between the health of a class and the number of liaisons who are present.[14] The teacher will want to learn the strategies to foster students into liaison roles. As a faculty member, the fastest way to increase one's own value on the staff is to increase one's liaison profile.

2-9

Fostered Leaders

(Why *foster* a student into a *leader*?)

There are certain ingredients, values, characteristics that the teacher wants present in a class (i.e., qualities like: A–punctuality, B–curiosity, C–kindness, D–ambition). Employing techniques such as *Class Values* assists the teacher in knowing which values are part of the classroom culture.

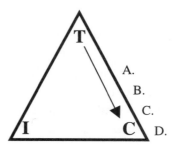

© 2000 by Michael Grinder & Assoc., ARR. AHC03 (360) 687-3238; FAX (360) 687-0595; http://www.michaelgrinder.com

If certain desirable qualities are absent, the teacher can look for members who do have these characteristics (e.g., quality D).

Then the teacher can foster these pupils to become leaders by giving the individuals attention.

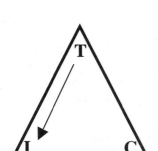

I with quality D

This only works after the teacher has rapport with the class. The class has to be drawn to the teacher for fostering to occur.

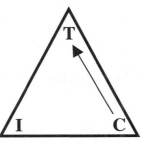

When the class sees the teacher giving selected individuals attention, and they, too, want the teacher's attention, the class tends to emulate the individuals who are being fostered. On the primary level the fostering is done openly. "I like the way Philip and Janet are ready." Because of peer pressure at the higher grades, the fostering has to be subtle.

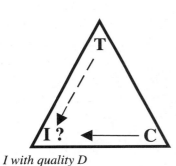

I with quality D

This results in the class exhibiting the quality the teacher is looking for in the class.

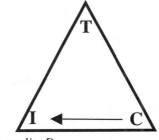

I with quality D

© 2000 by Michael Grinder & Assoc., ARR. AHC03 (360) 687-3238; FAX (360) 687-0595; http://www.michaelgrinder.com

Vignettes: Conspiracy of Love

Pete Petree has been teaching science at the high school for fifteen years. He is known to be demanding of his students. Over the years the word has spread that although he is a task master, students leave well prepared for college. What the pupils don't know is his conscious formula of group dynamics. His fourth period chemistry class has diligent students but lacks something. Besides having the class be ready for university rigors, he wants them to be curious about the world around them. Pete privately learns that two of his students who are shy but respected by their mates are really into skateboarding. Using the Internet, Pete discovers the patented protected ingredients of the latest skateboards. He then shares this information with the IT instructor, Molly Modem. He then privately and casually talks to the two skateboard aficionados: "I wonder what they put into the boards to make them so durable, flexible and lightweight?" They ask Mrs. Modem if they can use the computer to investigate some information. Molly, as rehearsed, makes sure the boys will have to do some hunting but will be successful. The next day two boys burst into the classroom with enough energy to power the lights of the whole city. Mr. Petree makes sure class time is given to the sharing of their discoveries. As a student in the back of the room says in a catty manner, "Do they get extra credit for that?" Pete, with a look as if he was thinking about the question for the first time, replies, "I guess so." Within a week the majority of the class members are seeking permission to research things they are personally interested in. The goal of having the students connect what they are learning inside the classroom with reality has been achieved.

Abigail Acumen always enjoys teaching the highest readers of the fifth grade. This select group doesn't need motivation–just time to do what they enjoy. This year is much like other ones—the group is so serious. They just want to read and write book reports. Abigail knows the importance of educating the full person. While these top students are not comfortable with open-ended activities such as creative writing and role play, it is these flexible skills that they need most. Outside of class, Abigail accidentally overhears Randy Recluse, the raconteur. His humor is clever. Over the course of the next week, Abigail gradually makes Randy more comfortable. Initially, she "sandwiches" him with other people.[15] E.g., "I was impressed with Sally, Randy and

continued on next page

© 2000 by Michael Grinder & Assoc., ARR. AHC03 (360) 687-3238; FAX (360) 687-0595; http://www.michaelgrinder.com

Mattie's papers last night. Would Jim, Randy and Alice read aloud the next three paragraphs?"

It is early October and Randy Recluse is becoming familiar with the limelight. Ms. Acumen privately asks Randy to pick a friend and together read Abbott & Costello's, baseball farce, "Who's on First?" By the time Halloween arrives the class is more comfortable with skits and being humorous—all led by Randy Recluse's example—because "if he can do it, so can we."

Summary

This chapter demystifies the art of reading the class. The paradigm for the teacher is to stay outside herself and watch the class' response. This is the method for identifying the leaders. This informs the teacher, either directly or indirectly, with which pupils the teacher needs to have rapport. The teacher doesn't want to think about who her leaders are. She suspends her perception and instead notices the class' perception. Otherwise, she could manage a student whom the other pupils are not even noticing. By managing, the teacher calls the class' attention to the inappropriate student, and in so doing the teacher inadvertently creates an inappropriate leader. The concept of barometers allows the teacher to switch from an arduous template of reading every student to a much more manageable blueprint, one in which there are usually four to six leaders and three to five key barometers. Sometimes the same student is both a leader and a barometer. The competency of interpreting the collective voice patterns during cooperative learning activities hones the teacher's timing of when to intervene and bring the class' focus back to the teacher. And finally, the teacher can create the classroom micro-culture desired by fostering students who represent the qualities the teacher wants.

© 2000 by Michael Grinder & Assoc., ARR. AHC03 (360) 687-3238; FAX (360) 687-0595; http://www.michaelgrinder.com

Rubric for Chapter Two: Reading the Class

	Struggling Novice	Apprentice	Scientist	Artisan of Healthy Classroom
Class Leaders, pp. 58-65	The teacher operates from power, and therefore the only leaders are resistant leaders.	The only leaders the teacher perceives as leaders are the ones the teacher selects.	The teacher recognizes the class' perception of their leaders.	The teacher shares leadership with the class, and leaders change over time.
Class Barometers, p. 67	The teacher doesn't recognize that subgroups are formed. The teacher sees the class as a whole.	The teacher knows there are subgroups but doesn't recognize them.	The teacher can recognize subgroups in the room and know their memberships.	The teacher utilizes the barometers' reactions to proactively acknowledge the subgroups' reactions.
Class Values, p. 72	The inconsistency of the teacher is such that there are no values or culture.	The teacher's values are based on a philosophy which is inconsistently present. The teacher reinforces them with power.	The values of the classroom are based on the teacher's values and they are operational.	The teacher is aware of and can read the class' values; operates on the concept of the class as a culture.
Class Liaisons p. 76	There are camps in the room which are uncooperative with each other.	There are subgroups in the room which don't communicate with each other.	The pupils have a fluidity in that they have membership in many subgroups.	There are lots of liaisons, and the concept of leadership is blurred.
Fostered Leaders, p. 76	The teacher operates from dictatorship, and being a teacher's pet can change with the wind.	The teacher promotes students based on favoritism.	The pupils see teacher's fostered leader as a leader.	The teacher fosters leaders based on the values the teacher wants to add to the class culture.

Transcends the Educational Culture

© 2000 by Michael Grinder & Assoc., ARR. AHC03 (360) 687-3238; FAX (360) 687-0595; http://www.michaelgrinder.com

Chapter Two Post-its

Leaders

Who are the class' leaders? Are they different than the ones I would have liked them to select? Do I share leadership when appropriate?

Chapter Two: Reading the Class, pp. 58-65.

Values, the Class' and Mine

What are the class' values? Are they different than mine? Am I recognizing and adjusting to the classroom culture?

Chapter Two: Reading the Class, pp. 72-76.

Barometers, Identifying

Who are the barometers of the important subgroups?

Chapter Two: Reading the Class, pp. 67-68.

Liaisons

Who are the liaisons or potential liaisons? Are liaisons replacing leaders?

Chapter Two: Reading the Class, p. 76.

Barometers, Utilizing

How am I proactively utilizing the barometers?

Chapter Two: Reading the Class, p. 69.

Fostering Students

What are the values I want to add to the culture? Which students would it be helpful to foster?

Chapter Two: Reading the Class, pp. 76-77.

© 2000 by Michael Grinder & Assoc., ARR. AHC03 (360) 687-3238; FAX (360) 687-0595; http://www.michaelgrinder.com

End Notes

1. See the *Approachable-oriented Class*, p. 190.

2. See p. 173.

3. See the concept of *ABOVE (Pause) Whisper, ENVoY*, p. 18.

4. See p. 63.

5. See *ENVoY*, p. 18.

6. See details in *ENVoY II*.

7. A leader and a barometer are descriptions of different functions in a group. A student could be a leader, a barometer, neither or both.

8. Chapter Six, p. 173, has a list of students that the teacher wants to preventively manage; those categories of subgroups can be added to the above list.

9. For further information, read *Osmotic Learning*, p. 158.

10. These maneuvers are called *Decontamination* (*ENVoY* p. 58) and *Break and Breathe* (*ENVoY* p. 62).

11. These maneuvers are called *Decontamination* (*ENVoY* p. 58) and *Break and Breathe* (*ENVoY* p. 62).

12. See *The Value of a Liaison*, p. 76.

13. See p. 72.

14. Expanded in Chapter Five.

15. See *ENVoY II* for a further explanation of the sandwich technique.

© 2000 by Michael Grinder & Assoc., ARR. AHC03 (360) 687-3238; FAX (360) 687-0595; http://www.michaelgrinder.com

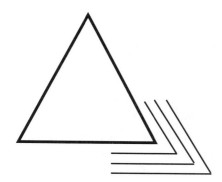

STAGES

Each student has an invisible number of coupons for raising their hands. If a student like the dog in the front row has exceeded her number, then the rest of the class begins to progress through stages of irritability. The dog in the back left corner is confused. The cat at the front left is annoyed. And the back right corner cat is bored/ignored. The teacher is aware that the dog with her hand up is in jeopardy of being emotionally removed from the classroom community. The teacher has his left hand extended towards the student indicating, "Not now!"

To be respectful of gender equality and yet provide the educator with a fluid reading style, in this chapter the teacher is referred to by the male pronoun and the student by the female pronoun.

Introduction

Changes in class dynamics are based on several factors. Chapter One deals with the formation of the class. One of the major indicators that the class is becoming a unit is each student becomes more familiar with her classmates. Chapter Two focuses on how to read the dynamics as it forms and after it occurs. Chapter Two extends Chapter One's concept of familiarity because the first students to emerge as being unique are the leaders.

Chapter Three expands the concept of familiarity to what happens when a student is seen as inappropriate. There are three stages a class progresses through when inappropriateness is perceived. In addition to a student being the source of the inappropriateness, the class itself or the teacher could be. Each stage warrants a different response from the teacher. These stages are often intuitively sensed by teachers. This chapter will remove the cloak of mystery and explain the sensory specific evidence of each stage and effective responses.

Utilizing the concept of three stages, many questions about classroom dynamics patterns are addressed. When can a teacher attempt to *save* a student from progressing through the three stages? What will happen if a teacher attempts to privately manage a student and the student doesn't comply? When is a student a *bully* and why can't a teacher explain to such a student how her behavior is detrimental to the class' learning? Under what circumstances can a teacher effectively protect a student from the class' feedback when the class is annoyed with the student? How can a teacher recognize which students' status needs to be increased or decreased because of the health of the class as a whole? And what are the techniques to increase or decrease a student's status?

Three Stages of Irritability

> What are the *three stages* a class goes through when behavior is seen as inappropriate?

There are three stages a class goes through as the class sees an individual student as inappropriate: shocked, confused and annoyed. The following are the descriptions of each stage with a sensory specific description of that pattern of classroom dynamics. This specificity of the evidence allows the teacher to make accurate observations for deciding which effective responses are warranted. These stages can occur very quickly, as is often the case in sixth through tenth grade classrooms, or over a period of time. When the teacher is part of the class from its inception, the teacher can chart the progression of the class' reaction from one stage to the next stage. However, if the teacher enters an environment where the

© 2000 by Michael Grinder & Assoc., ARR. AHC03 (360) 687-3238; FAX (360) 687-0595; http://www.michaelgrinder.com

dynamics are already set—the liability of substitute teachers—then it is likely that one or more students are perceived in the second or third stage. The teacher must recognize the physiological indicators of the three stages and respond appropriately.

Shocked

The first stage is when the class is shocked. The class will freeze and often physically pull back. The room is often very quiet. At this stage of the class' reaction to the individual, the suggestion is that the teacher politely respond. The rationale for the teacher responding with a great deal of politeness and gentleness stems from the concept of *Unique*.[1] When the class doesn't see the student who is acting inappropriately as different enough from them, the class thinks how the teacher responds to that particular student is how the teacher will treat everyone. For example, if a fourth grader tries to be funny but acts in a manner that is more common to second graders, the students might be shocked. As they pull their heads back and hold their breath, they turn and look at the student. However, if the teacher reprimands the student, the rest of the students often will hold their breath even more and look straight down. From Chapter Two the teacher knows that where the class looks is an indication of who provides the safety in the room. If the class is looking down then neither the teacher nor the class is providing the safety; hence, an unsafe classroom.

By understanding the stages, the teacher knows that in a very short amount of time the pupils will become familiar with each other and they will see certain students as different from the rest of them. Then how the teacher manages these students in no way indicates how the teacher would treat the rest of the class.

Confused

If the student continues with such inappropriate behavior, the second stage is entered, one in which the class is confused. The confusion is evidenced when the class freezes and their foreheads have wrinkles on them. If the teacher clearly sees that the class, collectively, is at this stage, the teacher may want to indicate to the student some form of "see me after class." The teacher is attempting a two-prong rapport: satisfying the class' need to not take the class' time, and simultaneously main-

Answer gently intervene

T

I   C

1st ——————————— Shocked:
• *head pulled back*
• *breath held*

3-1

Delay "See me after class"

T

I   C

2nd ——————————— Confused:
• *head pulled back*
• *breath held*
• *furrowed forehead*
• *slight turning toward each other*

3-2

© 2000 by Michael Grinder & Assoc., ARR. AHC03 (360) 687-3238; FAX (360) 687-0595; http://www.michaelgrinder.com

taining rapport with the individual student by attempting to manage the student privately.

It is essential that the teacher convey to the student the importance of "cease and desist." Sometimes this is done privately[2] and other times it is better to reprimand so that other students know the student has been managed. It is recommended the teacher do some form of *"See me after class."* As the class starts to distinguish the individual as somewhat different from "them," the class begins to think the teacher's reactions to that individual won't apply to how the teacher will treat the rest of the class.

> **The complexity of coordinating all three corners of the classroom triangle is the ultimate artistry of educational group dynamics.**

3-3

Annoyed

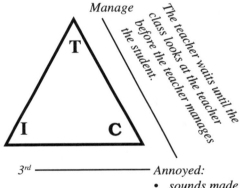

Manage

The teacher waits until the class looks at the teacher before the teacher manages the student.

3rd ——————— *Annoyed:*
- *sounds made*
- *full turning to look at each other*

If the student persists in the inappropriateness, the class transitions into the third stage of annoyance. Of the three stages, the annoyance stage has the clearest evidence because the class makes sounds such as "tsk" and "Oh..." Also, the class isn't frozen but moving; e.g., shuffling papers –resulting in background noises. The class is not safe unless the teacher manages the individual or at least indicates to the class that the teacher is cognizant that the individual student is inappropriate. Hopefully, the management is done in a location other than where the main content is dealt with. As management finishes, the teacher returns to the location of the main content and continues with *amnesia*.[3] If the teacher has *proactive* timing, the teacher is managing for the purpose of acknowledging to the class that the teacher, like the class, sees the student as acting inappropriately. If the teacher is *reactive,* the teacher is acting "fix-it."

The ramification of these three stages and the timing needed to effectively respond is the subject of the rest of this chapter. For example, if the teacher isn't stern enough with the student and the student persists and the class becomes *annoyed,* the teacher is caught. If the teacher does manage the student, which is what the class wants the teacher to do, the student is startled/upset because she feels there wasn't sufficient warning. On the other hand, if the teacher realizes that the student doesn't

© 2000 by Michael Grinder & Assoc., ARR. AHC03 (360) 687-3238; FAX (360) 687-0595; http://www.michaelgrinder.com

know the management is coming and the teacher has to warn the student, which is what the student thinks *is fair,* the class is upset because the teacher is out of synch with the stage the class is at.

Summary of Three Stages of Irritability

When a class sees an individual member acting inappropriately and that individual continues the behavior, the class goes through **three stages**:

1. Shocked

2. Confused

3. Annoyed

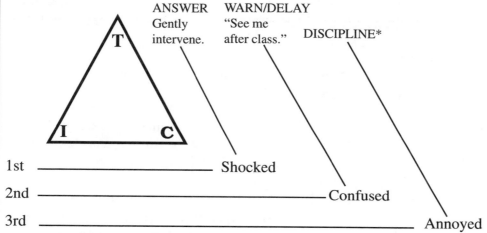

Physiological indicators of stages:

Shocked:
- head pulled back
- breath held

Confused:
- head pulled back
- breath held
- furrowed forehead
- slight turning toward each other

Annoyed:
- sounds made
- full turning to look at each other

_____
* Discipline has consequences. Management is preventive discipline..

© 2000 by Michael Grinder & Assoc., ARR. AHC03 (360) 687-3238; FAX (360) 687-0595; http://www.michaelgrinder.com

3-4

The purpose of a management-discipline system is to change the person. The purpose of just discipline is to isolate the person.

3-5

Ignoring–The Fourth Stage

If the student continues to act inappropriately, the class will progress through the three stages. There is a fourth stage that sometimes occurs—*ignoring*. The individual's behaviors innately attract attention; therefore, for the class to function, they ignore the individual. The class' non-verbal reactions indicate that the person is **not a member**. This is the stage after **annoyed**.

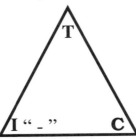 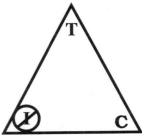

Individual is inappropriate.   *Class goes about what they are doing.*

While the first three stages are detrimental to the class dynamics, the fourth stage can be positive.

When a member of the class is placed in the category of *ignoring,* the entire health of the classroom suffers. This chapter speaks to preventing the student from being placed in the *annoyed* and *ignored* categories. In particular, the concepts of *Fairness, Saving* and *Protecting an Individual Student* address this. The teacher doesn't want to be lured into being *nice* to the student hoping that the student will change. As unhealthy as it is for the class to have a student in the *annoyed* and *ignored* dungeons, it is even more destructive for the teacher not to manage the student because the class will become confused or annoyed with the teacher.[4] The next concept addresses how to manage appropriately at these two stages.

> *Attention-Getting Behavior - Permission + Over Time = Class Ignores*

Fairness

When the individual's inappropriate behavior has continued and the class enters the *confused* stage, it is an opportunity for the teacher to be *fair* to the individual. The individual needs some form of warning that the teacher will be much harsher if the individual's inappropriate behavior continues. When the teacher says some form of *"See me after class...,"* the non-verbals of the teacher's face, voice and body need to convey the warning about what might happen if the student continues behaving inappropriately. A fair warning is very humane because the individual is in jeopardy of being excluded from the class.

© 2000 by Michael Grinder & Assoc., ARR. AHC03 (360) 687-3238; FAX (360) 687-0595; http://www.michaelgrinder.com

Many teachers operate with the criteria of kindness and rapport which was forged in the mold of a *one-on-one relationship*. Consequently, the teacher is uncomfortable being harsh to individuals. The teacher, based on classroom dynamics, will need to provide the class the safety the group deserves so that the class can function. By the teacher clearly indicating what the consequence is if the inappropriate behavior persists, the individual is behaviorally making a choice. *Fairness* can be measured by two parties: the individual and the class. It would be silly for teachers of certain grade levels to expect their managed student to approach the teacher afterwards and say, "Thank you for being fair; I deserved that consequence." Realistically, the teacher looks to the class for feedback on whether the teacher was fair when managing the student. Fairness has two ingredients: being consistent and letting pupils know the consequence is about to happen. When the class is at the confused stage and the teacher warns the student, the class sees the teacher as fair.

A yellow light is fair because it warns.

Vignettes: Stages

Amiable Aimie

Amiable Aimie is just *nice*. One couldn't find a *nicer* person. Until now her career has been exclusively on the primary level. She has been professionally raised to operate, "Let's love everyone into being the person they can become." This year for the first time, Aimie is teaching fourth grade and she has Naughty Ned, who thrives on attention. Aimie is inadvertently reinforcing Ned's inappropriateness. The more Naughty Ned acts out, the more Amiable Aimie gives him attention. Behaviorally, she has blurred the distinctions between the first three phases of the lesson and the fourth phase of a lesson. The first three phases are designed as being group-oriented; it is only after the class is occupied that the teacher gives the individual student attention. In essence, Naughty Ned is the lowest common denominator in the class and everyone's learning is suffering because the teacher automatically stops all reality to deal with him.

Bold Buddy

Bold Buddy has a teaching background mainly in junior high. It is early October of his first year in the third grade. When a student steps out of line, Bold Buddy is quick to step in. The teacher thinks putting his foot down creates order and high expectations. Just the opposite occurs; the students are afraid of his wrath. He may have control, but because of the students breathing high/shallow they are not learning as well as they could.

continued on next page

© 2000 by Michael Grinder & Assoc., ARR. AHC03 (360) 687-3238; FAX (360) 687-0595; http://www.michaelgrinder.com

Centered Cathy

Centered Cathy has taught long enough to have a repertoire of responses and yet is still very fresh in her enthusiasm and belief that she can make a difference–which she does. When Naughty Ned, who had Amiable Aimie last year, enters fifth grade, he thinks last year's ground rules apply–the teacher is gentle when intervening with him. By the time the class is in session for the third week, he is baffled by Centered Cathy. When he starts on his antics, the teacher, without even looking at him, says his name. As he looks up, the only attention he gets is a stop hand extended toward him. The teacher is talking about the lesson. If he persists, the teacher has a prearranged method of holding up one finger indicating a warning. (Centered Cathy once privately joked with an intern, "Now be prudent when selecting which finger to point toward the student–this is fifth grade.") If the second finger appears, Naughty Ned goes to the back corner and sits at an isolated desk to do his work. On the surface it seems like Centered Cathy is employing classic effective management techniques. And while this is accurate, what is important is to realize that the employment is based not on the individual student, but the timing of what stage the class is at.

Centered Cathy is gentle during the first two weeks of school because the class, which was a new composition from Naughty Ned's fourth grade classroom, had to develop an awareness that Naughty Ned is different from them. Consequently, anything the teacher does with him does not necessarily mean that that is how she would treat them.

3-6

Saving an Individual Student

(How does one save an individual?)

If the teacher tries to save an individual student from being ostracized, the following needs to be considered. The teacher's protection of a student needs to be done before the class is annoyed with the individual. If the teacher attempts to save an individual student after the class is annoyed with the student, there is a tendency for the class to associate the teacher with the individual, making the teacher guilty by association. For example, the class perceives that the individual is asking too many questions. The following diagrams illustrate the least-recommended and the recommended things the teacher can do when he wants to save an individual student from the class' input.

© 2000 by Michael Grinder & Assoc., ARR. AHC03 (360) 687-3238; FAX (360) 687-0595; http://www.michaelgrinder.com

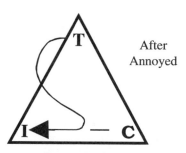

After
Annoyed

Least Recommended

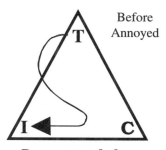

Before
Annoyed

Recommended

The class's tension is mounting as the individual asks the fourth question in a row. They are looking annoyed at the individual. The teacher says, "Shh, let's listen politely." The class rolls their eyes because they cannot believe the teacher.

The tendency is for the class to be annoyed with both the student and teacher. The classic case of "guilt by association."

The individual has just asked the third question in a row and the teacher notices the indicators of the class being in the "confusion" phase. The teacher says, "Sally, let's you and I talk about this after we start the assignment." The class is relieved.

This strategy of *when* to attempt to save an individual student has great ramifications for our current educational matrix of "least restrictive environment" for special needs students. While educators believe that all students can learn, many educational systems cannot financially provide what is needed to act on this credo. As a result, the class has a tendency, and sometimes the teacher has the same tendency, to see the special needs student as thwarting their academic progress. Understanding when to intervene will create a healthier classroom–intervene before the class is annoyed.

As long as the class knows a consequence is coming, the teacher is fair.

What are *saving* techniques? The *saving* techniques can basically be placed on a continuum which has one terminal labeled "private" and the other end "public." An example of the first type of technique is when a

© 2000 by Michael Grinder & Assoc., ARR. AHC03 (360) 687-3238; FAX (360) 687-0595; http://www.michaelgrinder.com

teacher sees Nat Inane—who, in the minds of the rest of the pupils, asks his fair share of questions—begin to raise his hand. The teacher privately signals Nat to put his hand down. Then later, during the Seatwork portion of the lesson, the teacher approaches Nat to assist him. Other times the class is aware that the teacher is teaching the student to avoid the classroom faux pas of receiving a disproportionate amount of attention from the teacher. For example, the teacher tapes four coupons on the student's desk. As the student asks a question, a coupon is removed. When there are no more coupons, no more questions are allowed. To *save* a student privately, the teacher must know ahead of time what is likely to happen. There are two levels of this. One level is knowing how the class will respond if the teacher calls on Nat. The other level, and one which is more sophisticated, is knowing when the student is going to act in such a manner that the class would activate the *stages*. In the above example, when the teacher accurately predicts that Nat is going to ask a lot of questions during a given lecture, the teacher could whisper to Nat before the presentation starts that he will help him in just a little while. The farther in advance the teacher knows the student will act a certain way, the more the teacher can privately manage.

Perception is the key to being proactive.

> **Foresight provides the opportunity for proactive management.**

3-7

Adolescents and Fairness

(What if the class isn't even shocked?)

In the eyes of the teacher an individual student is behaving inappropriately. However, the class is entertained by such action. In fact, the more bizarre the individual student acts, the more status the individual receives from the class. This is often the case with teenagers.

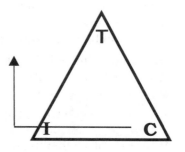

Since the teacher cannot wait for the class to progress through the three stages of *Shocked*, *Confused*, and *Annoyed*, the teacher switches to the concept of *Fairness*.

There are two ingredients of Fairness:

- The class perceives that the individual knows a consequence is coming.

- The teacher is seen as consistent.

© 2000 by Michael Grinder & Assoc., ARR. AHC03 (360) 687-3238; FAX (360) 687-0595; http://www.michaelgrinder.com

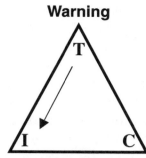

Warning

Teacher warns individual.

Awareness

The class is aware of warning.

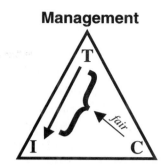

Management

Individual continues behavior; teacher manages and class thinks teacher is fair.

What is amazing about this process is that the individual student might protest that the teacher is *unfair* (e.g., "You *always* pick on me!"), and yet if the class sees the teacher as *fair*, the criteria of classroom dynamics have been met. The teacher wants to be aware of and interested in the class' perception. The teacher wants to distinguish between *fairness* and *popularity*. As teachers, we would all like to be seen as both *fair* and *popular*. In those situations where we cannot have both, in the long run, the former will serve the class and us better than the latter.

The teacher can be *fair* with the privacy of the individual preserved. For example, Frank inadvertently says an expletive and the group laughs. Frank enjoys the limelight and intentionally continues. The class looks at the teacher. The teacher non-verbally indicates a warning.

Two seconds before the end-of-the-class bell rings, the teacher says loudly enough for the class to hear and in a not-open-for-negotiation voice, "Frank, please stay after." The bell rings and the pupils file out while the teacher talks privately to Frank. The pupils out in the hallway are abuzz speculating on what is happening inside the room.

It is imperative that the teacher say, "Frank, please stay after," just as the class ends. The class sees the teacher as in charge *(proactive)*. If the teacher says, "Oh, Frank, may I see you," after the class ends, the group's perception often is less favorable towards the teacher. The class might wonder if the teacher, as an afterthought *(reactive)*, made the statement to Frank.

> **We want to put our foot down without it going in our mouth.**

© 2000 by Michael Grinder & Assoc., ARR. AHC03 (360) 687-3238; FAX (360) 687-0595; http://www.michaelgrinder.com

3-8

Rumors

When does a teacher manage a student publicly?

A corollary to *Adolescents and Fairness* is *Rumors*. Rumors occur when the teacher tries to keep the process of disciplining an individual private from the class. Although the teacher's motivation is positive by trying to respect the privacy of the individual, the strategy might backfire.

Warning

Teacher warns individual privately.

Awareness

The class is unaware of warning.

Management

Individual continues inappropriate behavior and is managed.

From a class dynamics viewpoint, the class might be surprised by the management and be *shocked.* This lack of knowledge (the teacher's *warning*) by the class could be compounded by the individual who thinks that the teacher has been unfair and spreads rumors as to the details of unfairness.

Shocked

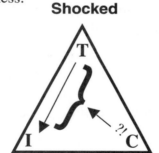

*Class surprised by **management** and therefore **shocked**.*

or

Individual tells class false impressions of previous interactions between teacher and herself.

The teacher wants to walk a tightrope of trying to preserve the dignity of the individual while, if appropriate, keeping the class abreast of the on-going development. Fairness is not determined by the teacher or the individual, but by the perception of the class.

Will the student comply?

If yes, manage privately.

If no, the class needs to know that management is occurring.

© 2000 by Michael Grinder & Assoc., ARR. AHC03 (360) 687-3238; FAX (360) 687-0595; http://www.michaelgrinder.com

Power vs. Influence

Whether or not a teacher's management is perceived as power or influence is often not determined by the technique employed but by the timing of when the technique is employed. And, in the case of *Fairness* and *Rumors*, does the class know that the employment is done?

Fairness can be measured by two parties: the individual and the class. If the teacher thinks the individual will change with the warning then it is beneficial that the class not be aware of the warning. If the individual isn't likely to change then it is beneficial for the class to be aware.

Individual Student as Bully

Why is a bully blind to her behavior?

3-9

The class sees the individual as inappropriate, but the individual has *power.* When the class reaches the annoyed stage, they dare not make sounds because they might be caught. The class rolls their eyes and quickly catches glances from neighbors to confirm that "we're all seeing it the same way."

The teacher is cautioned about meeting with the bully student in order to have the bully understand how her behavior is detrimental to the class' learning. When the teacher points out how her behavior is impeding the progress of the lesson, the student can counter with a variety of retorts. "I am just saying you are boring because everyone thinks so. I am just saying it aloud." "No I'm not, everybody likes me." "No one cares or is bothered by me." The teacher is at a loss to provide sensory specific evidence to the contrary—this is because the class is silent when they are annoyed.

It doesn't help to counsel a bully.

While the teacher perceives the class is silent because of their fear of reprisal from the bully, the bully's perception of the situation is very different and will likely remain set. Therefore, it is suggested that the teacher attempt to shift the student via behavioral conditioning instead of "insight/self-discovery" counseling.

For the safety of the class, the teacher uses the *power* of the teacher's position to handle the situation. Of course, *fairness* is always appropriate.[5]

Protecting an Individual Student

When does a teacher protect?

3-10

The class perceives an individual as inappropriate; for example, a "space cadet/nerd" who makes sounds and talks aloud to entertain herself. The

© 2000 by Michael Grinder & Assoc., ARR. AHC03 (360) 687-3238; FAX (360) 687-0595; http://www.michaelgrinder.com

individual is unable to learn from the class' criticism. The teacher intervenes and indicates non-verbally that this individual is off limits to class feedback. In order for this to happen, the teacher first must have the group seeking the teacher's respect and admiration.

Protect students who aren't ready yet to learn from feedback.

The operational difference between *Saving an Individual Student* and *Protecting an Individual Student* is where the burden of change of behavior is placed. In the first incident of *Saving*, the teacher is teaching the student to behave differently; the burden/responsibility is on the student to develop social and coping skills. In the second incident, *Protecting*, the burden is on the teacher to satisfy the student's needs. Essentially, the teacher is surmising that the student hasn't developed the appropriate social and coping skills yet. Hopefully, the teacher can satisfy the student privately so the class is less aware of the special protective status the student has.

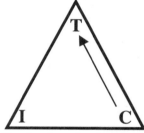

Teacher has class' respect.

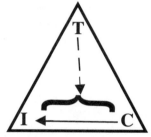

Teacher notices the class' reaction to an individual isn't effective.

Teacher indicates the individual is protected.

If a teacher inherits a classroom, the bane of all long-term substitute teachers, the dynamics are already set. In the eyes of the class, often one or more individual students have already progressed to the *confused-annoyed* stages.

Vignette: Patti Patient Protects

Patti Patient took time from her career to raise her two children. With both of them in school she is ready to work full time again. She anticipates a permanent position next autumn; for the remainder of this spring term she is a long-term substitute teacher. During the first week of taking over the class, every time Annoying Anthony even started to talk, the rest of the class moaned. It was obvious that it wasn't the content Anthony was talking about that irritated the class.

The desire of every new manager, which is what a teacher partially is, is to initially hide and observe. Once the teacher/man-

continued on next page

© 2000 by Michael Grinder & Assoc., ARR. AHC03 (360) 687-3238; FAX (360) 687-0595; http://www.michaelgrinder.com

ager has a sense of the classroom dynamics, the teacher's response can be much more appropriate and effective. By the end of the second week of teaching, Patti Patient has observed the pattern of the class' reaction to Annoying Anthony enough to know what to do. And yet, wisely, she realizes she doesn't have permission from the class to intervene. It is a wise person who can distinguish the difference between "knowing what to do" and "whether it would be effective to do it." It pained Patti daily to witness the class' treatment of Anthony. She knew she could intervene, but it would be a maneuver of power.[6] By the end of the third week the class is responding quickly to Patti's directives (e.g., "Take out your math book and turn to...." or "Look up here!" or "Quiet, listen to the announcements."), which indicates that she is seen by the class as reliable and dependable. This means, in turn, she can hold them accountable. Also, by this time she has established the necessary rapport with the leaders in the room. Patti Patient looks forward to next autumn when she will have her own classroom and will gain permission from the class much quicker than she has been able to in her present circumstances.

On Monday of the fourth week, when Annoying Anthony begins to speak, the pupils start their knee-jerk reaction of moaning but immediately the teacher interjects a "Sh!" The teacher is looking at Annoying Anthony while holding a frozen hand "stop gesture" toward the rest of the class. The class is quiet.

Increasing a Student's Status

3-11

(How does a teacher increase a student's status?)

The class isn't noticing an individual participant that the teacher wants the group to notice. This would be the case when the individual has some qualities that the teacher would like the group, as a whole, to exhibit more.[7]

The teacher sees that the pupil
is about to speak.

© 2000 by Michael Grinder & Assoc., ARR. AHC03 (360) 687-3238; FAX (360) 687-0595; http://www.michaelgrinder.com

Least Recommended

The individual doesn't want to be noticed (either shy or doesn't want to impose). The individual's pattern is to ask the teacher a question only when there is noise in the room. The class doesn't notice the individual or the qualities of this person. For example, the teacher says, "Class, take out your literature book and turn to page 75." It is during the rustling noise created by the books being opened that the student quietly says, "Are our reports due next Tuesday or Wednesday?" If the teacher answers the student's query while the class is still finding page 75, the class is not aware that the individual student has even asked a question, and they are not cognizant of the teacher's interaction with the student.

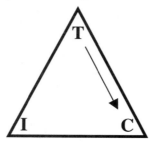

The teacher has just said, "Class, take out...and turn to page 75."

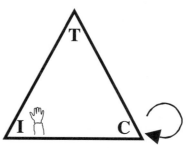

During the shuffle, the individual asks the teacher a question and the class is oblivious to the individual speaking.

Recommended

The teacher has just finished the announcement of "Class, take out...," the class is shuffling, the teacher sees that the individual wants to ask a question. The teacher verbally or non-verbally indicates "...in just a minute." Once the class has found page 75 and has settled down, the teacher entertains the individual's question and, in so doing, draws the class' attention to the person.

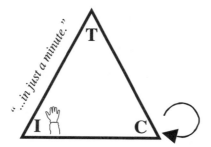

Class is shuffling. Teacher sees individual has a question.

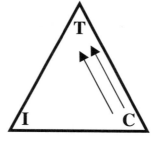

Class settles down and looks at teacher.

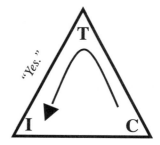

Teacher looks at individual and class follows teacher's eyes to the individual.

© 2000 by Michael Grinder & Assoc., ARR. AHC03 (360) 687-3238; FAX (360) 687-0595; http://www.michaelgrinder.com

Decreasing a Student's Status

An individual is a negative leader, and for the sake of the class' learning the teacher wants to decrease the status of the individual. The more bizarre the individual's behavior the more status the class gives the individual.

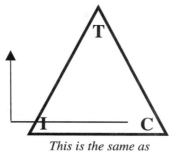

This is the same as
Adolescents and Fairness.

3-12

Since *noise* is associated with the class being annoyed with an individual, when the teacher anticipates the individual is going to talk (e.g., ask a question), the teacher artificially makes class noise and thereby creates the illusion of annoyance.

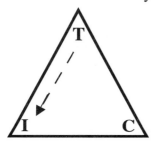

The teacher sees that the individual is about to speak.

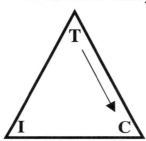

The teacher says, "Let's take our manuals and look at page 75."

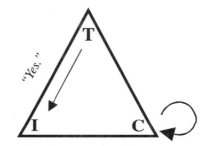

The teacher then calls on the individual, but few are listening because they are taking out their books and turning to page 75.

Summary

This chapter expands Chapter One's concepts of classroom formation and Chapter Two's template that certain students have major roles in the evolution of classroom dynamics. The model that a class progresses through the three primary stages of *shocked, confused,* and *annoyed* when irritated allows the teacher to select a response that fits the perception of the class. The fourth stage of *ignored* explains how a student's inappropriate behavior often has no effect on the group as a whole.

While the stages might be somewhat intuitively known to the educator, the spin-off classroom dynamics patterns are eye-opening. The construct of the classroom dynamics as a triangle forces the teacher to constantly consider how the class perceives the teacher when he attempts to either *manage, save,* or *protect* the individual student.

Much to the delight of the sixth through the ninth grade teachers, the adolescent view of stages is broached. Such educators know that often the class doesn't even enter the first stage of shocked when a student is

© 2000 by Michael Grinder & Assoc., ARR. AHC03 (360) 687-3238; FAX (360) 687-0595; http://www.michaelgrinder.com

inappropriate. In fact, the opposite condition is often present –bizarre behavior results in a higher status given to the student. Therefore the backup system to the three stages is the concept of being *fair. Fairness* has two ingredients: the teacher is consistent and communicates that a given consequence will follow any continuation of inappropriate behavior. *A Healthy Classroom* offers the junior high/middle school educators solace when managing students in that *fairness* is never determined by the managed student's perception but the class' perception.

Fairness is the backup system for when the *stages* cannot be accessed. It is also used with the concept of *rumors. Rumors*[8] is a valuable concept because it explains a curious phenomenon in which a teacher honors the student's dignity by managing the student privately and, in return, gets stabbed in the back by the student spreading *rumors* about how unfair the teacher is. The teacher's decision to manage the student privately needs to be based on the likelihood of the student complying. If the teacher misjudges that the student will comply and the student doesn't, the teacher is open to *rumors.* If the teacher prudently estimates that the student will not comply, the teacher needs to manage the student with the class somewhat aware of such action occurring. This is because the teacher can activate the backup system of *fairness.*

The concept of the *bully* student is most intriguing. Often the teacher cannot rationally talk to the student about how her behavior is interfering with class learning. The student who is a bully has a skewed view of what is occurring in the classroom. The student receives no feedback that she is *annoying* others because the other pupils are afraid to make sounds for fear of reprisals.

With negative leaders (bullies and inappropriate adolescents are in this category), the teacher wants to *decrease* these students' influence over the pupils. The techniques of *increasing* and *decreasing* empower the teacher to alter a student's status. The purpose is to increase the health of the classroom.

© 2000 by Michael Grinder & Assoc., ARR. AHC03 (360) 687-3238; FAX (360) 687-0595; http://www.michaelgrinder.com

The artistry of group dynamics is juggling all corners of the classroom triangle.

What stage is the class at in their reaction to the student? The stage describes the relationship between the class and the student.

What is the relationship between the student and the teacher?

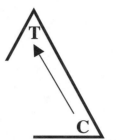

How does the class see the teacher?

© 2000 by Michael Grinder & Assoc., ARR. AHC03 (360) 687-3238; FAX (360) 687-0595; http://www.michaelgrinder.com

Rubric for Chapter Three: Stages

Transcends the Educational Culture

	Struggling Novice	Apprentice	Scientist	Artisan of Healthy Classroom
Three Stages of Irritability p. 84	The teacher is consistently surprised and rotates between shocked, confused and annoyed.	The teacher is inconsistent. The class doesn't know what to expect.	The teacher's responses are consistent. The teacher is seen as fair.	The teacher's response is based on the stage of irritability the class is in.
Saving a Student p. 90	The teacher is unaware that a student is in need of saving.	The teacher is inconsistent as to whether or not he will save a student.	The teacher attempts to save all students. The class sees the teacher as consistent and fair.	The teacher attempts to save the individual before the class is annoyed with the member.
Adolescents and Fairness p. 92	The class is either in chaos or the class walks around on emotional eggshells.	The teacher is inconsistent; the class cannot predict how the teacher will handle a given situation.	The teacher is consistent; everyone is managed in the same manner. "Fair is fair" is the axiom.	The teacher attempts to individualize how students are managed. The teacher is seen as fair.
Rumors (Public vs. Private Management) p. 94	The teacher is inconsistent; the class never knows what format management will occur in. The classroom is not safe.	The teacher either always explodes or always implodes.	Whatever the teacher's template, it is universally applied.	The teacher attempts to privately manage the individual unless the student is not likely to comply.
Bully p. 95	The teacher does not recognize that a bully is operating.	The teacher recognizes but has limited ways of responding.	The teacher employs power to create safety in the room.	The teacher employs power, decreases student's status and is fair.
Protecting a Student p. 95	The teacher never develops admiration from the class. The teacher is unaware a student needs protection.	The teacher is inconsistent; sometimes as a humanitarian he protects students whether they need it or not.	The teacher protects all students. The class sees the teacher as consistent and fair.	After the teacher has the class' admiration, the teacher protects the student who doesn't learn from the class' feedback. The student is given special status and is accepted as part of the class. Often this is the goal with *inclusion* students.
Changing a Student's Status pp. 97-98	The teacher is oblivious to the dynamics between individual students and the class as a whole. The teacher assigns status based on whether the teacher likes the student at the moment.	Teacher's "pets" are given special status.	The teacher operates based on the Golden Rule. Consistency is a hallmark of the classroom.	The teacher increases or decreases a student's status based on the dynamics of the class.

© 2000 by Michael Grinder & Assoc., ARR. AHC03 (360) 687-3238; FAX (360) 687-0595; http://www.michaelgrinder.com

Chapter Three Post-its

Three Stages

Am I recognizing the stages and responding based on the stage the class is in?

Chapter Three: Stages, pp. 84-87.

Rumors

Am I estimating correctly which students to manage privately and which ones, because of "rumors," I am having the class be aware that management is occurring?

Chapter Three: Stages, p. 94.

Saving a Student

Which student needs saving and am I doing it before the class has entered the annoyed stage?

Chapter Three: Stages, pp. 90-91.

Protecting a Student

When I have the class' respect, am I appropriately protecting a student with influence? And if not, am I protecting via power?

Chapter Three: Stages, pp. 95-97.

Adolescents and Fairness

Am I perceived as fair (warning ahead of time and consistent in consequence) by the class? Do I value being respected over being popular?

Chapter Three: Stages, pp. 92-93.

Bully and Changing a Student's Status

Am I changing certain students' status? If I cannot change a student's inappropriate behavior (e.g., "bully"), am I fostering "ignoring?

Chapter Three: Stages, pp. 95, 97-98.

© 2000 by Michael Grinder & Assoc., ARR. AHC03 (360) 687-3238; FAX (360) 687-0595; http://www.michaelgrinder.com

End Notes

1. See pp. 34-35.

2. This concept is the focus of *Saving an Individual Student*, p. 90, and *Rumors*, p. 94.

3. *Break and Breathe* (*ENVoY* p. 62).

4. See Chapter Five, *Managing a Healthy Classroom.*

5. In *Seasonal Giggles*, p. 115, if the teacher didn't have a sense of humor, the class' perception would be that the teacher is the bully.

6. See Chapter Five for further discussion of the difference between managing by power vs. managing by influence, pp. 139-140.

7. See *Fostered Leaders*, p. 76.

8. See p. 94.

© 2000 by Michael Grinder & Assoc., ARR. AHC03 (360) 687-3238; FAX (360) 687-0595; http://www.michaelgrinder.com

Chapter One: Class Formation could be misunderstood as a phenomenon that happens once. This chapter proposes that the group's cohesiveness is in a constant seasonal flux. Sometimes the class is close with both the teacher and each other. At other times there is a distance that is natural. *Seasons* increases the teacher's ability to not only recognize the change in the weathervane of the room but be able to predict ahead of time and thus modify both her teaching and management styles.

The above illustration is taken from the vignette on page 116. The story highlights the importance of the teacher having a sense of humor.

To be respectful of gender equality and yet provide the educator with a fluid reading style, in this chapter the teacher is referred to by the female pronoun and the student by the male pronoun.

Introduction

It could be argued that this chapter is a continuation and extension of Chapter One: Class Formation. Indeed, the educator wants to plant the seeds of certain management habits early in the school year so the habits will provide shade during those periods of the school year when the teacher needs them. Yet, Classroom Formation could be misunderstood as a phenomenon that happens once. This chapter proposes that Classroom Formation is in constant seasonal flux. It is especially important to both comprehend and predict how the degree of group unity is affected by such fluctuations.

Seasonal classroom dynamics addresses the sophisticated concept of *perception*. Perception can be interpreted as the ability to understand what is occurring at the moment. This definition of perception is misleading because there are things the teacher can do in September that work in September but sure make November difficult. The concept of Seasons broaches the more complex description of perception–understanding how what is occurring in the classroom at the moment will have ramifications over time.

This chapter opens with an understanding of when students identify with each other and the school as a whole and when they don't. The students' expansion and contraction of their identity with each other is reflected in distinctive voice patterns. By the teacher recognizing the students' closeness and distance with each other, the teacher can utilize the former and compensate for the latter.

> *Relationships are the foundation of organization.*[1]

Seasonal Giggles explains why certain humorous situations that occur in the classroom are not "retellable;" hence, the expression, "You would have had to be there to understand!" *Firsts* delineates the "halo effect" and why it is important for the teacher to be professional even after the teacher has established an excellent reputation with the class.

The second half of the chapter focuses on how seasons affect the teacher. As the class formation occurs, the teacher wants to recognize the lure of being a heroine of the class. *Teachership* challenges the educator to move beyond the dependency that occurs from being the center of safety and stability. This paradigm shift is critical for the concepts presented in the most sophisticated chapter–*Managing a Healthy Classroom*.

© 2000 by Michael Grinder & Assoc., ARR. AHC03 (360) 687-3238; FAX (360) 687-0595; http://www.michaelgrinder.com

The most important variable in a classroom is the relationship between the teacher and students. The single most influential variable in this dynamic is the teacher's well-being. There is no question that the teacher's well-being will be seasonally affected; the other question is what to do about it. The most powerful advice is to do the opposite of what is the human tendency. As the season becomes long, instead of decreasing one's physical exercise, increase exercise. Several classroom techniques are offered.

The single most influential variable in this dynamic is the teacher's well-being.

From Michael Grinder's previous book, *Righting the Educational Conveyor Belt*, the concept of *Right Brain Days*[2] is imported and examined. The summary chart of how to modify one's teaching styles is a godsend. The technique of *Hallway Noise*[3] will provide the reader with a comical way of viewing the difficult days of teaching.

The chapter finishes with a provocative treatment of the most vile situation of the school seasons—the students' acting as if they are *victims*. The difficulty of how to respond to the students' feeling seasonally put upon is compounded by the fact that the teacher is prone to the same ailment. While the symptoms of the students' falling into the seasonal hole of despair and the recommended strategies for the teacher are clearly outlined, it is wise to again repeat the necessity of the teacher to take care of herself, including exercising. Literally, the secret to a successful school year, from a physiological vantage point, is to have a different season than the students.

Students' Identity Size

4-1

What is a "class identity?"

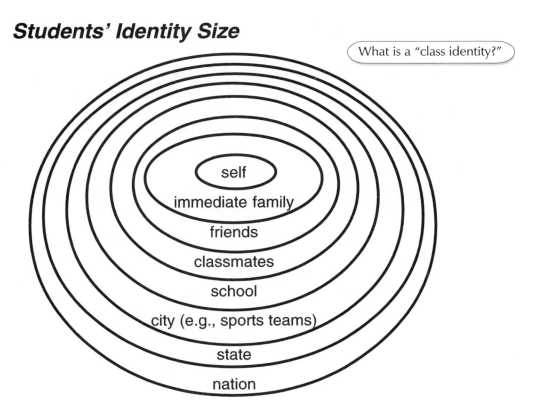

self

immediate family

friends

classmates

school

city (e.g., sports teams)

state

nation

© 2000 by Michael Grinder & Assoc., ARR. AHC03 (360) 687-3238; FAX (360) 687-0595; http://www.michaelgrinder.com

It is common parlance to use the term "identity" when referring to a person's feelings about oneself, character and goals (e.g., "That person's identity is….") We also use forms of the word: "I identify with…." As a group is formed, there is a "group identity." This pattern of classroom dynamics explores the interplay between the separate identity of individual members and the class identity. For instance, the preceding graphic shows a series of circles indicating a student's expanding levels of identity. Of course, each individual will have his own order/priority.

Collective Voice Volume and Identity Sizes

When classroom formation has developed and the day is a routine day, each individual person tends to identify with the other members of the class. "Our class" and "our school" are examples. When the members are doing small group work and the volume of the smaller groups remains at or below a certain collective maximum voice volume, the members identify with the large group as a whole.

Regular Day

Several small groups working quietly

As the season changes and the calendar shows that a *break in routine* (e.g., holiday) is nearing, the students tend to change to being more right-brain oriented. One of the effects is a *shrinkage* of individuals identifying as members of the class. The group's ability to function will be decreased. That is why cooperative groups don't work on some days. The increase in the noise level of the subgroups is evidence of the Identity Size Shrinking. This is because the pupils only have rapport with the immediate members of their small group and not the entire class.

As one smaller group (group X) talks loudly, it forces other groups (groups Y and Z) to talk louder because the speakers in groups Y and Z are being polite by talking louder so that the listeners can hear them. In turn, the loudness of groups Y and Z force the speakers in group X to speak louder, which results in groups Y and Z talking louder. It is important to consider this interpretation which says that the cause of the loudness is not impoliteness.

© 2000 by Michael Grinder & Assoc., ARR. AHC03 (360) 687-3238; FAX (360) 687-0595; http://www.michaelgrinder.com

Identity Sizes Shrink

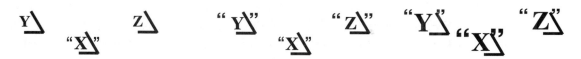

One small group talks louder than normal.	The other groups also talk louder in order to hear each other.	which dominos into ever increasing loudness.

For educators who are bus monitors, it is common for students to misbehave more while waiting for their ride than they do in the classroom because they don't have an identity with each other once school is out. During the first week of school, the teacher may want to have a party for those pupils who are going to be waiting for the bus and bond them together.

> **When there are breaks in routines, each student's identity shrinks.**

The collective contraction of groups identifying with each other is often caused by a change in routines. This change can be weather, approaching vacation and the status quo (e.g., new student is enrolled). Examples abound:

- the first snow fall
- the week before Spring Break
- reorganization of schedules; e.g., assemblies

Often the change in routine signals the individual pupils that their level of responsibility is going to be lowered. Students become:

- more short-term oriented
- more impulsive
- less left-brain linear and more right-brain creative
- shorter in concentration span
- more egalitarian; less authoritarian and hierarchical.

Right Brain Days[4]

4-3

Sometimes students' identity size changes because the break in the routine happens quickly. This is the case when pupils who are normal in the morning come back from lunch very different. Other times, the teacher can predict when these breaks in the routines will occur. When several

© 2000 by Michael Grinder & Assoc., ARR. AHC03 (360) 687-3238; FAX (360) 687-0595; http://www.michaelgrinder.com

days of other-than-normal student behavior is predictable, they are called Right Brain Days.

Proof that there are different seasons during the school year is found in the faculty lunch room. It is common to hear teachers bemoaning the fact that they can't get new, creative ideas from their students. At other times of the year, these same instructors are heard saying, "They're not listening. I told them, and they are just not listening." In the first case, the students are in their left brain and the teacher wants them in their right brain. In the latter case, the reverse is true: the teacher wants them in their left brain and the students are in their right brain. The following chart summarizes the attributes of each hemisphere.

Left Hemisphere	*Right Hemisphere*
Modes of consciousness	
• **Logical**	• **Intuitive**
• **Sequential**	• **Random**
• **Linear**	• **Holistic**
• **Symbolic**	• **Concrete**
• **Reality-based**	• **Fantasy-oriented**
Skills associated with	
• **Locating details and facts**	• **Being globally attentive**
• **Following directions**	• **Jumping to conclusions**
• **Listening**	• **Talking**
• **Analyzing from part to whole**	• **Analyzing from whole to part**
Student who is oriented	
• **Needs clear, specific, written directions**	• **Is distractible and seeks self entertainment**
• **Is uncomfortable with open-ended, unstructured assignments**	• **Loves self-selected assignments with creativity**

Apart from the teachers who have a 30% turnover rate of students and literally never leave September (they are trying to establish routines all year), most teachers have many days where established routines work. Days when the routines work are known as left-brain days. Those days

© 2000 by Michael Grinder & Assoc., ARR. AHC03 (360) 687-3238; FAX (360) 687-0595; http://www.michaelgrinder.com

when routines don't work are referred to as right-brain days because the students shift to using their right brain more. Some of these days can be circled on the calendar before the year starts, like the week before spring break, picture day, or homecoming. The teacher literally can design a curriculum that matches the pupils' learning styles. At other times, students become right brain-oriented due to drastic changes in the weather or vivid activities that occur during lunch (fights, injuries, when he finally asks her to be an *item*). This latter category of right brain days is more of a surprise nature and makes it more difficult for the teacher to modify a left-brain oriented lesson to be more right-brain oriented.

These right brain days are golden opportunities for integrated learning.

Since this is a book on management, and since a teacher can only successfully manage when the students can successfully do the work, it behooves the veteran educator to know the specific teaching methods which transform these right-brain days into golden opportunities for integrated learning. If the instructor doesn't know that fantastic learning occurs on these right-brain days, the teacher falls prey to showing videos to maintain control. The following chart illustrates which teaching styles to decrease and which teaching styles to increase.

Right Brain Days	
Decrease	*Increase*
reliance on teacher	group dynamics; interactive learning
reliance on authority	rapport
teacher lectures	manipulatives
new content	review of previous learned content
critical thinking	creative thought

Follow the axiom that all expectations/rules have to be visually displayed (i.e., *Exit Directions* and *Opening Visual Directions*[5]) and, if possible, structure the learning so that the class is deductively operating. Namely, have the pupils utilize known information holistically.[6]

© 2000 by Michael Grinder & Assoc., ARR. AHC03 (360) 687-3238; FAX (360) 687-0595; http://www.michaelgrinder.com

Vignette: JR's Bingo

Mr. Jr. (J.R.) High is a history teacher who always takes roll from a certain location in the room and begins his lesson from his podium. Because of his enthusiasm and instructional ability, his students are very attentive. Around the week before winter break, he realizes the students aren't responding in their usual way. If he continues, he runs the risk of contaminating his routines. He switches to a new location, expects to cover less content, emphasizes material from the last two chapters he has covered and creates a review unit.

To make the review unit far more interesting, he plans an academic bingo game for Wednesday of the last week. Using their books, the students brainstorm at least thirty-five concepts which have been covered over the last two chapters. The teacher lists the concepts on the board. Blank bingo sheets are distributed. The students fill in their bingo sheet by selecting twenty-five of the thirty-five concepts listed on the board. The teacher then asks either a matching, fill-in or a definition of one of the items on the board for a given column; e.g., column B. If the student has that item, the student puts a small "x" in the corner of the square. If J.R. wants to do a short review, he'll play bingo. If he wants more in-depth reinforcement, he'll play blackout (all squares are "x"ed).

Vignette: Role Play

Miss H.S. Lit has a regular routine: Monday is for doing vocabulary and an overview of this week's story. Tuesday is silent reading in class. Wednesday is a written review. Thursday, an oral discussion on plot, character and setting; and on Friday, a major test. Yesterday was Wednesday and school was closed due to bad weather; there was a two-hour delay in starting this morning. She anticipates the students to be "different" because of this change in routine. She intentionally starts the lesson in the usual way and is getting the lack of response she expects. Within three minutes, she purposely drops the book in exasperation, steps away from the board area and says, "Class, I hope you don't mind, I'd rather do something different today." Noticing the students shift to a surprised mental state, she suggests an alternative to their normal procedure: "In place of taking the test on Friday, those students who want an A for this week have the option of role playing the different characters in the story; those who want a B will...."

© 2000 by Michael Grinder & Assoc., ARR. AHC03 (360) 687-3238; FAX (360) 687-0595; http://www.michaelgrinder.com

Hallway Noise

4-4

The concept of seasonal energy is freeing because the teacher knows she is not the cause when the class is seasonally chaotic. The section on *Right Brain Days* proposed that certain seasons are predictable; but what about the spontaneous ones? The question arises, "Instead of hallucinating, how does the teacher verify that the season has suddenly changed?"

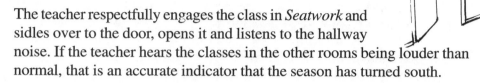

The teacher respectfully engages the class in *Seatwork* and sidles over to the door, opens it and listens to the hallway noise. If the teacher hears the classes in the other rooms being louder than normal, that is an accurate indicator that the season has turned south.

Vignette: "Yep, it isn't me!"

Vivian Verify is a fifth-year teacher of an inner city sixth grade. When the pupils went out to lunch, the class had had an average morning. But the way they came back in was anything but normal. After slyly noticing that her barometers indicated that something was definitely afoot, Vivian hurriedly put something on the overhead for the class to copy. Then she sidled over to the door and listened to the hallway sounds. Mrs. Thunder and Mr. Lightning were barking louder than usual. As Vivian slowly walked back to the front of a noisy room, she silently said to herself, "Yep, it isn't me. Knowing that, I know I will be OK with whatever I have to do."

Use of "I"

4-5

If the teacher realizes early in the day that she is off and vulnerably mentions to the class, "I need to ask a favor. I am not having the best of days and need …," this works because the teacher's person is proactively and vulnerably addressing the pupils as people.

There are other days when the teacher cannot ask a favor of the class because their identity is too small or limited and their concentration span is too short. They wouldn't remember what the teacher asked of them. The class is unruly and the teacher, as a person, is hurt by their behavior. Sometimes it works to share with the class that the teacher is offended. When it doesn't work, it is usually because the teacher is *reactively* expressing. Another way of saying this concept is: positions of authority can only effectively use "I" when there is a relationship between the sender and the receiver. Teachers want to avoid chastising a class using "I" (e.g., "I am really hurt by your lack of consideration when you ….") if there isn't a relationship between the teacher and the students.

© 2000 by Michael Grinder & Assoc., ARR. AHC03 (360) 687-3238; FAX (360) 687-0595; http://www.michaelgrinder.com

This not only applies when a reprimand is being given but also a compliment. Think of times when someone unknown to a faculty addresses them and says, "I appreciate/admire what a fine job ...." or when one woman compliments another woman on her outfit but the recipient doesn't value the compliment because it is not coming from someone who also dresses well.

It is difficult to have a relationship with a "position."

When the relationship from the student's side toward the teacher is low, using "I" may tarnish the longer term relationship. When a teacher gets mad and goes to her authoritarian position and says, "I want you to stop right now...," the class' reaction might not only be to resist the teacher's power but to damage the relationship level also. The teacher wants to use "I" when the relationship is high and the teacher is vulnerable so that the teacher's person is addressing the student's person. When the student's identity size seasonally shrinks, the relationship with the teacher is weak. The teacher wants to avoid using "I" because it implies there is a relationship when, in fact, there isn't.

When Relationship is Strong:

Teacher asks for a favor,

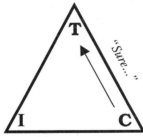

and the class responds.

When Relationship is Weak:

One would do well to reflect on the Thurston High School and Columbine High School tragedies with the concept of Identity Size *and* Crisis *in mind.*[7]

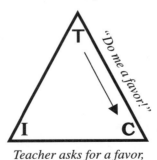

Teacher asks for a favor,

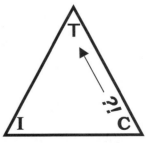

Class overtly or covertly indicates "Who are you?"

Crisis

There is one situation where group formation and identity is immediately expanded—a crisis. When there is a major catastrophe, people's identities can either expand greatly or withdraw incredibly. The expansion especially occurs when there is common meaningfulness in the cri-

© 2000 by Michael Grinder & Assoc., ARR. AHC03 (360) 687-3238; FAX (360) 687-0595; http://www.michaelgrinder.com

sis. Examples of this expansion are the San Francisco earthquake and Mississippi flooding. When the San Francisco earthquake occurred, there were several stages to the pattern of identity size:

- Fight or flight—the immediate response is one of personal safety.

- Those we love—the next reaction comes immediately after the first. A concern for those we love; a desire to protect those you care so much about—family.

- Expansion—either because those we love are secure or we abandon trying to reach/protect them, we expand to anyone we come in contact with. There is an outpouring of people's generosity and a bonding together. People open their homes, share their food, and freely give of their time and energy.

- If the hardship continues for a certain length of time, a different reaction sets in: people shrink their identity size and people horde their resources.

Seasonal Giggles

4-6

There are times when a class gets the giggles. Often this occurs when the class has been together for some time and the unisance of response is very high so that if initially some students giggle, in time, most of the room "gets the giggles." The class giggles are likely to happen at or just before a break. This would include holidays and first seasonal changes (e.g., snow, high winds, heavy rain, sunshine).

The difficulty with *Seasonal Giggles* occurs when the class' level of responsibility is decreasing while the teacher's levels are increasing. In other words, the teacher's sense of humor is probably low. The teacher's impulse is to *control* the situation. However, from a class dynamic standpoint, what is called for is *levity*.

Therefore, if the teacher recognizes the situation early enough:

- Set aside the non-verbals of presenting:

  - move from the presenting area;

  - leave behind the textbook, turn off overhead.

- Switch from the *position* of being a teacher to being a *person*.

The concept that a formed group develops their own brand of humor is not limited just to *Seasonal Giggles* as shown in the following vignette.

© 2000 by Michael Grinder & Assoc., ARR. AHC03 (360) 687-3238; FAX (360) 687-0595; http://www.michaelgrinder.com

Teacher Teaching

Some Giggle

Giggle Spreads

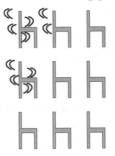

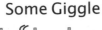

Teacher Joins while Stepping Away From the Presenting Area

Everyone Joins because Teacher Models that it is OK

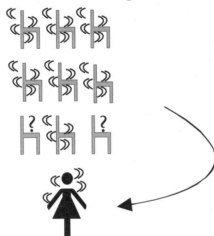

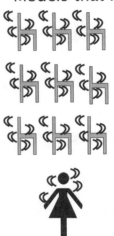

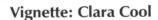

Vignette: Clara Cool

Clara Cool taught for thirty years and helps out once in a while as a substitute teacher. Her reputation is not only renowned but also delightfully tested by the younger brothers and sisters of former students who had Miss Cool. One spring day she was asked to cover an advanced writing class. While Clara, with her back to the class, was finishing up some written opening instructions on the chalkboard, the seniors crept into the room and silently organized to drop their books in unison. Clara slowly turns, drops her book and calmly said, "Sorry I was late."

© 2000 by Michael Grinder & Assoc., ARR. AHC03 (360) 687-3238; FAX (360) 687-0595; http://www.michaelgrinder.com

Firsts

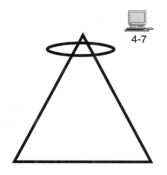
4-7

When a new class is still being formed, the teacher provides the *safety* for the members. It would seem then that after a group has gelled, the teacher has more latitude of response. In fact, this is usually true; if the teacher has done well enough there is a "halo effect." The illusion is that this is how the class will see the teacher throughout the duration of their relationship. This allows the teacher to be seen as doing fine even when the teacher at that particular moment might not be doing fine. The halo effect is true except when a *first* happens. A *first* is when something happens for the first time. Somehow the human brain has a special memory slot for *firsts*. Think of the first car you ever owned and compare how fast your memory comes back as compared to trying to remember the *second* or *third* vehicle you owned. It is no wonder that the firstborn has more pictures taken of himself compared to the number of photos of his siblings.

The Japanese have a saying that expresses the importance of a first: *"The good deeds of 100 years can be dashed in a second."*

In many ways how the teacher responds to the *first* sets the precedent of what the teacher sees as appropriate behavior for the class.

Categories of *first* include: humor, criticism, skepticism, compliment that is initiated.

For example:

- The *first* time someone pokes fun at the teacher.

- The *first* time someone criticizes the teacher, an individual, the content, the class, the process.

When a *first* occurs it isn't just the students figuring out how to act; it is also as if the students are sizing up the teacher for the first time. If it is an occurrence of an unusual circumstance (e.g., a student has a family emergency and asks for special consideration in order to submit a paper late), the whole class watches how the teacher handles the request.

Levels of Teachership

4-8

What is the lure of being a heroine?

A teacher can operate on at least two levels of leadership. The levels and the transition from one level to the next level parallel *the changing role of the teacher* as outlined in Class Formation.[8]

Level One Teachership

The first level is when the teacher is a heroine. This is done by developing rapport with the leaders in the class. If the class is only together for a

© 2000 by Michael Grinder & Assoc., ARR. AHC03 (360) 687-3238; FAX (360) 687-0595; http://www.michaelgrinder.com

short time, the rapport can be developed through a variety of means. Reputation (especially if the teacher is a "legend") and short-term rapport techniques such as mirroring[9] and acknowledging are two such techniques. If the students are going to be together for some time, the rapport is usually based on dependability and the satisfaction of the leaders' and the class' needs. In either case, the teacher is the hub through which attention and focus are given.

Vignette: Helen Hub

An example of the teacher being the hub of communication and dependence is when Helen Hub learns that Stella loves acting and she brings in a newspaper article announcing the formation of a local repertory company. Because Stella is a star and is loved by many other pupils, the teacher's relationship with Stella webs out to most of the class. Mrs. Hub also notices that Johnny is weak in hygiene and most of the class shuns him. Helen spends extra time with him before and after school. While the teacher's rapport with Johnny doesn't produce any ripple effect with the rest of the pupils, the teacher eventually reaches all the students directly or indirectly.

If the class is fragmented, then the teacher makes contact and satisfies the leaders of the individual diverse subgroups.

This level of teachership is completely appropriate for short-term groups; namely, under three day classes and at the beginning of the semester. Characteristic of this teachership level is the great demand for the teacher by the members. Members are honored by her papal visits/audience; hence, the heroine level.

Level Two Teachership

The advanced teachership level commences when the teacher begins to connect the leaders of the smaller groups to each other through the teacher. After individuals have been given status, they are then given status in a joining manner. Instead of recognizing, giving status or attention to individual leaders of separate smaller groups, these leaders are lumped together: "My compliments to both Thomas *and* Louise for the papers they

© 2000 by Michael Grinder & Assoc., ARR. AHC03 (360) 687-3238; FAX (360) 687-0595; http://www.michaelgrinder.com

wrote last night," or "If you get a chance, you may want to talk with Janet *and* Hank about how they are individually working on their projects." This level of joining is done by juxtaposition as characterized by the word *and*.

A greater level of bonding happens when the words "as," "during," "by," "while," etc., are used. "*As* Thomas and Louise demonstrated so well, good speeches can take a variety of forms." "*By* talking to Jane and Hank, you will find many options on how to respond to some of the difficult questions on the upcoming essay test."

The ultimate level of gluing the smaller groups together through their leaders is through a direct command. "Jane and Hank, you *will* want to see each other and swap your responses to some of Friday's essay questions."

> ***The three levels of joining are:***[10]
>
> 1. Juxtaposition = "…and…"
>
> 2. Cause and effect = as, while, by, during
>
> 3. Direct command = "…will…"

Vignette: Helen Hub (Continued)

On a routine day, Helen whispers to Stella, "I want to ask a favor. To help me out during math, I want to ask you to work with Johnny." Initially, Stella's face grimaced when Johnny's name was said but quickly relaxed when she realized what a special status she was being given.

Helen wisely whispers the same "special favor" message to Johnny, and while he was initially frightened and confused that Stella would need anybody of his social stature, he too quickly wanted to please his teacher.

Later during math, Helen smiled with pride because two people who would never associate with each other were interacting.

© 2000 by Michael Grinder & Assoc., ARR. AHC03 (360) 687-3238; FAX (360) 687-0595; http://www.michaelgrinder.com

Teachership One

Heroine: dependency can be power or just credible or relationship.

Teachership Two

Stella The Star

Snot-Nose Johnny

Teacher calls in emotional markers by asking Stella and Johnny separately, "I need a favor—would you help me by working with...."

The other form of *Teachership Two* is when the teacher defers/acknowledges/fosters an individual.

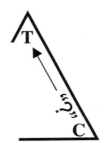

The class asks the teacher a question.

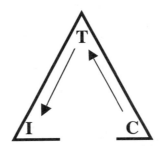

The teacher defers the question to an individual,

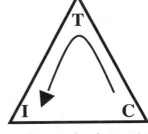

resulting in the class noticing the individual.

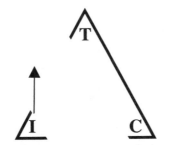

The individual's status increases.

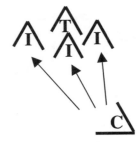

Over time the class recognizes many experts and the class is self-reliant.

Often the following educators have to either stay permanently at Teachership One or at least take longer to establish level one before progressing to Teachership Two: primary teachers, instructors of special needs groups (English language development, gifted and talented, special education), teachers who see a large number of students (specialists on the elementary school level), and secondary teachers who only instruct for fifty minutes.

© 2000 by Michael Grinder & Assoc., ARR. AHC03 (360) 687-3238; FAX (360) 687-0595; http://www.michaelgrinder.com

The Teacher's Seasonal Energy

4-9

People don't become teachers because of the money; culturally we are a most noble profession. When the United States government decided to send the first citizen into outer space, the guidelines for the selection included the following: the person must be someone seen as giving and as a good communicator—only teachers were asked to apply. In the author's opinion, the corollary of being so noble and giving is that we are very g-u-i-l-t ridden.

On those occasions when people from the corporate world switch professions and become teachers, the two most common descriptions of the difference between the corporate and educational cultures are:

- Educators financially subsidize their profession.[11]

- Educators are more prone to seasonally feel sorry for themselves.[12]

> *As much as the teacher resents someone having power over her, seasonally the teacher doesn't want to be empowered.*

"We keep saying that teaching is the most important profession, but we rarely treat it with respect."
Arthur Levine
President of Teachers
College, Columbia U.

We want to be appreciated and often don't feel like we are. The public will never love and appreciate us, as professionals, as much as we will always love our profession. Dr. Bill Sommers[13], involved with administrators' professional development, has an axiom, "If we don't feed our teachers, they will eat our students."

> What would be the evidence of that teacher's comfort with herself?

How does being noble and yet g-u-i-l-t ridden affect our comfort with ourselves? In addition to wanting to be appreciated, teachers want to be seen as kind instead of authoritarian. Since the teacher is innately comfortable with herself when giving and being kind, we want to observe the teacher assuming an authoritarian posture with a student or class. This is how we know how comfortable the teacher is with herself. The only reliable evidence is whether the teacher is breathing high/shallow vs. low/deep/abdominal. When one breathes high/shallow the person releases chemicals of fight or flight while chemicals of calmness are released when the person breathes low/deep/abdominal.

As a culture, teachers are emotionally affected by and define their self worth based on how others see them.

Simply put, if the teacher is in stress (high/shallow) while doing the authoritarian interaction or, more importantly, immediately following the exchange, the teacher isn't comfortable with herself. Seasonally we have to monitor our seasonal energy level.

© 2000 by Michael Grinder & Assoc., ARR. AHC03 (360) 687-3238; FAX (360) 687-0595; http://www.michaelgrinder.com

When the school calendar is between vacations, the lethargy of the educational doldrums sets in.

Statistically there are three kinds of jobs: working with people, ideas, and things (e.g., tools). For most of us, the first category, working with people, is the most stressful. As the seasons become long, specifically when the school is between vacations, fatigue starts to set in. This is when referrals to the office start to increase.

> *Success is really gained when the teacher has a different season than students.*

As humans, when our schedule starts getting crowded we tend to drop fitness. Statistically speaking, we really have to be OK with ourselves in order to be outside ourselves and focus on how the student is doing and facilitate the student as a *person*. The irony is that the days when we do have the energy to be magnanimous are those days when the students are OK also. It also seems as though our energy level influences how much outside ourselves we are. As we seasonally get run down we withdraw from being outside ourselves. We don't notice the developments (especially in terms of group dynamics) that are formulating. When *it* finally boils up, we are *surprised* = in a *reactive* posture.

Vignette: Joann Buff

Seven weeks is a long span between vacations. As Joann Buff drags herself to her car in the school parking lot, her body begged for a nap. She knew this morning the urge would be strong to go home and sleep– that's why she packed the bag of workout clothes that's in the back seat. Although she still felt sluggish as she opened the door to the gym, within 15 minutes of step aerobics Joann Buff could feel the chemicals change in her body. By the time she finished she was proud of herself for exercising. Once again she affirmed that 20 minutes of exercise is worth 40 minutes of sleep.

4-10

Associated vs. Dissociated [14]

A teacher's awareness of her internal state can be described on a continuum which has the word "associated" at the one end and "dissociated" at the other terminal. The more one is associated the more the person is aware of how she feels. This encompasses how one is in terms of sleep, food, security and need for privacy. Dissociated is a description of when one is not in touch with visceral inputs. It is more accurate to talk about the amount or degree of being associated and dissociated than to speak as if it is a switch activating one or the other condition. Every teacher wants to voluntarily be in control of her degree of association and dissociation.

© 2000 by Michael Grinder & Assoc., ARR. AHC03 (360) 687-3238; FAX (360) 687-0595; http://www.michaelgrinder.com

> *In general, the more difficult the situation,*
> *the more one wants to increase the degree of dissociation.*
> *Likewise, the more pleasant the moment,*
> *the more the enjoyment is experienced if the person is associated.*

Throughout the school year the teacher will experience aspects of fatigue. Since fatigue is usually a cumulative result, it is accurate to predict when the teacher is likely to be fatigued. In general, the teacher can seasonally expect a decrease in energy as the year progresses with a rejuvenation following vacations. It is during the seasonal fatigue times that the teacher is prone to feel sorry for herself.[15]

Fatigue skews a teacher's perception. The teacher wants to have a different season than the students.

While exercising is the best medicine for weathering the doldrums of the school year, there are coping behaviors which decrease the teacher's awareness of visceral experiences. The more the teacher slouches, the more the teacher goes inside; by contrast, the more the teacher is upright in body position the less she is aware of how she is. It is no small coincidence that visual-oriented teachers, famous for a posture that their grandmother would be proud of, are less in touch with themselves. And kinesthetic-oriented instructors, with a tendency to slouching, are more associated. There is also a correlation between the lower the grade level, the more associated the teacher, and the higher the grade level, the more dissociated.

Contracts with Our Body

4-11

In any kind of "extended" sport season (e.g., "the playoffs") the identity of everyone involved with the team is tremendous. As soon as the final contest is complete the tendency is for the people to become sick. A way of thinking about this phenomenon is to realize that they are not in touch with themselves individually. Some time after the final whistle blows the people become associated and, on some level, realize that they have been using their energy like an emotional weekend ATM—withdrawing energy (demanding a lot of their time, energy, and concentration) to focus and not putting anything back in (rest, downtime, etc.). Literally the body tells the mind, "I know you have found this experience very meaningful and without knowing it have become exhausted. I am closing us down for repair!"

© 2000 by Michael Grinder & Assoc., ARR. AHC03 (360) 687-3238; FAX (360) 687-0595; http://www.michaelgrinder.com

Vignette: Don't Touch the Furniture

Hugh has taught health for five years. He intellectually knows that his body's blood is commissioned to his digestive tract for the time period following lunch. Yet his professional commitment doesn't allow him to offer anything other than his best. So while his body is more suited for siesta than lecture, Hugh makes a point to stand more upright then normal. He is especially conscious of this when writing on the overhead so as not to lean on the machine.

4-12

Charlie Chaplin

Whenever a teacher expands her repertoire, there is an awkward time during the learning curve when she does not feel like she is being herself. This is especially true while the teacher is learning how to select the appropriate level of being associated and dissociated. After doing a new habit or skill for a while, the behavior feels familiar and we add it to how we define ourselves. There is a story that brings laughter and comfort to us as we learn to increase our self-image.

Charlie Chaplin, the famous silent film actor, was vacationing at the French Riviera. He learned that the Mediterranean resort he was staying at was hosting a Charlie Chaplin look alike contest. He entered and came in third place.

4-13

Pushing a Class

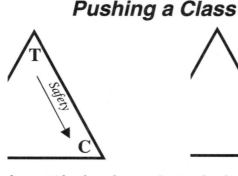

Initially teacher provides the safety.

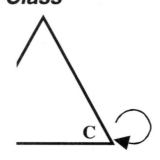

In time the class provides their own safety.

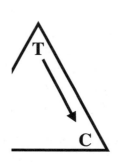

The teacher can push/demand more of the class.

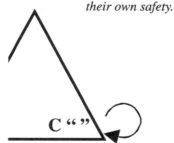

The class grumbles to themselves and yet

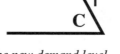

meets the new demand level.

© 2000 by Michael Grinder & Assoc., ARR. AHC03 (360) 687-3238; FAX (360) 687-0595; http://www.michaelgrinder.com

Once a class has been formed as evidenced by unisance of response and the members providing their own safety, the teacher has the option of pushing the class.

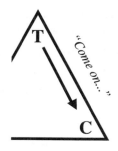 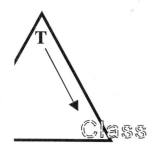 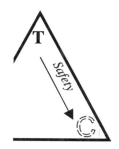

Teacher pushes class.   *Class's **Identity Size** is shrinking.*   *Teacher stops pushing and starts **Teachership One.***

However, if the safety is no longer provided by the class (e.g., because of seasonal shrinkage of *Identity Size*), the teacher has to return to *Teachership One*.

Victim

4-14

In my training by Carl Rogers and others of that ilk, one of the premises was that one could love another person toward finding and fulfilling that person's potential. The framework produced good results and yet there were some students for whom the Rogerian approach wasn't effective.

My search to understand what was occurring when I was not successful led me to study negotiation-mediation. Fisher and Ury[16] offer a perspective of the difference between people who play "win-lose" instead of the desired mode of "win-win." Their works are invaluable in offering some templates by which to view hostile interactions. Especially helpful is the concept of viewing the interaction from three levels: the *issues*, the *needs* of each party, and the *relationship* between the parties.

I intuitively know that some students can't be reached by a "system approach;" e.g., rewards and punishment. I was struck at how important the *relationship* was if the conflict could not be resolved on the *issue* level. One immediate application is working with the "difficult student" population. We have to have *relationships* with them. They are not deterred by consequences.

Still, I found myself in situations where a student would not let me form a *relationship*. The student was operating as a "victim" and was a master at sabotaging relationships.

© 2000 by Michael Grinder & Assoc., ARR. AHC03 (360) 687-3238; FAX (360) 687-0595; http://www.michaelgrinder.com

No one can put you down without your permission.
Eleanor Roosevelt

Then I stumbled upon Herb Cohen's concept[17] of the three variables of any negotiation: *P*ower, *I*nformation, and *T*ime. By extrapolating from Cohen, an insight emerged. Most negotiation methods presume that the student is either operating from a "win-win" or "win-lose" posture when interacting with you...but the "victim" operates "lose-lose." The student feels so hopeless that his desired outcome is to have others feel miserable also. The "victim" sees teachers as having *P*ower and, therefore, manipulates the other two variables of *PIT*...the student withholds *I*nformation and *T*ime. The victim plays "*IT*."

That is why most attempts at reaching the student who is stuck in his "victim" persona fail. The "victim" actually wants the teacher to attempt to reach him because then he has the distorted view of getting back at the teacher by passively withholding information and time. The picture scene is when a parent wants to talk to her teenager. The first thing he says is "How long is this going to take?" (=withholding time). This is quickly followed with "Can I go now?" (=withholding information).

Symptoms

Each of us has a persona inside that is a "victim." This persona surfaces during adolescence. The indicators of a student being a "victim" follow.

• He withholds information and time.

• He feels sorry for himself.

• He feels bad and wants others to suffer also.

• He wants "freedom from..." instead of "freedom to...".

• He is emotionally reactive instead of proactive.

• On one level, he wants to have someone in authority explode at him because that proves how others pick on him.

> *As much as the student resents the teacher having power over him, the victim doesn't want to be empowered.*

Strategies for Working with the "Victim"

• Point to the rules/expectations when managing[18].

• Make sure as a teacher you are OK; ignore any words or ploys that would tend to hook[19] you.

• Watch for times when the student isn't in his "victim" role and brainstorm a plan of action of how he wants to act and be treated during his temporary "victim" time.

© 2000 by Michael Grinder & Assoc., ARR. AHC03 (360) 687-3238; FAX (360) 687-0595; http://www.michaelgrinder.com

- Stay at 90° or side-by-side from the student and avoid eye contact.

- Figure out how to have the student seek or come to you.

- Understand that the "victim" hates pressure to do well; e.g., know when to use "encouragement" instead of "praise."[20]

- Keep looking for opportunities to develop a relationship with the student because it is through contact that the student develops hope.

- Try to let the student select choices within the guidelines that the teacher sets.

Summary

This chapter exposes what often are the mysteries of the school year. The ebb and flow of classroom formation and identity can be metaphorically understood from a concept in astronomy. The term that identifies when Earth is closest to an orbiting object is *perigee;* when Earth is at its farthest point, it is referred to as the *apogee.*

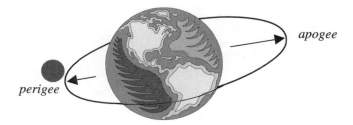

Perigee and apogee are analogies for the seasons of the school year.

Sometimes the class feels close to the teacher.

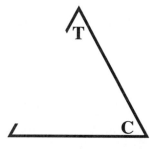

Other times the class operates with greater emotional distance from the teacher.

Sometimes the class feels close to each other.

Other times the class operates with greater emotional distance from each other.

© 2000 by Michael Grinder & Assoc., ARR. AHC03 (360) 687-3238; FAX (360) 687-0595; http://www.michaelgrinder.com

The concept of *Seasons* reveals that sometimes our profession does things instinctively well. For instance, statistically Friday is the day when the students least identify with each other and the school as a whole. (The exception is if there is a big sports event.) This is the day the students wear their school tee shirts, which automatically increases school spirit.

The concept of Teachership One exposes the well-intended but potentially unhealthy level of dependency of the students on the teacher. If the teacher needs the students to need her, the relationship is codependent. It is absolutely imperative that the teacher become adroit at creating Level One dependency for the purpose of moving the class towards Level Two. It is on Level Two that a healthy classroom is nourished and grows. It is equally important for the educator to realize when Level One is the best level the group dynamics can reach. Often this is the case in early primary, special education and high-turnover classes (over 30% turnover rate).

The emphasis has been on the teacher having a different season than her students. In order to accomplish this, the strongest recommendation is for the teacher to increase her exercise. It takes around two weeks for the middle aged teacher to receive benefits of increased exercises. For teachers who exercise regularly, the suggestion is to continue their fitness program and increase self-indulgence.

> *The needs of the class change with the season.*

© 2000 by Michael Grinder & Assoc., ARR. AHC03 (360) 687-3238; FAX (360) 687-0595; http://www.michaelgrinder.com

Rubric for Chapter Four: Seasons

Transcends the Educational Culture

	Struggling Novice	Apprentice	Scientist	Artisan of Healthy Classroom
Students' Identity Size, p. 107	Every day could be a "surprise day" for the teacher.	The teacher is often surprised at mysterious changes in the classroom and has a limited number of responses. Reactively responds.	The teacher intuitively senses that the collective interaction in the room is different on some days and has a limited number of responses.	The teacher can predict the identity size of the class and adjusts her style and approach.
Right-brain Days, p. 109	The teacher perceives the classroom as her domain of authority. Since every day is seen as the same, the teacher is constantly surprised.	The teacher is inconsistent; there are some good and some bad days.	The teacher can predict which days will likely be difficult.	The teacher successfully employs the right-brain days "Decrease/Increase Chart." The teacher selects her style of management based on the classroom dynamics.
Seasonal Giggles p. 115	The teacher is unpredictable; the lack of consistency means that the atmosphere of the classroom is left to the whims of the teacher.	The teacher lacks a sense of humor, especially when the class is more likely to have the seasonal giggles.	The teacher has a sense of humor.	The teacher maintains the class as a unit by joining the seasonal giggles.
"Firsts", p. 117	The teacher sees every day as the same.	The teacher sees days as different, but this is not based on dynamics.	The teacher senses that a *First* is a special occasion and operates intuitively.	The teacher recognizes a *First* and responds appropriately.
Teachership, p. 117	The teacher has no pattern as to a style of leadership.	The teacher operates either from power or pleading or vacillates between them.	The teacher operates from Level II.	The teacher selects the appropriate level based on the season and how the class dynamics are affected.
Teacher's Seasonal Energy, Associated-Dissociated, p. 121	The teacher has no pattern as to the teacher's degree of association-dissociation. There isn't a sense of seasons. The teacher feels victimized and sorry for herself.	The teacher has a gross sense of *seasons*. For example, "Don't smile until after Thanksgiving."	The teacher has a sense of her own well being and exercises regularly.	The teacher self-selects the degree of association-dissociation based on the seasons of the year and the difficulty of the class. Interprets the contract as "10 wellness days," thus staying home while the teacher can still easily recover; as a result, the teacher is absent less than other teachers. Has a different season than the class; especially increases exercise just before and during the more difficult seasons of the year.
Pushing a Class, p. 124	The teacher has no pattern as to expectations of the class.	The teacher vacillates between pushing the class and then not pushing the class; e.g., when the teacher wants to be popular/liked.	The teacher is consistent in terms of the degree that the teacher pushes the class. The class knows what to expect.	The teacher pushes the class based on the unity of the class.

© 2000 by Michael Grinder & Assoc., ARR. AHC03 (360) 687-3238; FAX (360) 687-0595; http://www.michaelgrinder.com

Chapter Four Post-its

Students' Identity Size

Am I recognizing and adjusting the seasonal changes in the students' identity size?

Chapter Four: Seasons, pp. 107-109.

Teachership

Am I selecting the appropriate level based on the season and the class' group dynamics?

Chapter Four: Seasons, pp. 117-120.

Right-brain Days—Predictable

Am I preparing for the predicting and recovery of the surprise unpredictable right-brain days? Do I check the "Hallway Noise" to verify that I am OK?

Chapter Four: Seasons, pp. 109-113.

Teacher's Energy

Am I having a different season than the class because of increasing my exercise during difficult seasons?

Chapter Four: Seasons, pp. 121-123.

Firsts

Do I give myself "grace" when a surprise "first" occurs and rehearse how I want to respond the next time it happens?

Chapter Four: Seasons, p. 117.

Pushing A Class

Do I change the degree of pushing the class based on the unity of the class as evidenced by the unisance of response?

Chapter Four: Seasons, pp. 124-125.

© 2000 by Michael Grinder & Assoc., ARR. AHC03 (360) 687-3238; FAX (360) 687-0595; http://www.michaelgrinder.com

End Notes

1. Margaret Wheatley, *Leadership and the New Science.*

2. See p. 109.

3. See p. 113.

4. For more details, see Chapter Eight, p. 169, of Michael Grinder's *Righting the Educational Conveyor Belt*, 1989.

5. *ENVoY*, pp. 28 and 48, respectively.

6. For a full discussion, see pp. 169-174 of *Righting the Educational Conveyor Belt.*

7. Utilizing Elizabeth Kubler-Ross' concept of grief, an understanding of community group dynamics can be gained. Those members immediately affected by the tragedy (e.g., parents of the deceased, those wounded, actual witnesses) grieve in a cyclical manner. Their support group caretakes these members. As the members operate with less emotional residue, the support groups feel good. Then occasions reactivate the raw emotions of the original event and the support groups feel unsuccessful and tire of trying to support. This splits the members from the support group. Frustrated that their support hasn't resulted in the grieving people *getting through it*, the supporters tire and shrink away. The grieving people feel abandoned. In essence, the grieving people have to rotate to a new group of supporters.

8. See Chapter One and specifically p. 39.

9. Neuro Linguistic Programming's term for one person's non-verbals being matched by another person; e.g., same facial expressions.

10. From John Grinder and Richard Bandler's NLP study of Milton Erickson.

11. It is a strange thing for an office worker to go to an office supply store and buy supplies for her desk. Yet teachers do this all the time. According to the NEA's 1997 report, U.S. teachers spent an average of $408 of their own money on their students during the 1995-1996 school year. Teachers in the West spent more ($477) than those in the East ($353). Teachers 40 to 49 spent more ($440) than teachers younger than 30 ($276). Elementary teachers spent more ($502) than secondary teachers ($323). Minority teachers spent more ($454) than white teachers ($400). And women spent more ($446) than men ($295). (*The Dallas Morning News*, "Out of Pocket" by Brian Boney, July 20, 1999.)

© 2000 by Michael Grinder & Assoc., ARR. AHC03 (360) 687-3238; FAX (360) 687-0595; http://www.michaelgrinder.com

12. The section on students being seasonally prone to feeling victimized, pp. 125-126, applies to teachers as well.

13. Principal and ENVoY trainer.

14. Being "associated" is correlated with Howard Gardner's Intrapersonal Intelligence. Being "dissociated" allows the teacher to increase her Interpersonal Intelligence (awareness of group dynamics).

15. A whole section on victims is presented on p. 125. The purpose is to have the teacher recognize and effectively respond to students who seasonally feel sorry for themselves. As educators, we can profit by understanding that administrators often have to handle teachers who feel victimized by the students acting like a victim.

16. Fisher & Ury wrote *Getting to Yes*, and Ury penned *Getting Past No*.

17. *You Can Negotiate Anything*.

18. *ENVoY*, Exit Directions, p. 28.

19. See *ENVoY II*. The two hooks, making eye contact and being verbal while managing, increases the likelihood of escalation.

20. For example, "You are a good math student" is praise while "You have four of the six problems finished" is encouragement.

© 2000 by Michael Grinder & Assoc., ARR. AHC03 (360) 687-3238; FAX (360) 687-0595; http://www.michaelgrinder.com

MANAGING A HEALTHY CLASSROOM

In the left illustration above, the teacher is explaining something that, based on the dog's facial expression, the dog is having difficulty grasping.

The scenario continues in the right illustration. Because of the cohesiveness of the class dynamics, the dog's cat tablemate is indicating that she will help the dog. The dog, who identifies strongly with her colleague, believes that she will be able to understand with peer help.

To be respectful of gender equality and yet provide the educator with a fluid reading style, in this chapter the teacher is referred to by the male pronoun and the student by the female pronoun.

"The essence of mastering systems thinking...lies in seeing patterns where others only see events and forces to react to." [1]

Introduction

A Healthy Classroom concerns itself with combining management strategies with an understanding of group dynamics.[2] This chapter focuses on how to manage a classroom so the atmosphere is "healthy." The definition of a healthy classroom is found by examining the various classroom cultures that are associated with different grade levels. Throughout this chapter the operational definitions of the *struggling novice*, *apprentice*, *scientist* and *artisan* are implicitly and explicitly present.

The Bell Curve of Classrooms

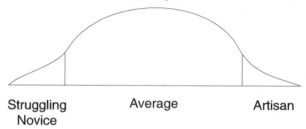

Struggling Novice   Average   Artisan

The average classroom is normal, meaning that most of the time the veteran teacher is a scientist of classroom management and seasonally reverts to the apprentice level of management. It would be wonderful if student teachers could be placed with artisans with the hope that the modeling would transfer. *A Healthy Classroom* contends that the artisan's philosophy of education, as well as artisan's conscious intention in the healthy classroom, is not enough to explain why the classroom is so healthy. This chapter suggests that a healthy classroom is a direct result of the artisan's utilization of group dynamics. Daily strategies that are behaviorally employed, often at an unconscious level, produce such results. The first purpose of this chapter is to reveal those strategies so that many average teachers in the "normal" classroom have a blueprint for becoming outstanding teachers in their own style of a healthy classroom.

Reshaping the Bell Curve

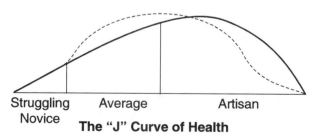

Struggling Novice   Average   Artisan

The "J" Curve of Health

© 2000 by Michael Grinder & Assoc., ARR. AHC03 (360) 687-3238; FAX (360) 687-0595; http://www.michaelgrinder.com

Secondly, by becoming conscious of what they do, the outstanding teachers can indeed assist student teachers.

One of the keys that the artisan becomes conscious of is that he manages the student's behavior in such a way that the student doesn't lose face. Where the teacher looks when managing is critical for addressing the student's behavior.

An even more sophisticated ingredient to a healthy environment is to understand the innate tendency for the class, as a group, to create niches for various members. While it is common for classroom stereotypes to include a "scapegoat," the teacher can employ several techniques to prevent scapegoats from appearing in his classroom.

Stereotyping is a natural phenomenon that can occur in both typical classrooms and healthy classrooms. Recognizing the former and fostering the latter is a daunting task. Tremendous optimism is given to a blueprint of preventing stereotyping and, instead, fostering full human beings. In particular, the technique of *sandwiching* is refreshing because of the ease of implementation. The chapter ends with the strategies that, when present, tend to create a healthy classroom. These descriptions can be used as a checklist/evidence of a healthy climate.

Classroom Cultures

5-1

While each classroom is a most unique and varied environment, it is helpful to examine some group dynamics patterns that the teacher molds. The lower the grade level, the more likely the individual student is highly valued. Literally, the classroom is centered around caring for the "I" corner of the classroom triangle. The teacher accepts every individual student and loves each into becoming the person the student is capable of being.

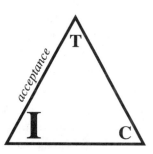

The higher the grade level the more the teacher leans toward focusing on the group as a whole and on moving as many students as possible into being all they can academically be. The teacher wants to demand individual accountability so that individual students don't hold up the class as a whole.

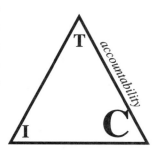

© 2000 by Michael Grinder & Assoc., ARR. AHC03 (360) 687-3238; FAX (360) 687-0595; http://www.michaelgrinder.com

These two modus operandi are the terminal ends of a continuum that is labeled "classroom cultures." The term *culture* is used to connote that there are many subtle ramifications.

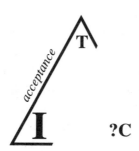

Employing the motto "a virtue when used to an extreme becomes a vice," each classroom style can become imbalanced. A classroom culture of acceptance is based on one-on-one rapport. The extreme end is one where all reality stops if one student is not OK with herself. The classroom culture of accountability is based on high productivity which, in the extreme, ignores the individual student for the sake of covering more content. Anything not written on the tight schedule is skipped.[3]

A Healthy Classroom suggests that while the culture of acceptance and the culture of accountability are admirable, neither is as healthy as a culture that balances both qualities. While the whole chapter expounds and expands the definition of a healthy classroom, a starting operational definition follows.

> **A healthy classroom is one in which the individual is accepted as a person and the individual is held accountable for her behavior.**

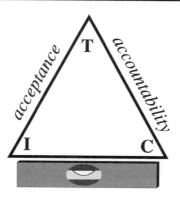

The carpenter's level illustrates this balance.

© 2000 by Michael Grinder & Assoc., ARR. AHC03 (360) 687-3238; FAX (360) 687-0595; http://www.michaelgrinder.com

Manage the Behavior, Not the Person

5-2

Employing management techniques that "blame and shame" a student has never worked well on the "at-risk" population. Historically, when there were only two to three students who were at-risk, a teacher could justify utilizing "blame and shame." While the methodology was not necessarily effective with the at-risk student being managed, "blame and shame" was a deterrent for the rest of the class who were witnessing the management. For certain grade levels (i.e., sixth through ninth grades) and with certain cultures (e.g., inner city), the "blame and shame" approach to management is an utter failure. For these students, if the instructor is disrespectful of the "person" part of the student when managing, the instructor's reputation as a manager and often as a teacher is gravely damaged.

A teacher fostering a healthy classroom commits himself to a culture of relationship.

The goal of the effective manager is to indicate that the student's behavior is inappropriate and needs to change without implying that the student as a person is "bad." The question is, "How does the teacher separate the student as a person from the student's behavior?" To answer that question, two definitions need to be introduced.

Two-point Communication

When a teacher is communicating, those students who are listening will most likely look where the teacher is looking. When the communication involves eye contact, the student is looking at the teacher because the teacher is looking at the student. Eye contact is referred to as *two-point* communication because there are two parties involved in the communication: the teacher and the student. Two-point communication is interpersonal in that the relationship between the parties is accessed. Two-point communication increases the emotions inside the parties who are looking at each other. This is true whether the emotions are positive or negative and whether the teacher is doing management or teaching. Sometimes unintended, but humorous, results can occur as illustrated in the following vignette.

Students follow teacher's eyes.

© 2000 by Michael Grinder & Assoc., ARR. AHC03 (360) 687-3238; FAX (360) 687-0595; http://www.michaelgrinder.com

---

Vignette: "Look Up Here!"

Violet Visual believes that she only knows if the class is listening to her when she sees their eyeballs. She is famous for demanding that everyone look at her when she is teaching. On this particular day, they have not been as attentive as she would like. By the afternoon Violet is very perturbed. She is standing at the board. While she is pointing to some written information, Violet is looking directly at the class. As she announces, "Look up here!" her patience is spent. She yells, "LOOK UP HERE!" She has all eyes now, but they are on her not the board. Being beyond her tolerance level she taps on the board and shrieks, "DON'T LOOK AT ME. THE ANSWERS ARE NOT ON MY FACE, THEY ARE ON THE BOARD." The students are breathing high, but not one of them dares to take his eyes off Miss Visual.

Three-point Communication

Since the student follows the teacher's eyes, once the teacher has the student's attention, the student will look where the teacher directs his eyes. If the teacher looks at the board, the student will follow his lead and look at the board also. Since the two parties, namely the teacher and the student, are looking at a third point, the communication is referred to as a *three-point* communication. Three-point communication is not as personal as two-point communication. Three-point communication is less emotional than two-point communication because the focus is on the issue level of the communication instead of the relationship level.[4]

Back to the question, "How to manage the behavior and not the person?" When managing, once the teacher has the student's attention, if the teacher doesn't look at the student the unconscious interpretation is that the teacher is only managing the student's behavior.

> *Three-point management = the student's behavior is addressed.*
> *Two-point management = the student, as a person, is addressed.*

The other correlations include:

- If the interaction is positive, two-point communication results in the parties breathing low/abdominal (i.e., comfort) and experiencing positive emotions.

© 2000 by Michael Grinder & Assoc., ARR. AHC03 (360) 687-3238; FAX (360) 687-0595; http://www.michaelgrinder.com

- If the interaction is negative, two-point communication results in the parties breathing high/shallow (i.e., stress) and experiencing negative emotions.

- If the interaction is negative, three-point communication results in the parties, instead of breathing high/shallow and experiencing negative emotions, breathing lower/more abdominally and experiencing more comfort.

Power vs. Inappropriate Power

5-3

A Healthy Classroom advocates that classrooms need to be run with influence instead of power.[5] And yet, for a teacher to be an effective manager by influence, the teacher has to be comfortable with power. Why? First, because there are many situations where influence wouldn't work. This is why Chapter One: *Class Formation* heads this book. In general, the teacher takes command of the classroom with power when the group dynamics are not functioning–this is when the teacher is the pilot of the airplane.[6] Formed groups are what allow the teacher to fully operate from influence instead of power.

The second reason that the teacher has to be comfortable with power is that if power isn't employed when it is necessary then the healthy results that were produced when the teacher was operating from influence are ruined.

Two questions arise: first, what is meant by power? The terms "power" and "influence" are described as follows:[7]

Category	Power	Influence
teacher is	in front of	off to the side
looking	at the student	at the student's work
physically	close	farther away
mode	verbal and non-verbal	mostly non-verbal

The second question is, "What is the difference between appropriate power and inappropriate power?"

If the student is off-task, the teacher's first choice is to try to shift the student to on-task behavior by employing influence.[8] For example, the teacher approaches the student from the side and looks at the student's desk while non-verbally pointing to the student's work. When the student notices the teacher's presence, the student will likely look up at the teacher. Once the student notices that the teacher is looking at the student's

Whenever possible, the teacher wants to operate from influence instead of power.

desk, the student will look down at her desk and begin to work. This is because the student follows the teacher's eyes. If the teacher is looking at the student's desk, the student will also. If the teacher's physical presence in an influential posture isn't sufficient to shift the student to on-task behavior, the teacher will switch to power management. This involves one or more of the following ingredients: the teacher says the student's name, comes in closer, shifts to being frontal, makes eye contact. Once the student shifts from being *off-task* to *neutral* the teacher shifts from power to influence. There are several reasons for doing this. Once the student is at *neutral,* she can only work if she is breathing low, and if the teacher is still using power, the teacher's eye contact alone won't allow the student to breathe well enough to concentrate. Secondly, the relationship between the student and teacher is damaged when the teacher continues to operate from power once the student is at *neutral.*

	OFF-task / Neutral / ON-task
1st choice	I n f l u e n c e
backup	P o w e r — I n f l u e n c e

The example of a teacher interacting with one student also applies to when the teacher is managing a whole class; for instance, saying something loud and brief, then pausing and then dropping to a whisper is a classic approach of getting a class' attention.[9] When the teacher is speaking loud (e.g., "CLASS, LOOK UP HERE"), the teacher only says the words until the class starts to shift to *neutral.* If the pupils start to shift when the teacher is halfway through the word "look" (i.e., "CLASS LO"), the teacher stops. Equestrians have a term to describe appropriate power: "equestrian tact"—only use the amount of power necessary.

> *Inappropriate power is when "neutral" is present and the teacher is still operating from power.*

A teacher has to be comfortable with power to manage from a frame of influence. What the teacher feels when employing power doesn't determine if the teacher will be doing appropriate or inappropriate power. It is how the teacher feels about feeling the emotions during the employment of power that determines if the teacher will stop the power posture once the student shifts from being *off-task* to *neutral.*

© 2000 by Michael Grinder & Assoc., ARR. AHC03 (360) 687-3238; FAX (360) 687-0595; http://www.michaelgrinder.com

Roots of Inappropriate Teacher Power

5-4

Accommodate, Accommodate, Explode [10]

Pretending that people are animals, they could be placed on a continuum of dogs at one end and cats at the other terminal.[11] The continuum is the *degree of accommodating* that the person extends to others. Like real animals, when one calls a dog, it comes—a high degree of accommodating; whereas when an owner calls a cat, it has a message machine. The dog operates under the golden rule of, "Treat others the way you want to be treated." The corollary is, "If I treat others the way I want to be treated, others will treat me the way I want to be treated." For example, if an adult dog asks an adult cat, "How was your weekend?" the cat might choose to talk endlessly or just say, "OK." In either case, the dog expects the cat to return the favor and ask, "And how was your weekend?" So, too, in the classroom, the dog teacher operates as, "If I accommodate the class and the individual students, they will accommodate me—our classroom will be an educational Camelot. Harmony and cooperation will reign."

The teacher's desire is to be a giving, caring person and often his tendency is to accommodate. The concept of accommodating spans a whole range of descriptions. It can mean the teacher is flexible and can change his expectations to accommodate the request from an individual student or the class as a whole. At the other extreme, "accommodating" includes situations when the teacher is not respected/appreciated. It is the latter that is referred to.

If the teacher repeatedly accommodates, each incident is like the proverbial straw that is laid on the camel's back, with the teacher being the camel. It is important to be cognizant of the cumulative nature of the "straws," especially seasonally. If the teacher continues to accommodate, he is likely to explode[12] when the final straw breaks the camel's back.

© 2000 by Michael Grinder & Assoc., ARR. AHC03 (360) 687-3238; FAX (360) 687-0595; http://www.michaelgrinder.com

---

Vignette: Scales of Justice

Long-Suffering Susan has a student teacher, Cathy Canine. Susan quickly realizes that her charge is a classic dog personality. Three years ago, Susan mentored a student teacher, Donald Dog. As a mentor, Susan wants to do even better this time. Susan wants to impart some wisdom that she learned the hard way: we can live the golden rule with the majority of students when we are interacting one-on-one. But with certain students, the cats, and often with the class as a whole, we want to operate with the platinum rule: treat others the way they need to be treated.

Long-Suffering Susan explains to Cathy Canine that as teachers we have an invisible "scale of justice" inside ourselves. When the class is mildly inappropriate, we set aside the fact that they are not respecting us; we accommodate. While in no way do we consciously keep track of the number of violations against us, a tally is being kept unconsciously. How do we know this? When the scales of justice are too tilted, Mount Saint Helens explodes. On the day when the emotional plume is raising in the air and the spewing of hot lava is flowing down the aisles, the actual incident certainly doesn't warrant the size of our explosion. Susan shares that she really embarrassed herself one day when she found herself at wit's end with an eighth grader and finished her harangue with, "And I had your sister too!" Talk about a *scale of justice* being kept a long time!! Long-Suffering Susan ends with, "As you learn to be attentive to the initial urges to accommodate, ask yourself, 'What do they need?' Resist the urge to manage when you feel a strong emotion, such as feeling violated. We don't want to justify our explosions. We want to avoid explosions by managing early, before we accommodate and start to feel."

Pupils' Perception

If the teacher explodes, how the class reacts and the teacher's style of exploding depend on several variables.

First, was the class witness to an imposition/disrespect of the teacher that the teacher accommodated? If yes, from the class' vantage point they are likely aware of the single straw that was just done. Depending on the age of the pupils, they may agree that what was just done shouldn't have happened, but they are mystified at the size of the teacher's reaction.

© 2000 by Michael Grinder & Assoc., ARR. AHC03 (360) 687-3238; FAX (360) 687-0595; http://www.michaelgrinder.com

The students are stunned because the explosion seems out of proportion to the specific incident that occurred. They are likely aware of the single straw but not the collective size of all the straws the teacher is responding to.

In addition, the concept of accommodating includes those times when the teacher has spent endless hours preparing a unit that was not well received. If the teacher explodes, the class will be *shocked* because they don't understand how the teacher could feel hurt because the disrespect/ imposition is based on the effort the teacher exerted when the class wasn't present.

The second variable that explains the class' reaction to the teacher's explosion is the frequency of the *Accommodate, Accommodate, Explode* syndrome. If the teacher repeats the pattern enough, the class will progress through the *stages* of *confusion* and *annoyance*.[13] In extreme cases, in order for the class to function, they will learn to *ignore* the teacher's harangues.

The third variable that influences the class' reaction to the teacher's outbursts is the teacher's style of releasing the weight of the straws.

If the teacher's style is the pattern of *Accommodate, Accommodate, Explode*, where does the pattern come from and what is the manner of the "explode?" This book is based on the concept of *culture*, with the corollary that a person often doesn't transfer the perception and competencies of one cultural context to another cultural context. The book opened with the example of the coach being totally aware of group dynamics while on the athletic field, and yet not having the same sensitivity in the classroom. The other example of how contextual cultural perception is was the principal who wouldn't think of responding to a teacher's request without taking into account how such a decision would affect the entire faculty. But that same administrator might begin a debrief of a classroom observation with, "There were two to three students over by the window not engaged." Such an opening might be totally insensitive to the ramifications if the teacher had attempted to engage such pupils. So while the teacher might be *personally* very healthy, the teacher's image of how a teacher releases the tension of the straws might be based on what was modeled for his by his own instructors. In essence, the healthy person might operate in a healthy way with his own current family and not transfer such healthy reactions to the *position* of a classroom manager.

For whatever reason we might *Accommodate, Accommodate, Explode*, there is no excuse for our infrequent counterproductive actions, nor is there a reason why we cannot choose to make the transition from a traditional culture of power to the new educational culture of influence.

We can make the transition from a traditional culture of power and create a new educational culture of influence.

© 2000 by Michael Grinder & Assoc., ARR. AHC03 (360) 687-3238; FAX (360) 687-0595; http://www.michaelgrinder.com

The solution is to manage early, before the teacher feels.

"When you go to pick up one thing, you find that it is hitched to everything else...."
John Muir

Accommodate, Accommodate, Explode usually happens when the teacher is in a fatigued, reactive state. This is not only innate to teaching, it is true in all professions. When we can't see something coming, partly because our own tolerance level is diminishing, our options are greatly decreased.

To be proactive, the teacher needs a model of healthy releasing before his patience is spent. The crux stems from the fact that the teacher is *accommodating* in the first place. A discussion of increasing the repertoire of teachers' coping behaviors misses the point. Instead of focusing on healthy ways to release the weight and tension of the straws, avoid putting the straws on the camel's back to start with. *A Healthy Classroom* proposes that the teacher not respond to the class and individual student based on how he feels, which is the tendency of the accommodating teacher, but on what the class and student need. *Manage early* before you feel. As Kendall Zoller[14] is fond of saying, "We are paid to feel when we teach, not when we manage."

Using Howard Gardner's Multiple Intelligence Model[15], the accommodating teacher is more intrapersonal and in touch with his feelings. The teacher behaviorally decides to intervene when there are enough straws on the camel's back to warrant the explosion and whereas successful group dynamics is a result of the teacher being interpersonal, attentive outside himself to the group dynamics. This is a more dissociated state. Perception of group dynamics involves being aware of the interaction between the class as a whole, the individual students who are present and the teacher. It is more sophisticated than just perception of the individual students or just perception of the class as a whole. Perception of group dynamics is understanding the ecology of people. The more the teacher progresses from just seeing the class as a collection of individuals to seeing the class as a whole as well as the individual students, the more the teacher has to change his way of viewing reality. This transition is similar to driving: the faster you travel the bigger the signs have to be so you can read them from a distance. The biggest road sign the teacher wants to read is his seasonal energy level. There are certain seasons that the teacher wants to be cognizant of and prepare for by exercising. One of the surest indicators of fatigue is the reduction in the teacher's sense of humor. By exercising, the teacher can have a different season than his class. He can remain dissociated and effective during times when students are seasonally prone to operating like victims.

One of the repeating themes in this work is that we, like all cultures, behave in habitual ways. One of them is our tendency to operate from an *Accommodate, Accommodate, Explode* template. We want to transcend our culture. "Traditions are like recipes. They are passed down forever. The trick is to know what to eat and what to leave on your plate."[16]

© 2000 by Michael Grinder & Assoc., ARR. AHC03 (360) 687-3238; FAX (360) 687-0595; http://www.michaelgrinder.com

"The child is the father to the man."[17]

Vignette: Mary Martyr and Don Doormat
(least recommended)

Mary Martyr and Don Doormat teach next door to each other. While each has a family of their own, they spend most of Sunday conscientiously preparing their classrooms for the upcoming week. They look forward to taking a snack break and visiting with each other. Their friendship, and with it their mutual trust, has increased over the years. Many times at the end of a long school day they stop by each other's rooms to comfort each other. Without fully realizing it, they have been saying, "These kids nowadays have no respect," and "They just don't appreciate what we do for them." They feel especially comforted when they share that they "lost it" during the day and yelled at the children and the other one says, "I know, I regretfully do that too." They jokingly describe themselves, "We are not *soul* mates but we are *sol*ace mates."

Vignette: Healthy Harry and Fitness Fran
(recommended)

Healthy Harry and Fitness Fran are former primary teachers who teach seventh grade. While at a "stress retreat" they recognized their tendency to pour themselves into their work. They have a pact to help remind themselves to live balanced lives. The time spent "after hours" on school work has to be equalized by a quarter of that amount spent on fitness. Since they started the agreement, they have been averaging 30 minutes three times a week at the gym or walking. They know that they feel bad when they read about the biographies of outstanding educators in the newspaper and when professional journals tell of all the neat stuff that these teachers are doing. They joke that they have yet to hear of a teacher who spends only the regular contract hours working being honored. They hope that the decrease in preparation time is more than compensated for by their being models of healthy adult human beings.

© 2000 by Michael Grinder & Assoc., ARR. AHC03 (360) 687-3238; FAX (360) 687-0595; http://www.michaelgrinder.com

5-5

Stereotyping

So far, *A Healthy Classroom* has defined a healthy classroom as one where the individual student is managed with respect. This involves the "teacher" corner interacting with the "individual student" corner of the classroom triangle.

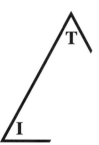

Of equal importance, but of a more difficult nature, is the interaction between the "class" corner and the "individual student" corner. It is an

innate part of group dynamics for a class to gravitate towards stereotyping the individual members of the class.

As previously mentioned,[18] initially the class stereotypes are based on physical characteristics like size, weight and general appearance. In time, the class notices internal traits like intelligence, competence, confidence, humor, skepticism and curiosity.

On the surface it would seem that the student would accept the image if the identity is positive, such as "best looking" and "very smart." But it seems that acceptance of the identity is not based on whether the image is negative or positive but on whether the identity is voluntarily accepted. If the student wants the identity, whether it is positive or negative, the person welcomes the role. When the identity is imposed on the student, the person may well resent the imposition.

Each corner of the classroom triangle is vested in maintaining the stereotyping. The individual is interested in maintaining the image because the student has an identity and a person would rather have an identity than no identity. This also explains why a student will continue to act in an inappropriate manner, because such behavior provides the security of a given identity. This explains why the majority of students who are abused at home and are counseled towards a different placement (i.e., foster home) will absolutely resist. The other two corners are drawn to stereotyping, because they know what to expect from different members of the class. The familiar is more comfortable than the new or the unknown.

© 2000 by Michael Grinder & Assoc., ARR. AHC03 (360) 687-3238; FAX (360) 687-0595; http://www.michaelgrinder.com

Scapegoat

5-6

One of the most common ways that stereotyping is detrimental to classroom dynamics concerns the creation of a classroom "scapegoat." This is a group dynamic process where one person[19] is in the lowest position in the class. Colloquially, the hierarchial order is represented by the ladder, and the student at the bottom is referred to as being on the lowest rung of the classroom ladder.

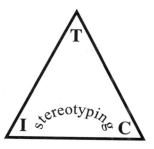

The ladder effect is especially present when inappropriate behavior appears. The bottom rung of the ladder is the "whipping boy."[20] In time, all the pupils expect such behavior from the individual student. Often the dynamics include the teacher subtly, and not so subtly, managing the person. This includes comments like, "Well, we all know that Joe is *always* late!" In certain classrooms the same student is at the bottom of the ladder regardless of whether it is the punctuality ladder, or the weak on reading ladder or the inattentiveness on listening ladder. Other classrooms have different ladders for different behaviors, so that a student who is *never* punctual might not be the same student who is *always* fiddling around instead of listening (e.g., "Sally, PLEASE LISTEN!!").

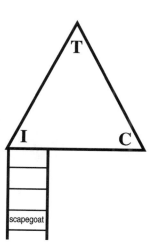

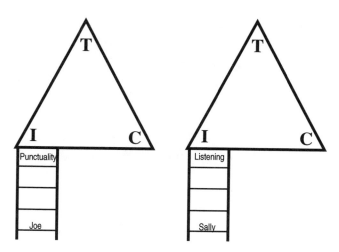

© 2000 by Michael Grinder & Assoc., ARR. AHC03 (360) 687-3238; FAX (360) 687-0595; http://www.michaelgrinder.com

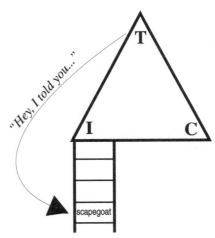

Because of the security of a given identity, the individual student often clings to a set of behaviors. The other two corners of the classroom triangle are also interested in maintaining the stereotyping because of predictability. From a management perspective, the teacher and class know and are comforted by knowing who will and won't need to be managed. For example, if several students are acting inappropriately and the scapegoat is one of them, it is likely the teacher will reprimand the scapegoat.

When the teacher, however inadvertently he might be doing so, reprimands one or two students more often than is actually warranted, scapegoats are created. Unusual as it might be, if the class is starting to be inappropriate and the teacher calls on a student who is perceived as liked by the teacher, then the class clearly distinguishes that the teacher is displeased with the behavior and not the person. This form of sorting assists the class to understand that the purpose of school is learning, management is done quickly, amnesia occurs and the class is back to learning.

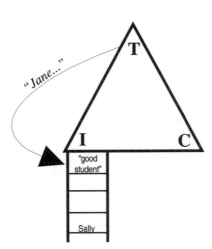

For a healthy classroom, it is imperative that the teacher find something that the teacher genuinely likes about the student that he will eventually manage. This breaks the cycle of the managed student feeling disliked (e.g., "You *always* pick on me.").

© 2000 by Michael Grinder & Assoc., ARR. AHC03 (360) 687-3238; FAX (360) 687-0595; http://www.michaelgrinder.com

---

Vignette: Pearl Proactive

Pearl Proactive attended a preschool workshop where Harry Wong presented.[21] Pearl has a gift of finding something positive about every student. Harry's concept added a missing piece to Pearl's puzzle—how to convey to the parents that she likes her students. She was very inspired to implement one of his suggestions. After the first day of school, she phoned all her parents. Just like Harry suggested, she reached 80% of her parents during dinner time. She followed his suggested script by briefly saying, "Hello, this is Mrs. Proactive. I am pleased to have (and she would mention the student's name) in my class." It was imperative to Pearl that she reach the parents of the students she will likely manage.[22] Pearl found the phone calls to be the best investment of her after-school hours for the whole year. It was effective because the parents of students who are often managed are only used to phone calls from school that are negative. Pearl Proactive also learned that the calls also produced some humorous results. When one parent ended the conversation with the teacher, she turned to her child and said, "That was your teacher. What did you already do wrong!?"

While the individual student finds it wonderful that the teacher likes her, from a classroom dynamics standpoint, it is even more important that the class perceive that the teacher likes those students he might manage. The reason is obvious. In the above example the teacher could afford to wait until a "good" student joined the misbehaving group. As previously mentioned, when the teacher manages a "good" student, the class knows the teacher is displeased with the behavior. However, there will be more occasions when the teacher cannot afford to wait for the "good" student to join in than when the teacher has the luxury to wait. Therefore, the teacher needs to be perceived as liking all students.

The question arises, "Why is the teacher managing the 'good' student such an uncommon practice?" The answer is found in the opposite direction, "What is the benefit of managing only the scapegoat?" The members, aside from the scapegoat, who are misbehaving improve their behavior while the relationship between the teacher and these students is preserved. In the true sense of the word, the scapegoat student isn't a goat at all

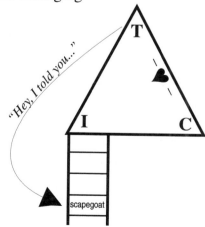

5-7

© 2000 by Michael Grinder & Assoc., ARR. AHC03 (360) 687-3238; FAX (360) 687-0595; http://www.michaelgrinder.com

but a sacrificial lamb, delivered up for the good of the teacher's relationship with the class.

How does a teacher know how much his inadvertent behavior is subtly reinforcing the scapegoat's inappropriate behavior? Let's examine two classrooms: Teacher A and Teacher B both have scapegoats in their rooms.

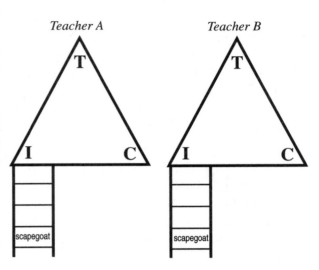

If the scapegoats are removed, what will happen?

If no new scapegoat appears in Teacher A's classroom and this is a pattern for several years, then Teacher A's classroom is a healthy classroom. If in Teacher B's classroom another scapegoat appears and this is a pattern, then Teacher B's classroom is less than healthy. Although most teachers claim that the students determine the success and ease of the year, the specialists of elementary schools know the teaching personality of every self-contained teacher. But the teacher's behavioral and emotional signature imprints the class. Such characteristics are vivid to the PE, music, media center and computer lab specialists. The specialist looks at his schedule before school even starts and can predict what kind of school year the specialist will have based on the schedule of when certain teachers' classes are seen. The specialist hates to have Teacher B's unruly classes just before or just after lunch and at the end of the day. The specialist smiles if the angels of scheduling have Teacher A's class scheduled during these time slots.

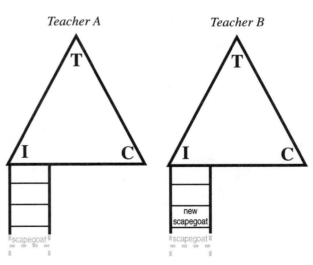

© 2000 by Michael Grinder & Assoc., ARR. AHC03 (360) 687-3238; FAX (360) 687-0595; http://www.michaelgrinder.com

Teacher's Efforts to Prevent Stereotyping

The goal of healthy classroom management is to recognize our cultural tendency to generalize from a student's behavior to the student as a person. This tendency is true apart from whether the student exhibits negative or positive behaviors. If the straight "A" student makes a mistake, the student is still a good person. And, equally true, if an at-risk student behaves well or does well academically, in no way does the student's value as a human being increase. From a classroom dynamics vantage point, the positive identity assigned to the individual is often as emotionally isolating as the negative identity. And, even more important, the existence of stereotypes deprives each student of a model of a full human being. It is the same as a major character in a novel or movie compared to a minor player. The reader learns the many complexities of the former while the latter is assigned just one trait to support the plot. So too, in the classroom, the more facets each student shows in the classroom, the healthier the individual and the healthier the classroom atmosphere.

The definition of a healthy classroom is when each individual student is accepted as a person and, at the same time, each person is held accountable for her behavior. "Accepted as a person" includes creating an environment where a person's many facets are encouraged. Stereotyping is a group dynamic process whereby members of a class are seen in predictable images. Predictable images allow everyone to be comfortable; the teacher can count on certain people to act in certain ways. Likewise, the group is able to know what roles and functions will be done by which members and, lastly, the individual person has an identity. In essence, the person's behavior and the person have been generalized together. As teachers we have the tendency to say, "Well, we all know Sally is 'smart.'" "Fred is such a 'clown.'"

For a teacher to move toward a healthy classroom, he has to switch his purpose from "educating the student" to "educating the whole person."

> **A healthy classroom is one where the student is known apart from her behaviors.**

In literature the main characters are described as "full" and the minor members of the story as "flat." Stereotyping results in flat human beings. The teacher wants to acknowledge the abilities and attributes that each member of the class displays and, at the same time, foster each student to be more than the student sees herself as being.

© 2000 by Michael Grinder & Assoc., ARR. AHC03 (360) 687-3238; FAX (360) 687-0595; http://www.michaelgrinder.com

Outside the home, school is the primary vehicle for socializing people into their self beliefs.

Examples of Preventing Stereotyping

If the class starts to see a student as...	The teacher...
asking a lot of questions	tries to decrease this behavior.
critical	notices when the student is complimentary and fosters the new behavior.
serious	watches for a glimmer of humor and endorses the humor.
a class clown	observes a sliver of seriousness and encourages this behavior.

Vignette: Structured Mistakes

Gloria Global views education as not just academic education but human education. She is a legend for achieving amazing results with unusual methods. Once she asked a straight "A" student to come to the back of the room and had him sit in a chair that was brought in from a classroom that was two grades lower than Gloria Global's classroom. The student was invited to write with his "off hand" and misspell two words during a spelling test. When asked by her colleagues for Gloria Global's rationale, she said, "I am as concerned for the 'better' students as for those who struggle academically. The 'perfect' students experience school life as a format of absolutes. They are pandered to because of their 'right' answers. They miss the opportunity to practice recovery or flexibility. That is only because they are still in school. They don't know that success in life after graduation is not composed of such a black and white format." Gloria Global explained that this particular student was ready to broaden his image. By having the student use the chair from a lower grade and write with his "off hand," Gloria Global is able to suspend the student's self-image and let him practice the concept that his *person* is not the same as his *behavior in* a safe environment.

© 2000 by Michael Grinder & Assoc., ARR. AHC03 (360) 687-3238; FAX (360) 687-0595; http://www.michaelgrinder.com

5-8

Standard-bearers Foster Full Humans

While the teacher wants to prevent stereotyping in his classroom so that the students become full human beings, it is precisely the early formation of stereotypes in the classroom that provides the teacher with grist for the mill to foster full humans. As *Group Formation* occurs, the uniqueness of each student begins to emerge. Statistically speaking, the students who are noticed are usually identified with one characteristic. If an individual student is seen as having more than one characteristic, then the traits tend to be correlated; for example, the straight "A" student is "serious." During the initial stages of stereotyping, certain students surface as standard-bearers of different traits. The noticeable standard-bearers, such as "the class clown" and "the brain," unconsciously mold the students into thinking that "in life each person finds her niche." These standard-bearers are critical in achieving one of the goals of a healthy classroom–fostering full human beings. How? Since the standard-bearers are the salient models of what human beings are, if they manifest a full range of traits then the students believe that it is normal for one's personality to include a full range of behaviors. The goal is for the teacher to elicit humor from the straight "A" student and a seriousness from the class clown. In the area of management, if there is a class "problem child," the level of healthiness that the classroom can arrive at is limited.

Vignette: Barbecue

Solomon Faire has been teaching for years on a variety of grade levels. He knows that often the teacher is a surrogate parent and, based upon certain home conditions, often is more effective than the biological parent. Solomon knows a teacher's priority is to care for the whole class and, secondary to this, the teacher tries to care for the individual students. About every other year Solomon will have one to three students who seek attention in inappropriate ways. He wants the class to ignore the student (Paul Pariah), because if the class is *shocked, confused,* or *annoyed*[23] by the student's behaviors, the student will only continue to act this way in order to get attention.

This year the class isn't showing the flexibility that Mr. Faire needs to individualize the rules. Every time Paul Pariah does the smallest infraction, the pupils call out, "Mr. Faire, Paul is doing it again!" Of course Paul Pariah loves it. Solomon reflects on how to convey the dynamics involved to the class.

Solomon Faire arranges to have Paul Pariah be in another part of the school for twenty minutes. Solomon Faire stands next to

continued on next page

© 2000 by Michael Grinder & Assoc., ARR. AHC03 (360) 687-3238; FAX (360) 687-0595; http://www.michaelgrinder.com

the bulletin board where the rules are posted and tells the following story. At the 4th of July family picnic, hamburgers are being served. The first three people receive one hamburger each, the fourth person receives three, and another person only receives the buns without the meat. Mr. Faire asks the class what they think of the server. There is a clear consensus that the chef is unfair. Then Solomon Faire explains that the fourth person who receives three hamburgers is on a college football scholarship, weighs 275 pounds and needs a lot of food to keep his weight up. The pupils' comments indicate an immediate change of view. Solomon Faire shows his innate patience and sure enough, someone asks, "What about the person who doesn't get any meat?" The question is followed with an immediate chorus of "Yeah!" They are satisfied when they learn the fifth person is a great grandpa who doesn't like to have his false teeth in his mouth and therefore can't eat meat, only the buns.

Solomon Faire then explains, "This classroom is like that picnic and the teacher is similar to the server." Pointing to himself, Solomon Faire continues, "That is why the cook has to treat each person differently." And, as the students nod, the teacher moves over to Paul Pariah's desk and says, "That's why someone is better served with different rules; let's ignore it when Paul acts that way. Let me decide what to do with him privately."

5-9

Sandwich

If students are both praised and reprimanded in clusters and the clusters are cross-stereotyped, health is increased. If Brian Brain is singled out ("In reading the papers last night, Brian's essay was excellent."), then the class unconsciously thinks, "Sure Brian can achieve such heights because he is 'the brain.'" If Brian's name is mentioned with two other smart students, then the classroom is fostering hierarchy. If Brian's name is mentioned with two of the class clowns, then everyone can be anyone. The term *sandwich* is used because the person who doesn't typically belong in the category of students being mentioned is placed in the middle of the students who, from a stereotypical standpoint, do belong there. In the management arena, by sandwiching the "scapegoat" with students who are seen as behaving appropriately, the caste system is broken. ("The discussion with Sally, Joe (the previous year's 'problem child') and Frank produces some interesting concepts.")

© 2000 by Michael Grinder & Assoc., ARR. AHC03 (360) 687-3238; FAX (360) 687-0595; http://www.michaelgrinder.com

> **Vignette: Michelangelo and the Sistine Chapel**
>
> (The following is a true and humorous example of sandwiching a "good" person among the "bad.")
>
> When Michelangelo was painting the Sistine Chapel, a particular Cardinal kept intervening. The nosy official not only would visit the work in progress and critique Michelangelo's work but also would complain to the Pope that he should direct Michelangelo to make changes. The artist finally drew the line and prevented the Cardinal from entering the building. When the chapel was finished there was an opening ceremony. Much to the Cardinal's chagrin, he found a facsimile of his face in the portion of the painting predicting hell.

Healthy Humor

As mentioned in Chapter One, *Class Formation*, laughing is one of the fastest ways to have a class breathe. When the humor is done so that laughter occurs in unison, instant health is gained momentarily. Humor is usually done at the expense of a person or subgroup. Someone once said that adult comedians would be lost for material if sex and drinking were off limits. Both as teachers and students, we have all experienced healthy humor. But what is it? It would be easy to say, "Healthy classroom humor happens when laughter is not at the expense of a student or group of students." But greater clarity is called for. If all three corners perceive that the humor stems from the student's behavior and not the student as a person, then it is healthy humor. This kind of humor is liberating because the individual student can laugh and the class can identify with the same behavior.

> *Healthy humor is when the class laughs "with the student" instead of "at the student."*

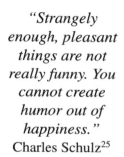

5-10

"Strangely enough, pleasant things are not really funny. You cannot create humor out of happiness." Charles Schulz[25]

Favoritism

5-11

Teachers have always known that showing favoritism towards certain students has negative consequences. *A Healthy Classroom* explains why favoritism is destructive–it splits the class. The educator wants to consciously try to avoid exhibiting partiality. Unconsciously the educator still will be indicating a bias.[25] The teacher's face, voice, body posture/proximity and breathing are communicating degrees of like or dislike. When a teacher calls on a student for academic purposes, the teacher physically comes closer to the student he likes compared to the student

© 2000 by Michael Grinder & Assoc., ARR. AHC03 (360) 687-3238; FAX (360) 687-0595; http://www.michaelgrinder.com

he dislikes. The reverse is also true. When the teacher calls on a student for management purposes, he stays farther away from the student he likes and moves closer to the student he dislikes.

5-12

Leaders, Barometers and Liaisons Over Time

Since *A Healthy Classroom* implies that a healthy classroom does the opposite of stereotyping by fostering full humans, it follows that the leadership in such an environment might well change. The antithesis of stereotyping is an atmosphere of flux. One evidence of a class in flux is that different tasks warrant different leadership qualities, which means that the leadership is shared. Some of the teacher's techniques to broaden the base of ownership in the classroom have been previously mentioned; namely, *Fostered Leaders* and *Levels of Teachership*.[26] Sometimes the leadership changes because of the characteristics of the leader. Initially, the external auditory may be a leader, but within two days the person's status declines. Over time the dynamics of leadership in a healthy classroom change. There is a blending of who does what; the words *always* and *never* (e.g., "Sally *always* gets to help the teacher." "I *never* get to read aloud.") are markedly absent. The term "committee" is a popular and effective way of getting things done in the room.

"Life's a dance you learn as you go. Sometimes you lead, sometimes you follow."[27]

Over the course of the school year, in addition to the leaders being affected by time, so are the barometers. In a healthy setting several variables influence who the barometers are. The more stereotypical the classroom, the more certain students are barometers for the class as a whole. The healthier the classroom, the more students' full personalities come out. This means that there are many subgroups, and each student belongs to several subgroups. Often the barometers for subgroups don't change, but over time the importance of the subgroups changes. Time affects barometers differently than leaders. For example, at the beginning of the year the subgroup of skeptics ("Let's check out the teacher.") might be influential but in time the subgroup's influence fades.

Any discussion of leaders and a healthy classroom must include the concept of *liaison*. This student floats between several subgroups. A liaison is a student seen by some of her peers as being credible-oriented; she values productivity and sees the class as more important than the individual students. She is perceived by other classmates as being approachable-oriented; she is committed to high morale and relationships with individual members of the class. A liaison's flexibility is such that sometimes she is a "lead" and other times a "support." The varied views of this student indicate that the liaison is not in a given mold. The liaison shatters the confines of stereotyping. In essence, liaisons supercede and therefore replace the concept of *leaders* and *barometers*.

© 2000 by Michael Grinder & Assoc., ARR. AHC03 (360) 687-3238; FAX (360) 687-0595; http://www.michaelgrinder.com

> ***In a healthy classroom, there is a larger
> number of liaisons than in the average classroom.***

Vignette: "Why didn't you say Allison's name earlier?"[28]

As the classroom phone rings, Malcolm quickly points to two math problems on the board and indicates for the pupils to practice them. Since Malcolm has fewer students in his eighth grade class than the other instructors, the office was notifying him that a new female student would be sent immediately to the room. As Malcolm hangs up the phone, he plans to pull three students out into the foyer and give them a "heads up" on the new member of the class. As he starts to say, "Can I see Sally..." the class stiffens a bit, "... and Nicole and Allison out in the foyer," the class relaxes. Julie, the class' external auditory student says, "Why didn't you say Allison's name earlier?" Curiously, the teacher asks, "Why?" And Julie, ever ready to volunteer information pipes up, "Because she's never in trouble!" Instantly Malcolm realizes the class assumed the phone call meant someone was in trouble. However, when Allison's name was mentioned the pupils knew the assemblance was going to be positive because Allison is always "good."

That night at home as Malcolm shared his day over the dinner table, he realizes that until he broadens the base of the leadership in the classroom, Allison must be the first name mentioned for all neutral or positive gatherings of students.

Management Positively Affects Curriculum

The ENVoY trilogy programs[29], while they emphasize management, positively affect the curriculum:

1. Since effective management techniques are quicker than ineffective management methods, the ENVoY trilogy provide the teacher with more time for curriculum.

2. Since the approach is based on the student being more attentive to *visual* clues, and since being *visual* is the key to academic success, the approach influences the student to develop her visual modality. If the teacher writes "5 x 5 = " on the board and says, "Class, what is five times five?" the class can answer without looking at the board.[30] Lessons taught orally inadvertently increase inattentiveness, whereas if the teacher says, "Class, what is five times this number?" and taps on the board, the class has to visually be attentive.

© 2000 by Michael Grinder & Assoc., ARR. AHC03 (360) 687-3238; FAX (360) 687-0595; http://www.michaelgrinder.com

Likewise, *A Healthy Classroom* focuses on how healthy classroom dynamics positively affect the management arena. The next several pages delineate specifically how.

One of the greatest academic challenges has been finding ways to accommodate the needs of the "inclusion students." The first three phases

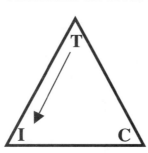

of a lesson are class oriented; the teacher helps the individual student only during the fourth phase. The teacher can be very skilled at individualizing instruction and still may be shackled by the lack of time to assist these students. Since the teacher has a limited number of ways to stretch time, the answer to assisting these students might well lie in the other corner, namely the class, aiding these students. This would only happen when the class is unified— which is what occurs when *A Healthy Classroom* is implemented.

Osmotic Learning

5-13

A Healthy Classroom produces an interesting phenomenon. When the class has been sufficiently formed, students can learn osmotically.[31]

There are several levels of this kind of learning. One is "ownership." When a student says to the teacher during the *Teaching* phase of the lesson,

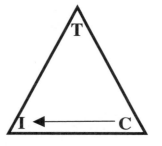

"I don't get it," and a table mate immediately volunteers to help, the teacher covers more content for the group as a whole with the class owning the learning for those who need assistance.

The "ownership" level is common in many healthy classrooms. Another level, much less common, is when the teacher checks for understanding during the presentation of new material—"Does that make sense?"— and most students congruently nod their heads. But sometimes a small number of students nod their heads "yes" while having furrowed foreheads. This incongruency can be interpreted as they consciously "don't

© 2000 by Michael Grinder & Assoc., ARR. AHC03 (360) 687-3238; FAX (360) 687-0595; http://www.michaelgrinder.com

get it" and yet, viscerally, believe they will. It is almost like these students are non-verbally saying, "Since I am a part of this larger organism called the 'class,' and the majority are 'getting it,' I will also!" It is as if the minority has confidence based on future competence. Being a member of a larger body allows one to accomplish more than what one could alone.

An even stranger level of osmotic learning is when the student can unconsciously perform a task. Based on the grade level, it might be finding the vowels in the alphabet, converting fractions to percents, or researching and writing papers. The phrase "osmotic learning," while a curious one, is an accurate description of students learning indirectly, instead of directly. Some possible explanations are offered.

The first is the research on "accelerated learning."[32] The popular phrase used to describe a classroom of accelerated learning is *relaxed alertness.* On the surface the term might seem like a paradox. Translating the phrase in *Healthy Classroomese,* we would find the pupils breathing low and on-task. The question is not whether the student "gets it" or not, but whether the student breathes high/shallow vs. low/abdominal when not understanding.

The second explanation comes from a model[33] that describes a person's learning as progressing through the stages of:

5-14

1. Unconscious incompetence. The student doesn't know she doesn't know/can't do something; e.g., the student has never heard of converting fractions to decimals and therefore is unaware of her ignorance.

2. Conscious incompetence. The student knows that she doesn't know or can't do something; for example, the student is introduced to the concept of decimals being a different way of expressing fractions but is unclear about how to do the conversion.

3. Unconscious competence. The person has been practicing a new learning or skill and doesn't realize that she is more competent than she is aware of. For example, the student says she cannot remember whether the numerator or the denominator becomes the dividend but instinctively makes the numerator the dividend.

4. Conscious competence. The person can not only do the new learning or skill but is aware that she can do it; the student knows for sure that the numerator becomes the dividend and can explain the skill.

5. Unconscious competence/habit. Since the conscious mind can only simultaneously hold five to nine items at a given moment[35], anything a student consciously can do (stage four) will in time become a habit. This means the student automatically does it without thinking, thus

It takes considerable knowledge just to realize the extent of your own ignorance.[34]

© 2000 by Michael Grinder & Assoc., ARR. AHC03 (360) 687-3238; FAX (360) 687-0595; http://www.michaelgrinder.com

allowing one of the five to nine conscious slots to be assigned to something new that will be learned. The difference between this level and level three, which has the same title, is the following. The student is doing conversion of fractions to decimals and becomes confused. If the student is at the third stage of development, she is lost. If she is at the fifth stage, she can easily recreate the fourth stage and arrive at a conscious understanding. As Jerry Seinfeld says, "When you're not doing well and don't know why, it is scary. If you know, it's not so scary!"[36]

A Learning Model

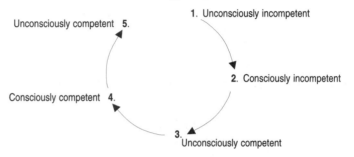

1. Unconsciously incompetent

2. Consciously incompetent

3. Unconsciously competent

4. Consciously competent

5. Unconsciously competent

Osmotic learning is when the third stage is reached in an accelerated manner because of the group dynamics.

5-15

Other Positive Effects

There are three other intriguing academic advantages from *A Healthy Classroom*. They foster thinking.

1. In the curriculum tube, the desire for years has been to switch the teacher from a "dispenser of knowledge" to a "facilitator of thinking."

CURRICULUM

This is parallel to the ENVoY movement in the management tube of switching from a style of "management by power" to "management by influence."

MANAGEMENT

© 2000 by Michael Grinder & Assoc., ARR. AHC03 (360) 687-3238; FAX (360) 687-0595; http://www.michaelgrinder.com

And while it is possible for a teacher to operate as a facilitator of thinking while managing from a power position, it is unlikely. It makes more sense to switch from a dispenser of knowledge to a facilitator of thinking at the same time the teacher changes from managing from power to managing through influence.

In fact, the management tube leads the curriculum tube.

2. The curriculum concept of fostering thinking could be done with the teacher working with the individual students; however, this may be an impossibility because of the amount of time such an approach would take. Another alternative is for the teacher to facilitate the class as a whole—which is what happens during the *Teaching* phase of the lesson. Thinking is part of the larger activity of reflection and verbally clarifying which is best done with smaller groups or one-on-one. Thinking by this definition demands that the class have safety to accomplish this. This is what *A Healthy Classroom* accomplishes.

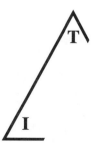

© 2000 by Michael Grinder & Assoc., ARR. AHC03 (360) 687-3238; FAX (360) 687-0595; http://www.michaelgrinder.com

3. "Dimensions of Learning"[37] and other curriculum modes say that relationships are the key to fostering thinking skills. This is true for no other reason than that dialogue usually is needed for thinking to occur. The curriculum tube has operated as if students cannot reach very high levels of sophistication without the much needed relationships and accompanying safety needed for thinking. The advocates of thinking are still waiting for the desired conditions. *A Healthy Classroom* develops the necessary group dynamics as a by-product of its management system.

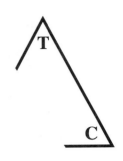

Vignette: Elsie Epiphany

Elsie Epiphany is devoted but not blindly committed to everything she does. She is a living example of Socrates' axiom, "An unexamined life is not worth living." In her mid-forties she signed up for a yoga class. Her colleagues, knowing she never missed a weekend church service, teased her, "Is this going to be your new religion?" One thing Elsie Epiphany immediately realizes in her yoga class is that breathing seems to be the key cause and indicator of how she is doing. She discovers that she often prays with high/shallow breathing. She had to laugh when she realized the contradiction of praying with the mental conviction that everything depended on her maker while physically acting like it depended on her. It took some concentration to remind herself to breathe low/abdominally when praying. She found much more peace from prayer and attending devotional services. The insights from the yoga class didn't stop with her spiritual life. She realized that every time a student wasn't "getting" a concept in the classroom and she was assisting the student, she was breathing high/shallow. In time, she learned that the more possessive she was about the outcome of the student "getting it," the higher/shallower she breathed; and, conversely, the more relaxed she stayed the more she actually achieved her outcome. It was as if the child's lack of understanding caused the child to be tight (breathed high/shallow) and Elsie Epiphany's concern showed in her breathing, as well. When she stays calm, her breathing positively affects the student. Elsie Epiphany wrote a private note to herself, "What we get is a by-product of how we breathe."

© 2000 by Michael Grinder & Assoc., ARR. AHC03 (360) 687-3238; FAX (360) 687-0595; http://www.michaelgrinder.com

Summary

This chapter presents strategies for preventing stereotyping in the classroom and fostering full humans. These strategies include, but are not limited to, the following:

- The absence of

  - scapegoats

  - students being equated with their behaviors

  - "ladders" of students being ranked

  - favoritism

  - "accommodate, accommodate, explode." Ideally, the teacher manages before he feels.

- Standard-bearers model a full range of behaviors that the rest of the students follow.

- Teachers sandwiches students from different categories.

- The class perceives that the teacher likes the student he managed.

- Teacher appropriately transitions from the necessary dependency of Teachership One to the healthier self-reliance of Teachership Two.

- Healthy humor is frequently present, enjoyed by all, and often only understandable to the members of the class.

- Leadership is shared, is based on situations, and changes over time.

- Osmotic learning occurs.

- Liaisons are present.

- Students are realistic, optimistic and ambitious about their future.

- Thinking occurs because the following is present:

  - **Safety**. It is OK to risk, to be vulnerable and explore and change one's mind.

  - **Relationship**. If thinking was developed during the teaching portion of a lesson, then there would only need to be a relationship between the teacher and the pupils and among the students. Thinking requires dialogue among the pupils; the

© 2000 by Michael Grinder & Assoc., ARR. AHC03 (360) 687-3238; FAX (360) 687-0595; http://www.michaelgrinder.com

safety necessary for dialogue is accomplished via Teachership II. Healthy group dynamics is the term for such safety and relationship.

> *An increase in one's professional competence is a result of one knowing oneself better.*
> Gabriel Byrne

© 2000 by Michael Grinder & Assoc., ARR. AHC03 (360) 687-3238; FAX (360) 687-0595; http://www.michaelgrinder.com

Rubric for Chapter Five: Managing a Healthy Classroom

	Struggling Novice	Apprentice	Scientist	Artisan of Healthy Classroom
Classroom Culture, p. 135	The teacher neither accepts students as individuals nor holds them accountable for inappropriate behavior.	The teacher always either accepts the students or holds them accountable without doing the other.	The teacher has a good degree of consistency of accepting the students as individuals and holding them accountable for inappropriate behavior.	The teacher successfully balances accepting the students as individuals while holding them accountable for inappropriate behavior.
Managing the Behavior, Not the Person, p. 137	The teacher manages with a two-point communication and doesn't always employ a two-point when the interaction is positive.	The teacher is inconsistent in employing a two-point communication when interacting positively and a three-point when managing.	The teacher has a good degree of consistency of employing two-point communication when intervening positively with student and employs a three-point when managing.	The teacher employs two-point communication when interacting positively with student and employs a three-point when managing.
Power vs. Inappropriate Power, p. 139	The teacher is inconsistent in terms of the degree of power employed.	The teacher always uses either too little power or too much power.	The teacher has degrees of power, stopping most of the time when the student is at *neutral.*	The teacher stops employing power as soon as the student is at *neutral.*
Accommodate, Accommodate, Explode, p. 141	The teacher explodes over things the class doesn't comprehend; apologizes; pattern is repeated.	The teacher becomes seasonally fatigued and explodes over things the class doesn't comprehend.	The teacher recognizes when his internal scales of justice are starting to feel imposed upon and starts to manage.	The teacher, instead of managing on how he viscerally feels, manages based on what he sees and hears occurring in the classroom.
Scapegoat, p. 147	Any student could be the scapegoat.	Certain students are always the scapegoats.	The teacher rotates whose name is said; amnesia follows management.	Every student feels she is a *favorite.* The class manages itself.
Preventing Stereotyping, p. 153	Any student could be a scapegoat; there is no consistency.	The teacher is inconsistent as to who in the pool of students at the bottom of the classroom ladder could be the scapegoat. The length of time a student is in the *dog house* is not predictable.	The teacher knows that stereotyping limits each student's view of what she can be and has a few strategies that he employs.	The teacher actively employs strategies to prevent stereotyping. These include rounding the standard-bearers into fuller human beings, sandwiching students from different categories, healthy humor, fostering liaisons, sharing and rotating leadership.

Transcends the Educational Culture

© 2000 by Michael Grinder & Assoc., ARR. AHC03 (360) 687-3238; FAX (360) 687-0595; http://www.michaelgrinder.com

Rubric for Chapter Five: Managing a Healthy Classroom (cont.)

	Struggling Novice	Apprentice	Scientist	Artisan of Healthy Classroom
Standard-bearer Students p. 153	The teacher wants to be the only leader in the room. All leadership is in the form of resistance.	The teacher has favorites who are the leaders of the class. Their behaviors are not monitored, and at times a bully system develops.	The teacher recognizes that the class sees certain salient students in a definite way. The teacher has a limited number of strategies that he employs to foster them into fuller human beings.	The teacher actively fosters the standard-bearers into fuller human beings and in so doing creates an atmosphere that anyone can become anyone and do anything.
Sandwich, p. 154	No one gets compliments because no one is good enough for the "king's" attention.	The teacher gives "Yes, but..." compliments. Students hope they don't receive "left-handed" attention. The teacher's pets are exempted from accountability.	The teacher knows that he wants students to have an unlimited view of their future and instinctively does rudimentary forms of sandwiching.	The teacher recognizes the start of stereotyping and sandwiches students from different categories thus blending the categories.
Healthy Humor, p. 155	Any student could be the recipient of demeaning remarks.	There are certain students who are constant candidates for demeaning remarks.	The teacher recognizes what is healthy humor and allows it. If it isn't, he intervenes and halts it.	The teacher fosters the ingredients of healthy humor. Kindness and appropriate laughter prevail in the room.
Avoiding Favoritism, p. 155	There is no rhyme or reason to the whims of the teacher.	The teacher has certain favorites, and these students are not held accountable for their behavior. Predictability of a hierarchical system exists.	The pupils find it a little strange but very acceptable that the teacher likes the students he manages.	The teacher, via direct and indirect means, creates an atmosphere where everyone is accepted, and yet they are held accountable for their behaviors.
Leaders, Barometers, Liaisons Over Time, p. 156	There is either chaos or the teacher is the only leader and does so by power.	The teacher picks his own leaders and behaviorally fosters a hierarchical structure.	The teacher has a sense of the ever-evolving nature of a healthy class and supports such occurrences when they happen.	The teacher fosters students to fully blossom as human beings. Students belong to so many subgroups that the concept of barometers is blurred. Leadership is replaced with liaisons.
Osmotic Learning: Special Needs Students, p. 158	The teacher is oblivious to the special needs students in the room.	The teacher is aware of the special needs students but can't find time to assist them.	The teacher is trying his level best to assist the special needs students.	The class offers to assist the special needs students.
Osmotic Learning: Thinking, p. 160	The teacher teaches in a lecture format; correct answers are valued.	The teacher asks thinking questions but is the only source of the answers.	The teacher challenges the students to think, and they share their thinking with the teacher.	The students challenge each other to think, and they share their thinking with each other.

Transcends the Educational Culture

Chapter Five Post-its

Classroom Cultures

How does a student know that I care and like her as a person? How do I hold the student behaviorally accountable?

Chapter Five: Managing A Healthy Classroom, pp. 135-137.

Accommodate, Accommodate, Explode

Instead of operating based on feelings, do I manage based on what the students need? Am I managing early enough?

Chapter Five: Managing A Healthy Classroom, pp. 141-145.

Managing the Behavior

Am I systematically employing eye contact when the interaction is positive and a third point when managing because of my visual information?

Chapter Five: Managing A Healthy Classroom, pp. 137-139.

Scapegoat

Am I rotating which students are managed, or are there certain names I am using so much in a negative manner that I wouldn't give an offspring the same name?

Chapter Five: Managing A Healthy Classroom, pp. 147-150.

Power vs. Inappropriate Power

Am I halting any power employed as soon as the student(s) shifts to *neutral*?

Chapter Five: Managing A Healthy Classroom, pp. 139-141.

Preventing Stereotyping

Which of the following am I employing: rounding personalities, fostering liaisons, sharing and rotating leadership?

Chapter Five: Managing A Healthy Classroom, pp. 151-153.

© 2000 by Michael Grinder & Assoc., ARR. AHC03 (360) 687-3238; FAX (360) 687-0595; http://www.michaelgrinder.com

Chapter Five Post-its *(continued)*

Standard-bearer Students

Am I actively fostering standard-bearers into fuller human beings? Is there an atmosphere that anyone can become anyone and do anything?

Chapter Five: Managing A Healthy Classroom, pp. 153-154.

Avoiding Favoritism

Am I creating an atmosphere where everyone is both individually equal and at the same time unique?

Chapter Five: Managing A Healthy Classroom, p. 155.

Sandwich

Am I sandwiching students from different subgroups so that the distinctions between categories are blurring?

Chapter Five: Managing A Healthy Classroom, pp. 154-155.

Over Time

Do students belong to many subgroups, the concept of barometers is blurred and leadership is replaced with liaisons?

Chapter Five: Managing A Healthy Classroom, pp. 156-157.

Healthy Humor

Am I fostering a healthy humor when we are laughing with kindness *with* the student instead of *at* the student?

Chapter Five: Managing A Healthy Classroom, p. 155.

Osmotic Learning

Are the students *thinking* with each other? Are the *special needs* students being cared for by the class?

Chapter Five: Managing A Healthy Classroom, pp. 158-163.

© 2000 by Michael Grinder & Assoc., ARR. AHC03 (360) 687-3238; FAX (360) 687-0595; http://www.michaelgrinder.com

End Notes

1. Senge, Peter M., *The Fifth Discipline Field Book*.

2. *ENVoY* and *ENVoY II* are collections of management strategies.

3. This is the theme of Albert Cullum's book, *The Geranium on the Window Sill Just Died But Teacher You Went Right On*.

4. *Exit Directions* (*ENVoY* p. 28) preserves the relationship while seeking compliance on a behavioral level.

5. All three of the ENVoY Programs are built on this premise.

6. See p. 40.

7. *Influence Approach* (*ENVoY* p. 38).

8. The concept of *OFF/Neutral/ON* when coupled with the *Influence Approach* defines appropriate power (*ENVoY* ch. 1).

9. *ABOVE (Pause) Whisper* (*ENVoY* p. 18).

10. The author hesitates to include this section because although some readers will find tremendous insight, some will be confused and others will be offended. The hope is that whether you agree or disagree, the section extends a dialogue about the characteristics of our "culture."

11. *Dogs and Cats* is presented in *ENVoY II*.

12. *Imploding* isn't any healthier.

13. See Chapter Three: *Stages*, pp. 84-88.

14. *ENVoY* trainer and coach, California.

15. *Multiple Intelligences: The Theory in Practice* by Howard E. Gardner. Paperback, March 1993.

16. Denzel Washington in the movie *Mississippi Masala*.

17. It would have been nice if the William Wordsworth had said, "The child is the parent to the adult."

18. See Chapter One: *Class Formation*, p. 34 ("How well are the individual students known?")

19. While there may be more than one scapegoat in a classroom, the text will use the singular reference.

20. In Roman times, a child of wealth had a slave assigned to him as a muse-playmate. When the child was naughty the parents would likely whip the slave. Because the child won't want to see his "friend" hurt, he is likely to change.

© 2000 by Michael Grinder & Assoc., ARR. AHC03 (360) 687-3238; FAX (360) 687-0595; http://www.michaelgrinder.com

21. National Teacher of the Year, inspirational speaker and author of several books including *First Days of School*; the above suggestion is more palatable for self-contained classroom teachers.

22. See *Preventive Management Inventory*, p. 173.

23. Reference to Chapter Three: *Stages*, pp. 84-88.

24. Charles Schulz, *Charlie Brown, Snoopy and Me*.

25. The readers are strongly encouraged to receive training in TESA (Teacher Expectations and Student Achievement) and GESA (Gender Expectations and Student Achievement). These programs are excellent at increasing instructors' awareness of the teachers' non-verbal communication and the effect on individual students as well as the class as a whole. If you have trained in these approaches, you are encouraged to include these concepts in your professional development plan for the school year.

26. p. 76 and p. 117.

27. Song by John Michael Montgomery, "Life's A Dance."

28. This is a variation of *Sandwich*, p. 154.

29. *ENVoY, ENVoY II* and *A Healthy Classroom*.

30. *Getting Them to Seek You (ENVoY II)*.

31. The scientific definition of osmosis is the passive diffusion of water across a selective permeable membrane from an area of high concentration to an area of low concentration. The term "Osmotic Learning" is employed because as a result of group dynamics information flows from students who initially grasp a concept to those students who need assistance to grasp it. As Margaret Wheatley says, "Information only flows with (and because of) relationships."

32. The reader might want to investigate "Suggestopedia," Dr. Lazonov's research, Peter Kline's *Every Day Genius*, Super Camp (800) 228-5327, DePorter's *Quantum Teaching* and *Quantum Learning*, the SALT organization. A general source with many references is Vos & Dryden's *The Learning Revolution*.

33. Many readers are familiar with Albert Bandura's four-stage model. *A Healthy Classroom* adds stage three converting the model to a five-stage template.

34. Thomas Sowel, *Creators Syndicate*.

35. George Miller, "Seven plus or minus two."

36. May 19, 1998 interview with Bob Costas, NBC.

37. See ASCD "Dimensions of Learning" by Bob Marzano.

© 2000 by Michael Grinder & Assoc., ARR. AHC03 (360) 687-3238; FAX (360) 687-0595; http://www.michaelgrinder.com

Managing Cats

MANAGING
SPECIAL
SITUATIONS

This chapter could be subtitled, "When baffled, come here to confirm your sanity." We are most baffled when we are surprised by how the class is behaving. By greeting students at the door, not only can we set a welcoming tone but we can also check out the size of the chip on certain students' shoulders.

As teachers we often have to be a chameleon when greeting students. With most students the teacher can smile and make eye contact while greeting. With the at-risk population we often have more success if we don't seem too happy.

In the above illustration the first cat who enters indicates that it might be a rough day. Because the teacher has noticed it she won't be surprised. When we are not baffled we can proactively adjust.

To be respectful of gender equality and yet provide the educator with a fluid reading style, in this chapter the teacher is referred to by the female pronoun and the student by the male pronoun.

> *From a group dynamics standpoint we want to manage*
> *the individual student based on, and for the sake of, the class.*

Introduction

It is with much hesitation that this chapter is included in this work. This chapter will have more information that appears in other parts of the book than any other chapter. The final decision to have this chapter included was made for two reasons: first, it helps to have the reader see the concepts more than once; and secondly, some concepts are highlighted, woven together and summarized better here than scattered throughout the book.

Preventive Management Inventory identifies the five students the teacher is most likely to manage and offers specific strategies to respond. *Controlling the Microphone* explores the number one curriculum issue for new teachers—who gets to talk, what they are allowed to talk about and when they get to talk. This issue of who gets to talk about what and when plunges the reader into the controversial area of the *auditory-oriented student*. While every student has a right to learn, the auditory-oriented learner that will be introduced in *Preventive Management Inventory* doesn't mesh well with the group dynamics setting of the classroom. Time is devoted to list the three characteristics of such a learner and seven practical strategies that can be implemented.

The demographics of the classroom are rapidly changing. One population that is increasing is the *asocial* pupil. There are four separate entries for this problematic area. The *Temporarily Asocial Student* and *Chronic Asocial Student* sections make the distinction between the length of time the student has been asocial and what implications that holds for the teacher. *Greeting Them at the Door* is an age-old technique that provides the teacher with early information regarding which students might be temporarily asocial and what to do about the situation. When the teacher is unable to remove the *chronic asocial student*, the teacher can do brilliant modeling for the rest of the class on how to be emotionally mature when circumstances prevent the teacher from being actively effective. *Confirming the Class' Sanity* squarely addresses this issue.

Among the remaining competencies in this chapter, *Interpretation of Voices* will greatly assist the teacher in knowing the timing of when to call the class back from cooperative learning activities. And, finally, the concept of "Dog and Cat"[1] is applied to the broader picture of the educational culture and when a "dog" teacher would or wouldn't intervene compared to a "cat" teacher.

If lost, read this chapter.

This chapter will reaffirm your sanity. There are some situations beyond our influence.

© 2000 by Michael Grinder & Assoc., ARR. AHC03 (360) 687-3238; FAX (360) 687-0595; http://www.michaelgrinder.com

Preventive Management Inventory

6-1

The class' needs and the individual student's needs may be different enough that the teacher will do the group dynamics axiom of class first, then individuals. There are legitimate learning styles that don't mesh well in a group setting. The teacher knows that she is clear about these distinctions because the teacher can like someone who, as a member, is a pain. In general, the teacher wants to be attracted to "troubled students" in that the teacher has to establish a relationship with those she will eventually manage.

As the pupils enter the room, the teacher may want to do some preventive management by identifying students who are potentially troublesome for the class' learning and health. Think of students as dogs and cats. We mean this in a most respectful manner. In fact, professionals who work with horses and dogs claim that people are often more humane towards animals than they are toward fellow human beings.

Dogs are approachable, cooperative, and will operate win-win. Credible-oriented students are independent learners, like cats, and are often oblivious to the win-win paradigm. By understanding that dogs come when they are called and cats have call waiting, call screening and message machines, we are not offended by cats' independent behaviors. The students who are most potentially troublesome are stressed students, auditory-oriented students, "what about" learners, students different than your style, leaders, or captured students.

Stressed Students

Some students don't breathe. They are identifiable by lack of fluidity in movement, difficulty finding words, shoulders rising, high breathing and a stiff appearance. The more the culture of the classroom is credible-oriented, the less the student in stress will affect the rest of the class. This is because credible-oriented people are more productivity-oriented whereas an approachable-oriented culture is more people-oriented and will stop everything until each member of the class is OK.

Auditory-oriented Student

Some students ask a lot of questions. They are identifiable by neurological indicators[2] and friendliness. (They have never met a stranger.) Especially troublesome are auditory learners who don't breathe. The most dangerous situation is when a classroom has three or more auditory students because they activate each other. Picture each auditory student as a separate tracking station. Every time one student talks it activates all the other auditory students. This is why the sixth to ninth grade teachers have to be so careful when managing and doing preventive management.

© 2000 by Michael Grinder & Assoc., ARR. AHC03 (360) 687-3238; FAX (360) 687-0595; http://www.michaelgrinder.com

The letter "a" in adolescence stands for "auditory"—the whole class, on any given day, is auditory.

"What About" Learners

The average student thinks in terms of WHAT, WHY and HOW are we going to cover the topic. But certain students think differently from their classmates. These students are more right brain-oriented. They think in terms of "what about...." These students are identified by kinesthetic neurological indicators[3] and body shifts. They are mistake prone, impulsive, entertainment oriented, and self-selective. These are the students who may not be able to persevere through college but, if they do, will be very successful in graduate school.

Students Different Than Your Style

There are many models of how people think. The teacher who is aware of her own style of thinking will know how to compensate for those students who think differently than she does.

The author is very kinesthetic and globally-oriented. He thinks about WHAT and HOW we are approaching the next topic. He forgets to say WHY the topic is important. His approach can confuse students who are notetakers, exhibit visual neurological indicators[4] of being linear-oriented, want details and are motivated by a logical sequence. As a compensating device, the author will periodically say, "Now WHY are we doing this?" By asking this question aloud and then answering the question, the author remembers to satisfy students who think differently than he does.

Leaders

Who are the leaders? Leaders are those individuals who pupils give attention to. Sometimes that attention is not for positive behavior.

Captured Students

If a student feels he is involuntary in attendance, which is often the case with adolescents, it is likely the teacher will manage the student.

What To Do

How does a teacher respond?

Once a teacher has identified the five categories of students she tends to manage (stressed, auditory, what about, different, leaders), the following are suggestions:

1. Establish rapport.

© 2000 by Michael Grinder & Assoc., ARR. AHC03 (360) 687-3238; FAX (360) 687-0595; http://www.michaelgrinder.com

2. Set up a location for questions.

3. Teach the class to raise hands.

4. Find areas of high interest for right-brain participants and incorporate the items into the presentation.

5. When answering questions, increase the length of time before calling on the person. This requires the teacher to remember to call on the person later or approach the person during a break.

6. When asking for questions or calling on a questioner, be precise as to the frame around the questions that are pertinent; e.g., "Only ask those questions needed in order to do this exercise."

7. Acknowledge resistant students.[5]

Controlling the Microphone

6-2

In the classroom the control of "who speaks, when and on what topic," is essential to the teacher's control of the format. When teaching or releasing a class to do work (the *Teaching* and *Transition* phases of a lesson) and a question arises, the teacher has to be careful because the teacher is dealing with an individual student during a group-oriented time slot. Because there are several considerations that come into play,[6] the following techniques will add to the teacher's repertoire of responses.

Increase the Student's Manners

When a student, without raising his hand, blurts out a question[7], the teacher is in a bind. The worst time this occurs is when the teacher has her back to the class, such as when writing on the board. If the teacher doesn't answer the query, the class might think the student is disrespected or the class might see the teacher as appropriately rude. The student becomes the class' pariah, in which case unhealthy stereotyping sets in. The teacher's initial task is to foster the student who asks a lot of questions into raising his hand. When the student raises his hand, the teacher has more choices as to when to call on, or even if to call on, the student. When students raise their hands, the teacher's timing is more proactive.

Satisfy, Satisfy, Delay[8]

The concept of *Satisfy, Satisfy, Delay* immediately applies. If this is the first time this student has asked a question, answer very respectfully. However, if the class sees the student as uniquely capable of asking a lot of questions, the teacher may want to delay answering the question. Examples include the teacher actually looking at the student while gesturing with just the index finger extended to indicate "in just a moment."

© 2000 by Michael Grinder & Assoc., ARR. AHC03 (360) 687-3238; FAX (360) 687-0595; http://www.michaelgrinder.com

Increase the Student's Patience

Once a student senses that the teacher will eventually satisfy his query, the teacher can condition the student to be patient. For example, during question and answer time, the teacher could call on other students while peripherally watching the student who has raised his hand but often blurts out. As the student makes sounds of anxiousness, the teacher gauges how long he can keep his hand raised. As the student nears his frustration tolerance level, the teacher calls on him.

If the student in question is the only one with his hand raised while the teacher is teaching, the teacher can look at the student and signal with a gesture, "I will be with you in just a minute," and then continue instructing the class.

Location for Questions

Since 80% of communication is nonverbal, the need to control the microphone can be done by having two locations: one for the presentation and the other for handling/encouraging questions. Have a different *face*, *voice* and *body* for each location. For example, the teacher could address the class in the following manner. Standing near the overhead projector, the teacher says, "Today we are going to introduce a new idea. To make sure we are all clear about this concept, after we finish the concept (teacher steps away from the overhead), we will have time for questions (teacher points down at his feet indicating that when the teacher is in this location the class can ask questions)." This establishment of two locations is often critical for a difficult content lesson. Sometimes the students need to know "what is in it for them" to wait to ask questions. One possible preface that the teacher can say while introducing the questioning location is, "By waiting until later to ask your questions, your questions will be even more intelligent."

Once the teacher has established the two locations, the teacher's consistency stabilizes the two locations. The artistic level of this is to quickly notice which students are likely to ask questions, calibrate what they individually look like when they begin to raise their hand, and immediately go to the question location before they actually raise their hands. In this manner the teacher is conditioning the pupils to think they are asking the question because the teacher is standing in the location for questions when, in truth, the teacher is standing there because he knows that certain students will have questions.

© 2000 by Michael Grinder & Assoc., ARR. AHC03 (360) 687-3238; FAX (360) 687-0595; http://www.michaelgrinder.com

---

Vignette: Puppy Training

Patty Poodle teaches French. As a hobby she breeds and trains dogs. She says that people are often more humane to animals than they are to humans. Pet owners take their dogs to training schools because the adults need to be conditioned. If the owner is consistent, the dog receives clear directions and will follow directives. The same thing is true in the classroom. When the teacher is clear and consistent, the students are relaxed because they know what to expect. The way Patty Poodle explains the two locations to her teaching colleagues is interesting. She says you can power manage dogs/pupils or influence manage them. In the former, you tell the dog to sit, and while saying the word "sit," you push the dog's rump down. If you want to use influence, you run the dog around the block twice. As the dog, out of fatigue, starts to sit down, say the word "sit." In the classroom, as the students start to have a question, move to the question location and say, "Any questions?"

Location for Future Questions

For a particularly long unit, which is more likely the case in the upper grades, it may take the teacher several days to fully explain the large concept. An example of this level of sophistication is a "term paper." When the student has a valid question that cannot be answered until later in the unit, the teacher is likely to respond with, "We will cover that later." The verbal acknowledgment that the student will be satisfied later will work for a couple of times. By the time a fourth student has asked a question and received the standard reply, "We will cover that later," those students who asked the first three questions start to wonder, "How is she going to remember all our questions?!" The solution is to have a location where the questions being asked can be written down and answered later. Often a bulletin board will be titled with the unit's name, and all questions that are raised out of sequence are written out. As the questions are covered, the teacher checks off the questions. This visual representation of questions guarantees the inquiring student that his question will be addressed.

Vignette: Rearview Mirror

Freddie Farsight teaches both Drivers Education and English. For years he was perplexed when a student would ask a valid question early in his term paper unit. The question usually had to do with requirements and how the student could earn a high

continued on next page

© 2000 by Michael Grinder & Assoc., ARR. AHC03 (360) 687-3238; FAX (360) 687-0595; http://www.michaelgrinder.com

grade for the upcoming assignment. Freddie Farsight could appreciate the ambition behind the question but Freddie Farsight couldn't answer it on two counts. First, the question was complex enough that answering it would take the whole period and, secondly, the concept of the question would make perfect sense in two days when the concept was scheduled to be covered. This year when Freddie started the term paper unit he began in the following manner, "Class, many of you have your driving permits and have been practicing driving. Initially, your focus is on the mechanics of starting the car: brake engaged, seat belt buckled, ignition turned on. Next your attention is given to what is ahead of you as you drive. As you scan the road ahead you are very attentive to what is coming up. At some point you are startled to discover a vehicle directly in front of you that previously wasn't there. As you start to recover your breathing, you realize that the car isn't in front of you but appearing in the rearview mirror." As the pupils laugh, Freddie Farsight continues, "Now why didn't we notice the vehicle behind us earlier? It is because when we are learning something new there are only so many items we can be attentive to. As that which is new, such as the mechanics of starting the car, becomes more familiar, we then notice what was present all along but out of our awareness, such as the car in the rearview mirror. Initially, our minds weren't ready for the rearview mirror; it would have just overwhelmed us.

"So too in this unit there will be things that you will want to know about that we are not ready for yet." Freddie Farsight walks to the bulletin board with a title "Term Paper." "As you can see, this chart has all the individual assignments and their due dates. These are steps in the path to writing a term paper. To the right is a blank flipchart paper with the title 'Rearview Mirror.' When a question comes up that cannot be answered now because it would only overwhelm you—like the car in the rearview mirror—we will write the question here and then check it off as we come to that section of the term paper unit where the question fits. You are assured that the question will be answered because it is listed here as a reminder that we will cover it. When the question is addressed, the question will be checked off." Freddie Farsight walks back to the front of the classroom and begins the introduction to the unit. Hidden inside his lectern is a real rearview mirror. When a student asks a question that will be answered later, Freddie Farsight holds up the actual mirror and points to the bulletin board. Everyone laughs as the student walks over and writes out her question.

© 2000 by Michael Grinder & Assoc., ARR. AHC03 (360) 687-3238; FAX (360) 687-0595; http://www.michaelgrinder.com

Employing a Credible Voice Pattern and Specificity

The approachable voice pattern (rhythmically rolls up and down and ends with the intonation curling up) signals that the speaker is seeking input. This is what that teacher is doing when the teacher says, "Any questions?" There are days, however, when the teacher wants to decrease the number of questions that are likely to be asked. This can be done by employing the credible voice pattern of a flatter voice with an intonation that curls down. This often causes the class to think about how important their questions really are. This results in the pupils self-monitoring and prioritizing their questions. Of course, the more specific the teacher is, the more guidance the pupils have on how to screen out frivolous questions. "Any questions about how to convert single-digit fractions to decimals?" is very different than "Any questions?"

Auditory-oriented Student

6-3

(How does a teacher spot an auditory-oriented student?)

Identifying

The previous section, *Controlling the Microphone*, emphasizes the importance of controlling "who gets to talk when about what." The auditory-oriented student is at the cross hairs of such a discussion. The auditory-oriented adult is the least common modality style in an educated population. They are so misunderstood that they are often an emotional minority amongst intelligent people, and yet their IQ's cover the full range of average to brilliant. This section will explain why such a student is much maligned. At the same time, from a group dynamics standpoint, educators will want to limit the auditory-oriented student's innate, yet unconscious, tendency to monopolize the microphone. This is because an unchecked auditory-oriented student in a group setting will alienate his classmates and prevent the class from obtaining higher levels of a healthy classroom. Because of the importance of this concept there will be references to adults as well as to students.

It is important to make the distinction between someone who is *oral* and someone who is *auditory*. An *oral-oriented* person is verbal; the person can be interrupted and concentrate on the new focus. The first characteristic of an *auditory-oriented* person is the person's need to finish the verbal. If interrupted, the person is still concentrating on what he was saying and cannot hear what is being said. The auditory-oriented person operates much like a phone message machine. Once the mechanism is overloaded with information, it has to speak in order to release information, thus opening up slots for new, incoming information.

An auditory-oriented student talks in order to think. A visually-oriented student thinks before talking.

© 2000 by Michael Grinder & Assoc., ARR. AHC03 (360) 687-3238; FAX (360) 687-0595; http://www.michaelgrinder.com

The second characteristic of the auditory-oriented person is the need to talk in order to clarify. The person lacks an internal monitoring system that can silently listen to his thoughts. Visually-oriented people have this system which organizes their thoughts so that when they speak, the information is delivered in a succinct manner.

The third habit of an auditory-oriented person is the tendency to think in whole cassettes. The person cannot easily fast forward to the point that is pertinent—the listener feels captured to listen to the entire tape. Often the listeners feel like the speaker is talking without any awareness of who the speaker is talking to. The listeners feel violated and used.

Our definition of an auditory-oriented person is someone who

- has to speak to release his internal focus of concentration;

- clarifies aloud; and,

- is long-winded.

It is painful to witness an auditory student who talks to gain social acceptance and yet his incessant talking drives him further from the social contact he craves.

The auditory-oriented student monopolizes conversations; operates as if there is no group; loses permission to speak because the class unconsciously operates as though everyone receives a certain number of coupons to speak, and once his coupons are all used up, he loses permission to talk. The visually-oriented student is motivated by productivity, the auditory-oriented by sociability, and the kinesthetic-oriented student by morale. It breaks a teacher's heart to see an auditory student with a core need to be socially liked and accepted. The student's lack of social skills drives people away, which in turn urges the student to try harder using the same strategies that offended his classmates before.

Group Dynamics

From a group dynamics standpoint, visually-oriented listeners get frustrated with auditory-oriented people because "they cannot get to the point." The exception is the female adolescent. The sixth through ninth grades put a premium on the ability to soliloquize. This is why it is better for a teacher to be on three committees run by visually-oriented chairs than one committee chaired by an auditory-oriented person (especially if the person is from the district office). In essence, auditory-oriented members of a group slow down the speed of productivity and, as a result, the group is split. Translated, this means the auditory-oriented person is a threat to the health of the group.

Formality Levels

If the group is large, has been together only a short time, and doesn't know each other, it is likely that the level of formality is high. For in-

© 2000 by Michael Grinder & Assoc., ARR. AHC03 (360) 687-3238; FAX (360) 687-0595; http://www.michaelgrinder.com

stance, the students are likely to raise their hands before speaking. This advantage allows the chairperson/teacher to figure out if it is appropriate, from the group standpoint, to allow the auditory-oriented person microphone time. If the level of formality is low, people don't raise their hands. If the chair is *surprised* by people speaking out, the chair is in a reactive position. If the chair wants to be proactive, the chair calibrates what behaviors the auditory-oriented participant exhibits before speaking. Examples of signals that indicate that someone is about to speak include:

- Touching his mouth area with his hand

- Shifting his body

- Eyes widen.

A common *surprise* occurs when the chair is in the process of turning her back to the group; e.g., to write on a white board or flip chart. If the chair has her back to the group and the auditory-oriented individual speaks out, the chair misses the group reaction to the individual and, therefore, responds void of group dynamics input.[9] The chair wants to check out the likelihood of the auditory-oriented participant's need to speak out before the chair turns her back to the group. The best way to "check out" is indirectly—without looking directly at the participant in question.[10]

Strategy for the Linear-Auditory Participant

> How does a teacher respond to an auditory-oriented student?

(Must be done with permission which is gained by non-judgmental feedback.)

1. Help the student become aware of his linear way of thinking.

2. Have the student become aware of his physiology when he realizes he is confused.

3. Ask the student to write down his question in the margin and leave a space on his notes so that he can write the answer later.

4. Have the student look around and notice the class as he raises his hand for the question to be heard.

It is respectful to offer several distinctions. There is a huge difference between an externally vs. an internally-oriented learner. A student could be an internal-oriented auditory learner and would be privately talking to himself. This style of processing information is completely acceptable to the classroom environment. It is the external-oriented auditory learner that causes concern for the teacher because he takes more than his turn at

© 2000 by Michael Grinder & Assoc., ARR. AHC03 (360) 687-3238; FAX (360) 687-0595; http://www.michaelgrinder.com

the microphone. The external-oriented person is someone who, in order to think, has to talk. This style is the bane of all committees because "thinking" and "talking" are inseparable. The style of learner that is most admired by classmates and appreciated by the teacher is the visually-oriented student—one who talks only when the thinking is done. While there is no correlation of intelligence between the auditory and the visual learners, there is a difference in terms of group acceptance. There is no question that educated groups love the visual-oriented person.[11]

Interventions

The following interventions are provocative and are often done, not because of the individual, but because of the group.

Double Dutch

Sometimes when the auditory-oriented person is already pontificating, it can be a task to *time* the teacher's intervention. Having six sisters, we spent a lot of our childhood jumping rope. When we advanced to two jump ropes turning in the opposite direction ("Double Dutch"), we would move our head and hands in synch with the ropes as we readied ourselves to enter the center of the action. So, too, the chair/teacher wants to get in a flow with the auditory-oriented person. If the person-in-charge nods her head in rhythm with the auditory-oriented person's speaking pattern, the speaker's head comes forward when the person is talking and goes back when the person inhales—the in-charge person's intervention is better timed. The person-in-charge wants to intervene while the auditory-oriented participant is inhaling.

Repeat of Cassette

If it is the first time the auditory-oriented person has articulated the information, try to let him talk because he doesn't know what he is saying until he actually hears himself aloud. To find out if this is the first time the auditory-oriented person is sharing this information, the person-in-charge can ask, "Have you told this to anyone else?" If the auditory-oriented individual says, "No," the audience is usually more tolerant when it is the *first* time something is shared.[12] If the auditory-oriented individual says, "Yes," the person-in-charge has more permission from the individual and definitely more from the group to intervene. The rule of thumb is that if it is a repeat of the tape then it is more OK to stop the individual or at least shorten the amount of time the individual gets the microphone.

© 2000 by Michael Grinder & Assoc., ARR. AHC03 (360) 687-3238; FAX (360) 687-0595; http://www.michaelgrinder.com

Fast Forward

If the auditory-oriented person has said this information before, the person-in-charge could say, "What are you learning as you share this information for a second time?" A similar, and even more dangerous question is, "If I/we have more time to listen what would I/we particularly want to note about this information?" These queries are invitations for the auditory-oriented participant to scan forward on his cassette and obtain a meta-cognition of the data then, hopefully, the person speaks more succinctly.

Steal the Thunder

If the auditory-oriented person is going to make a negative sound/ disagreement and if the person-in-charge indicates, in a jovial manner, that the person-in-charge expects the auditory-oriented person to utter something, the person-in-charge steals the auditory-oriented person's thunder in terms of the attention that he normally gets from his peers. An example is, "Now, Hank, get ready to groan/whine as we announce ...." In the eyes of the group, the person-in-charge is proactive.

Switching to Relationship

The person-in-charge can say, "Tell me/us what is it about me/us that makes you want to share this with me/us?" This switches the focus from the *issue/content* level to the *relationship* level of the communication. Advantages include:

- More options are available on the *relationship* level including forms of *Delay*[13] such as, "Could we talk about ... later."

- Forces the auditory-oriented individual to be outside himself and lets the listener know the auditory-oriented individual is aware of the listener. This removes the possible insult that many people feel when the auditory-oriented person drones on.

Acknowledgments

When the person-in-charge visually displays (e.g., on a flip chart) what the auditory-oriented person wants to contribute, the time spent on the auditory-oriented person's position is much shorter. There is a second purpose to acknowledge: the person-in-charge wants the group to know the person-in-charge is aware of the auditory-oriented person.

© 2000 by Michael Grinder & Assoc., ARR. AHC03 (360) 687-3238; FAX (360) 687-0595; http://www.michaelgrinder.com

Visual Information

The advantages of visually representing information are endless. This includes the format used to gather input from the group and put it on a flip chart. When information is displayed visually, the person-in-charge has the option of employing the visually displayed information as a third point. When the auditory-oriented contributor makes the same comment a second time, the person-in-charge can softly say, "Heather, is what you are saying any different than this (person-in-charge points to the visual representation of what the auditory-oriented person said the first time)?"

Some of the above techniques are very provocative and are not done for the auditory-oriented individual but more for the group's sake. At all times the person-in-charge wants to be seen by the group as *fair.*[14] In Chapter Three the concept of a group going through *shocked, confused,* and *annoyed* was detailed.[15] Many of the seven maneuvers mentioned can cause *confusion.* Confusion shakes up people. The following axiom clarifies the dynamics that occur when confusion is employed.

> *Confusion + permission = person-in-charge leads*
> *Confusion - permission = participants withdraw*

Vignette: Cross-cultural Colleen

In her twenty-plus years of secondary teaching, Cross-cultural Colleen has taught in inner city and rural settings. She often jokes that the kids attending school who are not attending in order to learn act out differently based on density of population. In the rural culture they are passive compared to the aggressive nature of the uneducated parts of the metropolitan area. Now she is teaching suburbia. While the cultural lines based on geography are blurring, she is curious to see what her new student from the inner city will be like. Danny Downtown is noticeable the first day. When he walks, one leg is extended differently than the other and he bends his hands at the wrist with certain fingers extended farther than the rest. When he socially talks, his head vacillates from looking at the listener with intense eye contact to flinging his head to the side and looking off in space. By the end of the second day he has been sent to the office twice for "disrupting the learning atmosphere."

Having studied Ruby Payne's *A Framework for Understanding Poverty,* Cross-cultural Colleen knows that in poverty, which is

continued on next page

© 2000 by Michael Grinder & Assoc., ARR. AHC03 (360) 687-3238; FAX (360) 687-0595; http://www.michaelgrinder.com

often the case in inner cities, the auditory person who can entertain is highly valued—much to the chagrin of the middle class
educator. Employing the concept of Dog & Cat,[16] Cross-cultural
Colleen recognizes that Danny is a "cat," and Colleen has to
indirectly establish a relationship with him by having him select
her, because he would shy away from any direct overtures from
her. Colleen knows she will have to be patient for such a relationship to develop.

Be careful to separate the oral/linear learner from an auditory student.
On the surface, the two people may operate very similarly, but they are
actually very different. The auditory student has difficulty turning off the
"play" button of his cassette when talking. The oral/linear learner when
talking can be interrupted and focus on the new content. He has to understand the process, so watch the person during the participant's input time
period. The linear person seems like an auditory person when asking
about a point that was missed (especially when the content is new, emotional or difficult). On the other hand, the auditory individual is unstop-
pable even with old content.

Temporarily Asocial Student

6-5

An individual student is acting in such a way that
the class is actively annoyed. The difficulty is
the student is temporarily unaffected by the peer
pressure. The teacher recognizes that the individual student is willing to socially self-destruct.
Later the class may not easily forgive the individual member for how he acted, so it is better

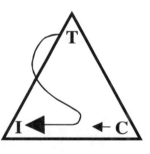

for the teacher to step in and manage the individual and not let the class
give the person their input.

This intervention is best done before the group moves from the *confused*
stage to the *annoyed* level. Remember, the teacher can only save an individual if the teacher intervene's before *annoyance* sets in.[17]

Chronic Asocial Student

6-6

The class perceives that an individual student
consistently acts inappropriately. The individual is immune to class pressure and the
teacher cannot establish a relationship with the
individual; consequently, the teacher has to use
power instead of influence. The teacher's ob-

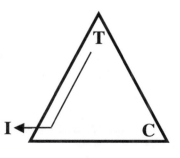

ligation is to try to remove the individual because the collective classroom health is at stake.

© 2000 by Michael Grinder & Assoc., ARR. AHC03 (360) 687-3238; FAX (360) 687-0595; http://www.michaelgrinder.com

6-7

Confirming the Class' Sanity

What can a teacher do when her relationship is too low with the student to use influence and yet the teacher doesn't want to employ power or legally can't exert enough power over the student?

Since one of the main goals of classroom dynamics is to make the class right, if the class knows that the teacher knows that the class views the individual as inappropriate, the teacher has accomplished her task. For example, the individual wants to dwell on a point that the class perceives as irrelevant. The teacher uses a hand gesture that sweeps from the individual through the entire class and says, "If (optionally add "you think") there is enough interest in that subject, we can spend more time on it...."

In essence, if we can't change the individual, at least we can confirm the class' sanity of perception.

You win some and you lose some, but you have to suit up for all of them.
Casey Stengel
(famous baseball coach)

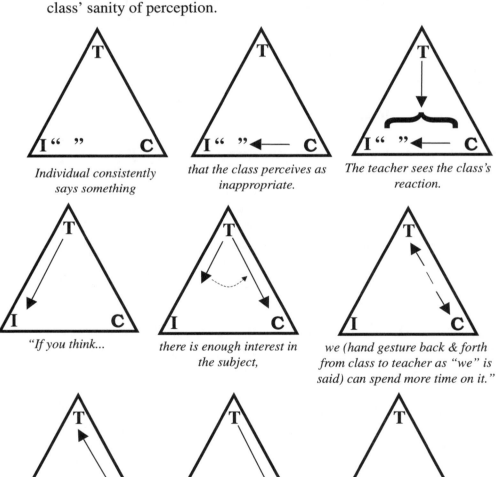

Individual consistently says something

that the class perceives as inappropriate.

The teacher sees the class's reaction.

"If you think...

there is enough interest in the subject,

we (hand gesture back & forth from class to teacher as "we" is said) can spend more time on it."

Let the class know

that you know

how the class sees the individual.

© 2000 by Michael Grinder & Assoc., ARR. AHC03 (360) 687-3238; FAX (360) 687-0595; http://www.michaelgrinder.com

Greeting Them at the Door

Greeting students at the door has been a tradition of educators for a long time. In the past, the educator did so to set the tone of the room. Greeting them at the door allows the teacher to know how to respond to the students. Now, the educator wants to greet the students for an additional reason—to check out the size of the chip on certain students' shoulders. The teacher wants to be a chameleon when greeting the students at the door. With most students the teacher can smile and make eye contact while greeting. But the teacher can't be too happy when greeting the at-risk population.

The teacher needs to know early in the day/lesson how the at-risk student is doing. There are days when the teacher cannot be a successful manager because the two prerequisites can't be met, either because the student can't do the work and/or he won't allow rapport with the teacher.

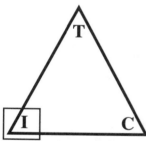

The teacher isolates the student.

When the teacher greets the students at the door, the teacher might suspect that a given student (e.g., Sam; of course there are Samanthas also) for that day is approaching the asocial end of the human continuum. The teacher wants to give the student a wide berth because he can't be reached on a human basis. What if the teacher cannot isolate the student and he wants to be self-destructive on this given day?

The teacher cannot allow the class to criticize their classmate for inappropriate behavior because it is more damaging than if the teacher were to criticize Sam.

Why is it more detrimental for the class and individual to be at odds

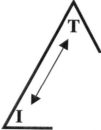

than for the teacher and individual student?

© 2000 by Michael Grinder & Assoc., ARR. AHC03 (360) 687-3238; FAX (360) 687-0595; http://www.michaelgrinder.com

Since the teacher has more emotional control than the pupils, it is better for the teacher to receive the brunt of the student's anger. The teacher better understands that the acting-out student is really frustrated with himself and life in general and not his particular teacher or classmates. If the teacher has orchestrated high group rapport and the class criticizes the student, his retort may damage his relationship with the class, adversely affecting the health of the group dynamics. It is better for the teacher to intervene, even if the intervention is done with power, and manage the student.

6-9

Keeping Them Away/Let Mikey [18] *Do It*

Just like at home with parents, students will send a student as an advance guard named "Mikey" to test the waters of whether a "yes" to the request is likely. If the adult doesn't bite Mikey's head off, the rest will swarm to the adult. The two mostly likely times when the teacher really doesn't want to get caught one-on-one and most likely that Mikey will be sent are:

- when the teacher wants to get underway and is just about to ask the class for their attention

- when the teacher releases the class to do their seatwork.

In fact, many teachers find that in the first case they may have been available for the last five minutes and no one really seemed to need them, and then all of a sudden there is a rush. It is similar to what happens in retail businesses. As they get near closing time, there is often an actual increase in customers. "The store is closing." Teachers want to be group-oriented during transitions. Teachers want to keep individual students away from them.

6-10

Interpretation of Voices

When the pupils are doing small group work, teachers often wonder what the clues are to determine when to bring them back to the next lecture portion of the presentation. Listening to the collective voice patterns can provide the teacher with invaluable information. When the collective sounds are flat, then the members are still learning, processing or concentrating = credible. If the collective voices are more rolling and rhythmic with varying pitches, the class is socializing = approachable. So when the collective voice patterns in the room start to change from the flat, credible voice pattern, indicating on-task, to the more rhythmic, approachable, the teacher can call them back to attention. Offering a warning that such a transition is about to occur is helpful. This is usually done by employing a flat, draggy voice while moving slowly and deliberately and saying "O-n-e m-o-r-e m-i-n-u-t-e." [19]

© 2000 by Michael Grinder & Assoc., ARR. AHC03 (360) 687-3238; FAX (360) 687-0595; http://www.michaelgrinder.com

Cultures and Intervention

6-11 &
6-12

The art of managing includes proactive perception and timing. The strategies of intervening reflect a teacher's perception and timing. When does the teacher intervene in general and specifically with the auditory-oriented student? It is not the teacher's style of intervention that determines the teacher's effectiveness; it is the interplay between the teacher's style and the class' style. There are many variables to consider:

- The auditory-oriented student wants to think aloud. The auditory-oriented student doesn't want to be interrupted. In fact, if interrupted, the auditory-oriented student will often have to start over to get *into the script*. When the auditory-oriented student finishes his cassette, there is a tendency for him to start to repeat himself. There will be a physiological change (e.g., a change in the gaze in his eyes, body shifts, voice tones are different) as the cassette is starting for a second time. If the teacher intervenes just at the start of the repeat, the auditory-oriented student tends to be very receptive.

- The class wants to have everyone speak with clearly thought out, succinct statements.

In time, the class distinguishes the auditory-oriented student as different from the rest of the pupils. As the class starts to progress through the *Three Stages*[20], the teacher has permission from the class to intervene. It is likely that the auditory-oriented student's *timing* of when he is ready for the teacher to intervene is after the class is ready for the intervention. It is recommended that the teacher follow the class' *timing*.

If the class is highly *credible*, they will want the teacher to intervene quickly (e.g., when the class is initially *shocked*). If the class is highly *approachable*, the class will want the teacher to intervene late, often after the class is actually *annoyed*.

In general, the teacher's style is reflected in the timing of her intervention.

> *Credible teachers intervene early and approachable teachers late.*

When the credible-approachable style of the teacher is different than the class, the timing of when the teacher intervenes is often a disaster. When the style of the teacher is the same as the class, the match is quite harmonious. When a credible class has a credible-oriented teacher, the timing of the teacher's intervention with an auditory-oriented student is perfect.

The question is, "Is an approachable class with an approachable-oriented teacher also a perfect fit?" The answer isn't a simple "yes" or "no." While

© 2000 by Michael Grinder & Assoc., ARR. AHC03 (360) 687-3238; FAX (360) 687-0595; http://www.michaelgrinder.com

the pupils individually like the teacher re-establishing order by intervening with an auditory-oriented student, the pupils are culturally offended. On the surface it sounds like a contradiction that the members are simultaneously appreciative and offended by the teacher's intervention. Pupils have different levels of their *persona*. Sometimes approachable-oriented students will publicly express disapproval when the teacher intervenes and their cultural norms of acceptance are violated. At the same time they are privately pleased class time was used well because of the intervention.

> *People publicly declare based on cultural norms before sharing, if at all, personal reactions.*

The Credible-oriented Class

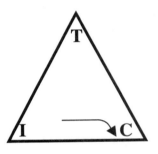

The more the culture of the class is "task-oriented," the more the sounds will remain flat or credible. If the sounds become approachable sooner than the teacher anticipated, the possible interpretation is that the pupils were not given enough content to handle and, as a result, the teacher could lose the class' permission to lead. This would be true for science, math and other left-brain oriented subjects.

Usually small groups (dyads, triads, cooperative learning groups) will finish their assigned tasks at different speeds. From a class dynamics standpoint, how does the teacher know when to bring the class back to a focus on the teacher? If the teacher asks for the class' attention when the very first small group finishes their task, it may prevent some of the other groups from finishing their assignments. Yet, if the teacher waits until the last group finishes their task, those groups that finished early may become irritated waiting for the smaller groups. As the teacher listens to the collective voice patterns in a room, the teacher may want to get their attention not at the beginning of the first change from the credible voice pattern to the approachable voice pattern, but at the second change.

The Approachable-oriented Class

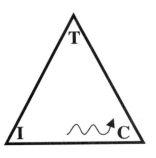

The more the culture of the class is gregarious, the sooner the approachable voice patterns emerge. The normal pattern of college-bound students is to do the tasks assigned. This is evidenced by collective credible voice patterns in the room. Then the future university students might socialize. This can be heard by the switch to the ap-

© 2000 by Michael Grinder & Assoc., ARR. AHC03 (360) 687-3238; FAX (360) 687-0595; http://www.michaelgrinder.com

proachable voice patterns. However, approachable cultures often have to do the socializing (share something social such as, "How are you?") before doing the task. Often the teacher will build in these *introductory activities* as part of the task so that it seems the groups are on task while socializing.

The teacher who knows that the smaller groups will need to socialize before going on task will release the class, and when the first of the smaller groups have finished their socializing and are starting to address the task at hand, the teacher interrupts and announces an additional condition of the task. For example, "Check with your group and make sure everyone has worksheet number four." "Your group should be discussing the second question." If done with effective timing, this maneuver will encourage all the remaining groups to close their *introductory/social* portion of the group work and focus on the task.

In summary, the *timing* of all classroom dynamics is based on the beginning of the second wave/change of the class dynamics voice pattern.[21]

Summary

This chapter described the students the teacher is most likely to have to manage: stressed, auditory-oriented, "What about…", those different than the teacher's style, leaders and those who feel captured in school. An essential part of managing these students is the ability to control who gets to talk, what can be talked about and when they get to talk. The strategies that can assist the teacher in controlling the microphone include fostering students to raise their hands, operating from the axiom of *Satisfy, Satisfy, Delay*[22] (Chapter One) to increase the student's patience while waiting his turn to talk, creating locations for present and future questions, employing a credible voice pattern and increasing the specificity of the questions the teacher will entertain.

There are many sections of this book that address the student who is not a "learner." This chapter devotes a special section to the auditory-oriented student who is a learner but can be most difficult to the classroom dynamics. Seven provocative strategies for intervening are presented. These are often done to preserve of the health of the class.

Chapter Six grapples with some of the most difficult situations that the teacher finds herself in. These are times when the interaction between the class and an individual student isn't healthy. For example, there are times when the student is either temporarily or chronically asocial, and when the teacher has to protect the student from criticism from the class. These are circumstances in which the teacher is often asked to intervene with power.

© 2000 by Michael Grinder & Assoc., ARR. AHC03 (360) 687-3238; FAX (360) 687-0595; http://www.michaelgrinder.com

Power management occurs when the teacher has to have results. Influence management is when the teacher seeks results. The purpose of influence management is to seek compliance from the individual student corner of the classroom triangle. Even more importantly it is to confirm to the class that their perception of the individual student is sane.

The more a teacher recognizes her innate intervention style, the more the teacher can adjust to circumstances. A credible-oriented teacher can be herself while dealing with a credible-oriented class but must increase her patience when with an approachable-oriented class. When working with a credible-oriented class, a teacher who is naturally approachable needs to increase the speed with which she intervenes. Both styles of teacher have to understand the ambivalence that an approachable-oriented class will have when the teacher intervenes. They will view the teacher as too harsh and yet will privately appreciate that the intervention was done.[23]

Credible Culture

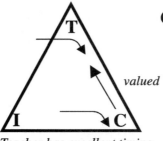

valued

Teacher has excellent timing.

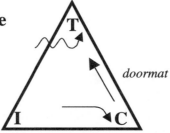

doormat

Teacher seen as "soft" needs to intervene sooner.

Approachable Culture

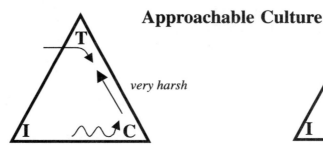

very harsh

The teacher seen as harsh needs to be patient. Teacher won't be bothered by the class privately criticizing her.

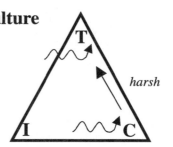

harsh

When the teacher who is naturally patient finally intervenes, she is bothered by the class' private criticism of her.

Credible-oriented teachers want to increase their awareness of the individual students.

Approachable-oriented teachers want to notice the class as a group.

When the class is an approachable culture, the teacher is seen as harsh when managing the individual. The credible ("cat") teacher isn't bothered by the class' reaction whereas the approachable ("dog") teacher is.[24]

© 2000 by Michael Grinder & Assoc., ARR. AHC03 (360) 687-3238; FAX (360) 687-0595; http://www.michaelgrinder.com

Rubric for Chapter Six: Managing Special Situations

Transcends the Educational Culture

	Struggling Novice	Apprentice	Scientist	Artisan of Healthy Classroom
Preventive Management, p. 173	The teacher is seen as angry and frustrated.	The teacher is constantly surprised that students don't respond to her requests (done via power or pleading) to comply.	The teacher employs the indirect strategies to establish rapport.[25]	The teacher has early perception of the students likely to be managed and, via influence patterns of direct and indirect approaches, establishes rapport. The teacher is seen as liking such students.
Auditory-oriented Students, p. 179	The teacher and class go off on tangents; productivity is very low in the classroom.	The auditory-oriented students are either squelched or allowed to control the classroom microphone and endlessly ramble on.	The teacher intervenes based on the needs of the class.[26]	The teacher balances the needs of the auditory-oriented student and the needs of the class. The teacher can switch the student to a visual mode and intervene when the student has finished the tape for the first time. The student remains a member of the class.
Asocial Students, p. 185	The teacher is not in control and the "inmates run the asylum."	The teacher either allows the student to be asocial (teacher is kind to a fault) or intervenes with power and squelches. Teacher is inconsistent.	The teacher recognizes that the class is frustrated with the student but consciously doesn't know what to consistently do.	The teacher intervenes when the class' feedback to the student won't affect the student and when the class' relationship with the student will be damaged by the student not letting the class' criticism in.
Confirming Class' Sanity, p. 186	The teacher daily models what not to do emotionally. For example, the teacher always ignores or defends.	The teacher is frustrated and feels she is letting the class down. The teacher is inconsistent in responding to the student.	The teacher accepts that she cannot do anything about the student.	The teacher recognizes that she cannot affect an inappropriate student; she encourages the class to ignore. The teacher models emotional maturity.
Greeting Them at the Door, p. 187	There is no system of the teacher greeting or not greeting the students at the door.	The teacher greets the students at the door on the easy days.	The teacher greets the students on the hard days and recognizes their individual moods.	The teacher greets the students and has a lot of ways to stay away from those students with "chips on their shoulders."
Cultures and Intervention, p. 189	The teacher has no style and class is unsafe because they don't know when the teacher will do what.	The teacher is inconsistent.	The teacher has a flexible style of when to intervene.	The teacher can recognize the culture of the class and times her interventions based on the culture. The teacher is OK when seen as harsh.

© 2000 by Michael Grinder & Assoc., ARR. AHC03 (360) 687-3238; FAX (360) 687-0595; http://www.michaelgrinder.com

Chapter Six Post-its

Preventive Management

Am I doing early perception of the students that I most likely manage, and am I seen by the class as liking those students?

Chapter Six: Managing Special Situations, pp. 173-175

Confirming Class' Sanity

When I can't change an inappropriate student, am I confirming the class' perception and encouraging ignoring the student? Am I modeling emotional maturity?

Chapter Six: Managing Special Situations, p. 186.

Auditory Students

Do I see auditory students as intelligent as the rest of the class and like the students, but place the needs of the class before the students, and try to keep the students as full members of the class? Am I increasing the visual capacity of the class by visually communicating (e.g., *Exit Directions*)?

Chapter Six: Managing Special Situations, pp. 179-185.

Greeting Them at the Door

Am I greeting them at the door on hard days and staying away from students who have "chips on their shoulders?"

Chapter Six: Managing Special Situations, p. 187.

Asocial Students

Do I recognize and intervene when the class' feedback to an asocial student will not change the student and will damage the class' relationship with the student?

Chapter Six: Managing Special Situations, p. 185.

Cultures and Intervention

Am I recognizing my style and attempting to intervene based on the class' culture? Do I value being respected more than being popular?

Chapter Six: Managing Special Situations, pp. 189.

© 2000 by Michael Grinder & Assoc., ARR. AHC03 (360) 687-3238; FAX (360) 687-0595; http://www.michaelgrinder.com

End Notes

1. This is the central theme of *ENVoY II*.

2. *Righting the Educational Conveyor Belt* by Michael Grinder, 1989, pp. 19-21.

3. Ibid.

4. Ibid.

5. The "A" of EASY, pp. 44-48.

6. In the section *Preventive Management*, the four kinds of questions, What, Why, How and "What about ...," are presented. Since that section explains the ramifications for dealing with the "What about..." student, see p. 173.

7. See *Auditory-oriented Student*, pp. 179-185.

8. See p. 35.

9. See *Three Stages of Irritability*, Chapter Three, pp. 84-88.

10. See Michael Grinder's Pentimento Pattern "Peripheral Sight" in *The Science of Non Verbal Communication*.

11. The visual learner has a much easier time in school than does the auditory learner. For further exploration of the author's views, see Chapters Five and Six of Michael Grinder's *Righting the Educational Conveyor Belt*.

12. See *Firsts*, p. 117.

13. See *Satisfy, Satisfy, Delay*, p. 35.

14. See *Adolescents and Fairness*, p. 92.

15. See Chapter Three, pp. 84-88.

16. Methodologies from *ENVoY II*.

17. See *Saving an Individual Student*, p. 90.

18. Years ago, a TV commercial featured a member of a family named Mikey whom the other siblings field tested new food on.

19. See *Yellow Light, ENVoY*, p. 66.

20. See Chapter Three, pp. 84-88.

21. First introduced to the idea by John Grinder.

22. See p. 35.

© 2000 by Michael Grinder & Assoc., ARR. AHC03 (360) 687-3238; FAX (360) 687-0595; http://www.michaelgrinder.com

23. Two researchers, Friesen and Ekman, found the a person's cultural norm will be display in public. This is was true even when the individually privately felt the opposite way. The researchers showed a video of a horrific industrial accident to two groups: all Americans and all Japanese. The Japanese, who place higher value on masking one's emotion than Americans, showed less facial reactions than the Americans. This was true, even if only one Japanese paticipant saw the footage in the presence of a single official-looking, white-coated experiementer. However, if a Japanese participant was left completely alone in the room to watch the film s/he showed a range of distressed facial expressions that was similar to the Americans. Applying this concept of "public image when in public" to the classrooms cultures of credibility and approachability, individual members from both groups may privately appreciate a teacher intervening with an individual who is disrupting the class, but only the credible culture encourages public display of the appreciation." Gottman, John **The Relationship Cure,** 2001, Crown Publishers, NY page 174

24. See *ENVoY II.*

25. Primarily the strategies are those employed with a Cat. See *ENVoY II.*

26. The employment of MITS (*ENVoY* p. 32) assists the teacher.

© 2000 by Michael Grinder & Assoc., ARR. AHC03 (360) 687-3238; FAX (360) 687-0595; http://www.michaelgrinder.com

Appendix A: Summary of a Healthy School

The summaries in this book are usually in a prose format. The following summary is done in a checklist format to encourage the educator to employ the checklist as an inventory. Based on such an inventory, she can select certain items for future professional growth. *ENVoY* and *ENVoY II* delineate competencies that, while not strategies for a healthy classroom directly, are prerequisite to creating a healthy classroom.

ENVoY and forthcoming ENVoY II

- ❑ **Two prerequisites to management**: teacher only attempts to manage a student who can do the work and with whom the teacher has a relationship at the moment.

  - ❑ Detection: teacher greets a student at the door who has an attitude. If possible, the teacher tries to avoid physically being around the student because of the chip he has on his shoulder—the relationship is too low.

- ❑ **Visual atmosphere**: teacher pauses, communicates visually and has the students *seek* her.

- ❑ **Teacher manages non-verbally**:

  - ❑ Minimal verbiage (e.g., student's name is said) and then the teacher switches to non-verbal communication.

  - ❑ Third-point management: rules, expectations, and directions (e.g., *Exit Directions*) are visually displayed and referred to when managing.

  - ❑ Decontamination: teacher systematically employs the ingredients of decontamination—*pausing* with the *frozen hand gesture* and *Break & Breathe.*

- ❑ **Fairness**: teacher employs the ingredients of early warning and consistency of consequence for inappropriate behavior.

- ❑ **Off/Neutral/On** and **Power to Influence**:

  - ❑ Teacher breathes low when she approaches a student to be managed.

    - ❑ Teacher's head is not looking at the student's head; instead, her head is tilted so as to be looking at the student's desk or even farther away.

To be respectful of gender equality and provide a fluid reading style in the Appendices, the teacher is referred to by the female pronoun and the administrator and students are referred to by the male pronoun.

© 2000 by Michael Grinder & Assoc., ARR. AHC03 (360) 687-3238; FAX (360) 687-0595; http://www.michaelgrinder.com

- ❑ Teacher stops when the student changes from *off-task* to *neutral* to see if the student progresses to *on-task*; if the student doesn't proceed to *on-task* but reverts to *off-task,* the teacher breathes low and employs power techniques until *neutral* is obtained and immediately switches to influence techniques.

- ❑ If there is under 30% student turnover rate, teacher operates with a *stair step down* on regular days, and a jump up the stairs on the hard days. (See forthcoming ENVoY II.)

- ❑ Fish Hooks: once the teacher has obtained the student's attention, teacher avoids the hooks of being verbal and making eye contact .

- ❑ Teacher employs the *stairs up and down* based on the day and season.

- ❑ The teacher appropriately employs *dog* and *cat* strategies for establishing relationships.

A Healthy Classroom Strategies:

- ❑ Teacher enjoys teaching and appropriately exhibits her "person" as well as her "position."

- ❑ Teacher holds the student accountable for his behavior while accepting the student as a person.

  - ❑ Physical positioning: adults in the hallway stand at 90° or side by side when managing a student.

  - ❑ Amnesia: management is not an end itself but a means to support the curriculum tube; management is brief and then immediately the focus is on the student being academically successful.

  - ❑ Dog House: following management, the student has full rights as a member of the class.

- ❑ Meta-emotional: teacher is comfortable when employing power techniques as evidenced by low/abdominal breathing either during management or, at least, following management.

  - ❑ Teacher attempts to have a different energy level than the students during educational doldrums and during predictable right-brain days by exercising.

  - ❑ Teacher has self-honesty as to her intervention style and appropriately adjusts to the culture of the group dynamics.

- ❑ Classroom dynamics:

  - ❑ Management is only done when the perception of the class is taken into account.

© 2000 by Michael Grinder & Assoc., ARR. AHC03 (360) 687-3238; FAX (360) 687-0595; http://www.michaelgrinder.com

❏ Teacher can fluidly move between credibility and approachability based on the situation; especially based on the degree of class formation. When appropriate, teacher employs the four ingredients (i.e., **EASY**) of blending a class into a group.

❏ Teacher does preventive management and establishes relationships.

❏ Teacher adjusts her management expectations and style based on *seasons* of the school year and the class' *stage* of reacting to the individual student.

❏ Teacher utilizes barometers to recognize and acknowledge possible resistance.

❏ Teacher effectively employs strategies to prevent stereotyping in the classroom and to foster full humans. This includes, but is not limited to (compared to the average classroom):

    ❏ The absence of:

        ❏ scapegoats;

        ❏ students being equated with their behaviors; "ladders" of students being ranked;

        ❏ favoritism;

        ❏ instead, the teacher manages before she feels.

    ❏ Standard-bearers model, and the rest of the class members follow, a commitment to develop their full personalities.

    ❏ Teacher sandwiches together students from different categories.

    ❏ The class perceives that the teacher likes the student she manages.

    ❏ Teacher appropriately transitions from the necessary dependence of Teachership One to the healthier self-reliance of Teachership Two.

    ❏ Healthy humor is frequently present; it is enjoyed by all, and it is often only understandable to the members of the class.

    ❏ Leadership is shared, based on situations and changes over time.

    ❏ Osmotic Learning occurs.

    ❏ Liaisons are present.

    ❏ Students are realistic, optimistic and ambitious about their future.

© 2000 by Michael Grinder & Assoc., ARR. AHC03 (360) 687-3238; FAX (360) 687-0595; http://www.michaelgrinder.com

Appendix B: Rubrics for Self-assessment and Professional Development

Because it takes years of implementation to arrive at a healthy classroom, the following is a way of assessing the reader's progress toward making the dynamics of a healthy classroom habitual. The criteria framework can be used as a self- or peer-assessment form. From such usage the teacher/coach/principal has a direction as to what the next phase might be. *A Healthy Classroom* becomes the source of understanding the dynamics of a healthy classroom and how to influence these dynamics.

In golf, you only have a skill at a habit level when you unconsciously know you are not doing something you want to be doing.

A = Aware of; the name of the skill is familiar.

U = Understand some or all of the components of the skill.

D = Doing the skill periodically.

H = Habit; most of the time I do the skill automatically.

In addition to listing A/U/D/H next to the skills, put an "F" next to the three skills the reader wants to focus on for the rest of the year.

Plan of Action

Every teacher has a right to grow—even the outstanding ones—and to be supported in that growth.

ENVoY was written to assist the majority of teachers to be both very effective managers and systematic. *A Healthy Classroom* can be read for conceptual understanding. You are encouraged to select rubrics for your professional development. Great teachers don't automatically remain great; they continually grow and as a by-product are great. *A Healthy Classroom* helps the great teachers grow and offers a blue print for the good teachers to accelerate their progress to becoming great.

Name of rubric—List three to five rubrics you want to emphasize. Often certain rubrics reinforce each other. It might be wise to invite other professionals, who are aware of your professional development, to offer input.

For what time period—State over what time period you plan to emphasize this. The length of time the rubric is emphasize is greatly dependent on the sophistication of the rubric and where you are in mastering the *artisan* level. More than one rubric can be selected for the same time period.

Plan of action—State where you are in your mastering of this rubric. Mention who and what can support you in your goal. Be realistic.

© 2000 by Michael Grinder & Assoc., ARR. AHC03 (360) 687-3238; FAX (360) 687-0595; http://www.michaelgrinder.com

Name of Rubric _____ Time Period _____

Plan of Action

Where you are in mastering this rubric (state evidence): _____

_____

_____

Your plan of action (state evidence you anticipate you will see/hear as you progress): _____

_____

_____

_____

Name of Rubric _____ Time Period _____

Plan of Action

Where you are in mastering this rubric (state evidence): _____

_____

_____

Your plan of action (state evidence you anticipate you will see/hear as you progress): _____

_____

_____

_____

Name of Rubric _____ Time Period _____

Plan of Action

Where you are in mastering this rubric (state evidence): _____

_____

_____

Your plan of action (state evidence you anticipate you will see/hear as you progress): _____

_____

_____

_____

© 2000 by Michael Grinder & Assoc., ARR. AHC03 (360) 687-3238; FAX (360) 687-0595; http://www.michaelgrinder.com

Introduction Rubric

Transcends the Educational Culture

	Struggling Novice	Apprentice	Scientist	Artisan of Healthy Classroom
R.S.V.P., p. 17	The teacher is missing most of the R.S.V.P. competencies, especially relationships.	The teacher has most of the competencies. Usually the R or the S is the last to be mastered.	The teacher has all four competencies.	The teacher knows how to employ the R.S.V.P. competencies towards a healthy classroom.
Group Dynamics, p. 17	The teacher operates on a blind philosophy of power and does not take into account the feelings of the individual students or the dynamics of the class as a group. Classroom is dysfunctional.	While caring about people, the teacher operates the classroom from the premise that it is the teacher's class.	The teacher has a sense of the interplay between the individuals who make up the class and the class as a whole; isn't able to articulate fully such understanding.	The teacher takes into account the class dynamics when assessing and making decisions. The students are held accountable for their behaviors, and yet they are accepted as individual people.
Teacher's Range of Behaviors and Behaviors Systematically Employed, p. 21	The teacher doesn't have a range of behaviors and is inconsistent with the behaviors exhibited.	The teacher is not *systematic*; the teacher is either too accepting (the "individual student" is always more important than the class) or the teacher is too strong on accountability (the productivity of the class is all-important).	The teacher employs patterns of influence.	The teacher has a range of behaviors and *systematically* applies the appropriate behaviors. The teacher is comfortable employing both Patterns of Power and Patterns of Influence.
Teacher's Consistency, p. 21	The teacher is inconsistent most of the time.	The teacher's inconsistency leaves the class unsafe a good portion of the time.	The teacher follows the Golden Rule: she treats students the way she wants to be treated. Students are held accountable for their behaviors and there are high expectations for productivity.	The teacher follows the Platinum Rule: teacher operates the way the class and individual students need the teacher to operate.
Teacher's Ability to Predict, p. 21	The teacher is constantly surprised.	The teacher is frequently surprised.	The teacher's perception is of what is occurring at the moment and not long-term.	The teacher can predict what is likely to happen over time if the individual student(s) or class continue to operate the way they are. The teacher knows whether it is actually appropriate to intervene and how to intervene.
Classroom Safety, p. 21	The class is unsafe most of the time.	The class is unsafe a good portion of the time.	The teacher provides the safety, and safety is present as long as the teacher is present.	Safety is provided by the class and is very present as evidenced by the students breathing low/abdominally.

© 2000 by Michael Grinder & Assoc., ARR. AHC03 (360) 687-3238; FAX (360) 687-0595; http://www.michaelgrinder.com

Rubric for Chapter One: Class Formation

	Struggling Novice	Apprentice	Scientist	Artisan of Healthy Classroom
Initial Class Formation p. 32	The teacher is inconsistent and oblivious to his effect on the class.	The teacher operates from a style and philosophy that isn't based on dynamics (e.g., does either "Satisfy" or "Delay").	The teacher knows that it is natural for the group to evolve and can articulate and foster some of the indicators of the formation.	The teacher knows, recognizes and accelerates the six indicators of class formation.
Eventual Class Formation, p. 32	For the teacher, "eventually" doesn't exist as a concept.	The teacher doesn't change when formation could be fostered with such a change.	The teacher knows the class formation is changing and implements some of the EASY strategies.	The teacher's perception allows him to be patient. Employs EASY strategies to accelerate the formation.
Changing Role of the Teacher, p. 39	The teacher is inconsistent.	The teacher operates only from power. Or, the teacher sometimes operates from power and sometimes is inappropriately kind.	The teacher is appropriately credible initially and gradually becomes approachable.	The teacher is appropriately credible initially and gradually becomes more approachable. Can select degrees of credible-approachable based on the degree of formation.

Transcends the Educational Culture

© 2000 by Michael Grinder & Assoc., ARR. AHC03 (360) 687-3238; FAX (360) 687-0595; http://www.michaelgrinder.com

Rubric for Chapter Two: Reading the Class

Transcends the Educational Culture

	Struggling Novice	Apprentice	Scientist	Artisan of Healthy Classroom
Class Leaders, pp. 58-65	The teacher operates from power, and therefore the only leaders are resistant leaders.	The only leaders the teacher perceives as leaders are the ones the teacher selects.	The teacher recognizes the class' perception of their leaders.	The teacher shares leadership with the class, and leaders change over time.
Class Barometers, p. 67	The teacher doesn't recognize that subgroups are formed. The teacher sees the class as a whole.	The teacher knows there are subgroups but doesn't recognize them.	The teacher can recognize subgroups in the room and know their memberships.	The teacher utilizes the barometers' reactions to proactively acknowledge the subgroups' reactions.
Class Values, p. 72	The inconsistency of the teacher is such that there are no values or culture.	The teacher's values are based on a philosophy which is inconsistently present. The teacher reinforces them with power.	The values of the classroom are based on the teacher's values and they are operational.	The teacher is aware of and can read the class' values; operates on the concept of the class as a culture.
Class Liaisons p. 76	There are camps in the room which are uncooperative with each other.	There are subgroups in the room which don't communicate with each other.	The pupils have a fluidity in that they have membership in many subgroups.	There are lots of liaisons, and the concept of leadership is blurred.
Fostered Leaders, p. 76	The teacher operates from dictatorship, and being a teacher's pet can change with the wind.	The teacher promotes students based on favoritism.	The pupils see teacher's fostered leader as a leader.	The teacher fosters leaders based on the values the teacher wants to add to the class culture.

© 2000 by Michael Grinder & Assoc., ARR. AHC03 (360) 687-3238; FAX (360) 687-0595; http://www.michaelgrinder.com

Rubric for Chapter Three: Stages

Transcends the Educational Culture

	Struggling Novice	Apprentice	Scientist	Artisan of Healthy Classroom
Three Stages of Irritability p. 84	The teacher is consistently surprised and rotates between shocked, confused and annoyed.	The teacher is inconsistent. The class doesn't know what to expect.	The teacher's responses are consistent. The teacher is seen as fair.	The teacher's response is based on the stage of irritability the class is in.
Saving a Student p. 90	The teacher is unaware that a student is in need of saving.	The teacher is inconsistent as to whether or not he will save a student.	The teacher attempts to save all students. The class sees the teacher as consistent and fair.	The teacher attempts to save the individual before the class is annoyed with the member.
Adolescents and Fairness p. 92	The class is either in chaos or the class walks around on emotional eggshells.	The teacher is inconsistent; the class cannot predict how the teacher will handle a given situation.	The teacher is consistent; everyone is managed in the same manner. "Fair is fair" is the axiom.	The teacher attempts to individualize how students are managed. The teacher is seen as fair.
Rumors (Public vs. Private Management) p. 94	The teacher is inconsistent; the class never knows what format management will occur in. The classroom is not safe.	The teacher either always explodes or always implodes.	Whatever the teacher's template, it is universally applied.	The teacher attempts to privately manage the individual unless the student is not likely to comply.
Bully p. 95	The teacher does not recognize that a bully is operating.	The teacher recognizes but has limited ways of responding.	The teacher employs power to create safety in the room.	The teacher employs power, decreases student's status and is fair.
Protecting a Student p. 95	The teacher never develops admiration from the class. The teacher is unaware a student needs protection.	The teacher is inconsistent; sometimes as a humanitarian he protects students whether they need it or not.	The teacher protects all students. The class sees the teacher as consistent and fair.	After the teacher has the class' admiration, the teacher protects the student who doesn't learn from the class' feedback. The student is given special status and is accepted as part of the class. Often this is the goal with *inclusion* students.
Changing a Student's Status pp. 97-98	The teacher is oblivious to the dynamics between individual students and the class as a whole. The teacher assigns status based on whether the teacher likes the student at the moment.	Teacher's "pets" are given special status.	The teacher operates based on the Golden Rule. Consistency is a hallmark of the classroom.	The teacher increases or decreases a student's status based on the dynamics of the class.

© 2000 by Michael Grinder & Assoc., ARR. AHC03 (360) 687-3238; FAX (360) 687-0595; http://www.michaelgrinder.com

Rubric for Chapter Four: Seasons

Transcends the Educational Culture

	Struggling Novice	Apprentice	Scientist	Artisan of Healthy Classroom
Students' Identity Size, p. 107	Every day could be a "surprise day" for the teacher.	The teacher is often surprised at mysterious changes in the classroom and has a limited number of responses. Reactively responds.	The teacher intuitively senses that the collective interaction in the room is different on some days and has a limited number of responses.	The teacher can predict the identity size of the class and adjusts her style and approach.
Right-brain Days, p. 109	The teacher perceives the classroom as her domain of authority. Since every day is seen as the same, the teacher is constantly surprised.	The teacher is inconsistent; there are some good and some bad days.	The teacher can predict which days will likely be difficult.	The teacher successfully employs the right-brain days "Decrease/Increase Chart." The teacher selects her style of management based on the classroom dynamics.
Seasonal Giggles p. 115	The teacher is unpredictable; the lack of consistency means that the atmosphere of the classroom is left to the whims of the teacher.	The teacher lacks a sense of humor, especially when the class is more likely to have the seasonal giggles.	The teacher has a sense of humor.	The teacher maintains the class as a unit by joining the seasonal giggles.
"Firsts", p. 117	The teacher sees every day as the same.	The teacher sees days as different, but this is not based on dynamics.	The teacher senses that a *First* is a special occasion and operates intuitively.	The teacher recognizes a *First* and responds appropriately.
Teachership, p. 117	The teacher has no pattern as to a style of leadership.	The teacher operates either from power or pleading or vacillates between them.	The teacher operates from Level II.	The teacher selects the appropriate level based on the season and how the class dynamics are affected.
Teacher's Seasonal Energy, Associated-Dissociated, p. 121	The teacher has no pattern as to the teacher's degree of association-dissociation. There isn't a sense of seasons. The teacher feels victimized and sorry for herself.	The teacher has a gross sense of *seasons*. For example, "Don't smile until after Thanksgiving."	The teacher has a sense of her own well being and exercises regularly.	The teacher self-selects the degree of association-dissociation based on the seasons of the year and the difficulty of the class. Interprets the contract as "10 wellness days," thus staying home while the teacher can still easily recover; as a result, the teacher is absent less than other teachers. Has a different season than the class; especially increases exercise just before and during the more difficult seasons of the year.
Pushing a Class, p. 124	The teacher has no pattern as to expectations of the class.	The teacher vacillates between pushing the class and then not pushing the class; e.g., when the teacher wants to be popular/liked.	The teacher is consistent in terms of the degree that the teacher pushes the class. The class knows what to expect.	The teacher pushes the class based on the unity of the class.

© 2000 by Michael Grinder & Assoc., ARR. AHC03 (360) 687-3238; FAX (360) 687-0595; http://www.michaelgrinder.com

Rubric for Chapter Five: Managing a Healthy Classroom

	Struggling Novice	Apprentice	Scientist	Artisan of Healthy Classroom
Classroom Culture, p. 135	The teacher neither accepts students as individuals nor holds them accountable for inappropriate behavior.	The teacher always either accepts the students or holds them accountable without doing the other.	The teacher has a good degree of consistency of accepting the students as individuals and holding them accountable for inappropriate behavior.	The teacher successfully balances accepting the students as individuals while holding them accountable for inappropriate behavior.
Managing the Behavior, Not the Person, p. 137	The teacher manages with a two-point communication and doesn't always employ a two-point when the interaction is positive.	The teacher is inconsistent in employing a two-point communication when interacting positively and employs a three-point when managing.	The teacher has a good degree of consistency of employing two-point communication when intervening positively with student and employs a three-point when managing.	The teacher employs two-point communication when interacting positively with student and employs a three-point when managing.
Power vs. Inappropriate Power, p. 139	The teacher is inconsistent in terms of the degree of power employed.	The teacher always uses either too little power or too much power.	The teacher has degrees of power, stopping most of the time when the student is at *neutral.*	The teacher stops employing power as soon as the student is at *neutral.*
Accommodate, Accommodate, Explode, p. 141	The teacher explodes over things the class doesn't comprehend; apologizes; pattern is repeated.	The teacher becomes seasonally fatigued and explodes over things the class doesn't comprehend.	The teacher recognizes when his internal scales of justice are starting to feel imposed upon and starts to manage.	The teacher, instead of managing on how he viscerally feels, manages based on what he sees and hears occurring in the classroom.
Scapegoat, p. 147	Any student could be the scapegoat.	Certain students are always the scapegoats.	The teacher rotates whose name is said; amnesia follows management.	Every student feels she is a *favorite.* The class manages itself.
Preventing Stereotyping, p. 153	Any student could be a scapegoat; there is no consistency.	The teacher is inconsistent as to who in the pool of students at the bottom of the classroom ladder could be the scapegoat. The length of time a student is in the *dog house* is not predictable.	The teacher knows that stereotyping limits each student's view of what she can be and has a few strategies that he employs.	The teacher actively employs strategies to prevent stereotyping. These include rounding the standard-bearers into fuller human beings, sandwiching students from different categories, healthy humor, fostering liaisons, sharing and rotating leadership.

Transcends the Educational Culture

© 2000 by Michael Grinder & Assoc., ARR. AHC03 (360) 687-3238; FAX (360) 687-0595; http://www.michaelgrinder.com

Rubric for Chapter Five: Managing a Healthy Classroom (cont.)

	Struggling Novice	Apprentice	Scientist	Artisan of Healthy Classroom
Standard-bearer Students p. 153	The teacher wants to be the only leader in the room. All leadership is in the form of resistance.	The teacher has favorites who are the leaders of the class. Their behaviors are not monitored, and at times a bully system develops.	The teacher recognizes that the class sees certain salient students in a definite way. The teacher has a limited number of strategies that he employs to foster them into fuller human beings.	The teacher actively fosters the standard-bearers into fuller human beings and in so doing creates an atmosphere that anyone can become anyone and do anything.
Sandwich, p. 154	No one gets compliments because no one is good enough for the "king's" attention.	The teacher gives "Yes, but..." compliments. Students hope they don't receive "left-handed" attention. The teacher's pets are exempted from accountability.	The teacher knows that he wants students to have an unlimited view of their future and instinctively does rudimentary forms of sandwiching.	The teacher recognizes the start of stereotyping and sandwiches students from different categories thus blending the categories.
Healthy Humor, p. 155	Any student could be the recipient of demeaning remarks.	There are certain students who are constant candidates for demeaning remarks.	The teacher recognizes what is healthy humor and allows it. If it isn't, he intervenes and halts it.	The teacher fosters the ingredients of healthy humor. Kindness and appropriate laughter prevail in the room.
Avoiding Favoritism, p. 155	There is no rhyme or reason to the whims of the teacher.	The teacher has certain favorites, and these students are not held accountable for their behavior. Predictability of a hierarchical system exists.	The pupils find it a little strange but very acceptable that the teacher likes the students he manages.	The teacher, via direct and indirect means, creates an atmosphere where everyone is accepted, and yet they are held accountable for their behaviors.
Leaders, Barometers, Liaisons Over Time, p. 156	There is either chaos or the teacher is the only leader and does so by power.	The teacher picks his own leaders and behaviorally fosters a hierarchical structure.	The teacher has a sense of the ever-evolving nature of a healthy class and supports such occurrences when they happen.	The teacher fosters students to fully blossom as human beings. Students belong to so many subgroups that the concept of barometers is blurred. Leadership is replaced with liaisons.
Osmotic Learning: Special Needs Students, p. 158	The teacher is oblivious to the special needs students in the room.	The teacher is aware of the special needs students but can't find time to assist them.	The teacher is trying his level best to assist the special needs students.	The class offers to assist the special needs students.
Osmotic Learning: Thinking, p. 160	The teacher teaches in a lecture format; correct answers are valued.	The teacher asks thinking questions but is the only source of the answers.	The teacher challenges the students to think, and they share their thinking with the teacher.	The students challenge each other to think, and they share their thinking with each other.

Transcends the Educational Culture

© 2000 by Michael Grinder & Assoc., ARR. AHC03 (360) 687-3238; FAX (360) 687-0595; http://www.michaelgrinder.com

Rubric for Chapter Six: Managing Special Situations

	Struggling Novice	Apprentice	Scientist	Artisan of Healthy Classroom
Preventive Management, p. 173	The teacher is seen as angry and frustrated.	The teacher is constantly surprised that students don't respond to her requests (done via power or pleading) to comply.	The teacher employs the indirect strategies to establish rapport.[25]	The teacher has early perception of the students likely to be managed and, via influence patterns of direct and indirect approaches, establishes rapport. The teacher is seen as liking such students.
Auditory-oriented Students, p. 179	The teacher and class go off on tangents; productivity is very low in the classroom.	The auditory-oriented students are either squelched or allowed to control the classroom microphone and endlessly ramble on.	The teacher intervenes based on the needs of the class.[26]	The teacher balances the needs of the auditory-oriented student and the needs of the class. The teacher can switch the student to a visual mode and intervene when the student has finished the tape for the first time. The student remains a member of the class.
Asocial Students, p. 185	The teacher is not in control and the "inmates run the asylum."	The teacher either allows the student to be asocial (teacher is kind to a fault) or intervenes with power and squelches. Teacher is inconsistent.	The teacher recognizes that the class is frustrated with the student but consciously doesn't know what to consistently do.	The teacher intervenes when the class' feedback to the student won't affect the student and when the class' relationship with the student will be damaged by the student not letting the class' criticism in.
Confirming Class' Sanity, p. 186	The teacher daily models what not to do emotionally. For example, the teacher always ignores or defends.	The teacher is frustrated and feels she is letting the class down. The teacher is inconsistent in responding to the student.	The teacher accepts that she cannot do anything about the student.	The teacher recognizes that she cannot affect an inappropriate student; she encourages the class to ignore. The teacher models emotional maturity.
Greeting Them at the Door, p. 187	There is no system of the teacher greeting or not greeting the students at the door.	The teacher greets the students at the door on the easy days.	The teacher greets the students on the hard days and recognizes their individual moods.	The teacher greets the students and has a lot of ways to stay away from those students with "chips on their shoulders."
Cultures and Intervention, p. 189	The teacher has no style and class is unsafe because they don't know when the teacher will do what.	The teacher is inconsistent.	The teacher has a flexible style of when to intervene.	The teacher can recognize the culture of the class and times her interventions based on the culture. The teacher is OK when seen as harsh.

Transcends the Educational Culture

© 2000 by Michael Grinder & Assoc., ARR. AHC03 (360) 687-3238; FAX (360) 687-0595; http://www.michaelgrinder.com

Appendix C: ENVoY and ENVoY II vs. A Healthy Classroom

The introduction to *A Healthy Classroom* indicated that a scientist of classroom management needs the four competencies of

R—the teacher has established *relationships* with the students, especially the hard-to-reach ones.

S —the teacher individualizes instruction so that the students, especially the inclusion students, are academically *successful*.

V—the teacher *visually* communicates.

P—the teacher *pauses*.

The first letter of the italicized words spell out the acronym *RSVP*. You are invited to *A Healthy Classroom*, and our four prerequisite competencies are your *RSVP*.

The next four pages detail which skills from *ENVoY* and *ENVoY II* directly address the *RSVP*.

© 2000 by Michael Grinder & Assoc., ARR. AHC03 (360) 687-3238; FAX (360) 687-0595; http://www.michaelgrinder.com

Establishing *Relationships*

ENVoY II addresses the oversight of *ENVoY*. While *ENVoY* preserves relationships while managing, *ENVoY II* directly delineates the components of establishing relationships. The concept is "Dogs & Cats." Because of the importance of this concept, some of the information that follows is repeated in parts of *A Healthy Classroom*. Dogs are students who accommodate and operate from a win-win template. Cats are pupils who expect others to accommodate them. It is not that cat students would intentionally impose, presume or insult. They are just being themselves. A relationship with a dog is established by spending time and giving attention. The cat has to choose a relationship with the teacher. How the teacher behaves so that the cat would opt for a relationship with the teacher is the extensive focus of the first chapter of forthcoming *ENVoY II*. Suffice it to say the teacher has to have something the cat wants and then teases the cat so that the cat is drawn to the teacher.

In summary, dogs and cats are different warranting different strategies for establishing a relationship with each. With a real dog, you throw a ball and the dog retrieves it—you give the dog what it wants. With a cat, you find something the cat wants and then keep the item out of reach—you tease the cat. If the strategies are reversed they backfire. When a dog is teased it becomes a mean animal; when a cat is given what it wants it is bored. The concepts of Dogs and Cats from ENVoY II is essential to interpreting group dynamics. On the surface, a classroom of dogs will seem more formed and cooperative than a classroom of cats. We need to examine this more closely because a teacher can herd dogs but not cats.

© 2000 by Michael Grinder & Assoc., ARR. AHC03 (360) 687-3238; FAX (360) 687-0595; http://www.michaelgrinder.com

The Teacher *Pauses*

Examples from *ENVoY* include:

Description	Term
When getting the students' attention.	Freeze Body (from *ENVoY II*, Frozen Hand Gesture)
If a loud voice is employed to get their attention, the teacher pauses before dropping to a whisper.	ABOVE (Pause) Whisper
When asking the class to raise their hands.	Raise Your Hand vs. Speak Out (also known as "increasing think time").
When releasing students to begin working.	Most Important Twenty Seconds (MITS)
After assisting a student, the teacher pauses and surveys the room.	Mini MITS
When walking around the room the teacher walks slowly—a form of pausing.	Walking Speed
After a stressful message, the teacher pauses before shifting quickly with one or more steps	Part of Break & Breathe and Decontamination (the latter is the most popular *ENVoY* skill).
When a student is off-task and as the teacher approaches, the student shifts from off-task to on-task or at least "neutral," the teacher pauses.	Part of OFF/Neutral/ON
When a student is off-task and the teacher approaches, if the student is still off-task, the teacher employs some power techniques (e.g., is in front of, makes eye contact, physically close and says name). As the student shifts to "neutral," the teacher immediately switches to the influence techniques (e.g., is to the side, looks at student's desk, physically moves farther away and is silent).	The Influence Approach

© 2000 by Michael Grinder & Assoc., ARR. AHC03 (360) 687-3238; FAX (360) 687-0595; http://www.michaelgrinder.com

Students *Successfully* Do the Work

This is a curriculum arena, outside the covenants or parameters of the ENVoY programs.

The Teacher *Visually* Communicates

Examples from *ENVoY* include:

Description	Term
When the students enter the room or begin the lesson, the teacher has information visually displayed.	Opening Visual Instructions (This is why "Daily Oral Language" is so successful.)
When the teacher finishes presenting the material (i.e., Teaching) and the students are ready to begin reinforcement work (i.e., Seatwork), the teacher has information visually displayed and refers to it when explaining what is expected.	Exit Directions (most of the skills in *ENVoY* need to be done on difficult days or with difficult classes. Exit Directions is the only one that HAS to be done every day). The most important *ENVoY* skill.
When the teacher has finished explaining the Exit Directions and asks, "Any questions?" the teacher answers the questions and has the information visually displayed.	Part of Exit Directions
When managing, once a teacher has the student's attention, the teacher avoids eye contact and being verbal.	Based on Exit Directions being present and (from *ENVoY II*) Avoiding the Hooks of Escalation.
When a student is off-task and the teacher, who is across the room, says the student's name and when the student looks up, the teacher points to the Exit Directions.	(From *ENVoY II*) They Follow Our Eyes

© 2000 by Michael Grinder & Assoc., ARR. AHC03 (360) 687-3238; FAX (360) 687-0595; http://www.michaelgrinder.com

Summary Chart

Category	ENVoY/ENVoY II	A Healthy Classroom
Ease of understanding	Easy	More sophisticated
Level of Management	Science	Art
Implementation	Immediately	Over the school year
Orientation	Process	Perception
Perceptual question	Short: What is occurring in the moment?	Long: What effect will what is occurring now effect the two months plus?
Level of competencies	Skills, interventions,	Concept-oriented
Work sheets	Self reflection and peer reinforcement forms	Self reflection and peer reinforcement forms
Level of observation	Observe either the teacher's interaction with individual students or the class as a whole	Observe the interactions between the teacher, the individual student and the class as a whole
Level of relationship	Establish and preserve the relationships the teacher has with individual students and the class as a whole	Foster group dynamics so that the teacher via leaders has a relationship with the class as a whole and individual students. And that this relationship is transferred to among and between the students themselves
Power Techniques	Teacher prefers influence techniques. If necessary, the teacher employs power techniques	The full impact of the influence techniques can only be accessible via a unified group. The teacher has to be comfortable with employing power techniques
Proactive anticipates	Anticipate the management needs of the individual students and the class	Anticipates the management needs of the group dynamic: how is the group effected when individual is managed? And how is the individual effected when class managed?
Criteria of successful management	Get results	Get results based on the level of relationship
By-product of management	Teacher respects and is respected	
Focus	Management	Management and the curriculum by-products

© 2000 by Michael Grinder & Assoc., ARR. AHC03 (360) 687-3238; FAX (360) 687-0595; http://www.michaelgrinder.com

Appendix D: Bibliography

Ackerman,Diane, (1990) **A Natural History of the Senses**. New York: Random House

Armstrong, Thomas. (1993) **7 Kinds of Smart**. New York: A Plume Book.

Bandler, Richard and Grinder, John. (1982) **Reframing**. Moab, Utah: Real People Press.

Barth, Roland S. (1990) **Improving Schools from Within.** San Francisco: Jossey-Bass

Bennis, Warren. (1997) **Managing People is like Herding Cats.** Provo, UT: Executive Excellence Publishing Company.

Briggs, John. (1992) **Fractals – The Patterns of Chaos.** New York: A Touchstone Book.

Brilliant, Ashliegh. (1990) **I have Abandoned My Search for Truth, and Am Now Looking for a Good Fantasy.** Santa Barbara: Woodbridge Press.

Buckingham, Marcus and Coffman, Curt. (1999) **First Break All the Rules.** New York: Simon & Schuster.

Buckingham, Marcus and Clifton, Donald O. (2001) **Now, Discover Your Strengths.** New York: The Free Press.

Cashman, Kevin (1998) **Leadership from the Inside Out.** Provo, UT: Executive Excellence Publishing.

Catford, Lorna, and Ray, Michael. (1991) **The Path of the Everyday Hero.** Los Angeles: Jeremy Tarcher Inc.

Cohen, Herb. (1980) **You Can Negotiate Anything.** New York: Bantam Books.

Covey, Stephen R. (1990) **Principle-Centered Leadership.** New York: Simon & Schuster.

Covey, Stephan. (1989) **Seven Habits of Highly Effective People**. New York: Simon & Schuster Adult Publishing Group.

Crum, Thomas F. (1987) **The Magic of Conflict.** New York: Touchstone Book, Simon & Schuster Inc.

Cullum, Albert. (1971) **The Geranium on the Window Sill Just Died But Teacher You Went Right On**. New York: Harlin Quist.

De Bono, Edward. (1995) **Six Thinking Hats**. New York: Harper & Row.

© 2000 by Michael Grinder & Assoc., ARR. AHC03 (360) 687-3238; FAX (360) 687-0595; http://www.michaelgrinder.com

DePorter, Bobbi and Hernacki, Mike. (1992) **Quantum Learning: Unleashing the Genius in You.** New York: Dell

Dryden, Gordon and Vos, Jeannette. (1994) **The Learning Revolution.** Rolling Hills Estates, CA: Jalmar Press.

Fisher, Roger and Brown, Scott (1988) **Getting Together.** New York: Penguin Books

Fisher, Roger and Ury, William. (1981) **Getting to YES.** Penguin Books.

Frankl, Viktor E. (1959) **Man's Search for Meaning.** New York: Beacon Press.

Fullan, Michael. (2001) **Leading in a Culture of Change.** San Francisco: Jossey-Bass.

Gardner, Howard. (1993) **Multiple Intelligences: The theory in practice.** New York: Basic Books.

Glasser, M.D., William. (1990) **The Quality School.** New York: Harper & Row.

Goleman, Daniel. (1995) **Emotional Intelligence.** New York: Bantam Books.

Gordon, William J.M. (1961) **Synectics.** New York: MacMillan Company.

Gray, John. (1992) **Men are from Mars, Women are from Venus**. New York: Harper Collins.

Grinder, Michael. (1993) **ENVoY: Your Personal Guide to Classroom Management.** Battle Ground WA: MGA & Associates

Grinder, Michael. (1989) **Righting the Educational Conveyor Belt.** Portland OR: Metaphorous Press.

Grinder, Michael. (2000) **The Science of Non-verbal Communication**. Battle Ground WA: MGA & Associates

Johnson, Barry. (1992) **Polarity Management.** Amherst, MA: HRD Press, Inc.

Johnson, M.D., Spencer. (1998) **Who Moved My Cheese?** New York: Penguin Putnam.

Joyce, Bruce and Showers, Beverly. (1988) **Student Achievement Through Staff Development.** While Plains, New York: Longman, Inc.

Joyce, Bruce, Weil, Marsha and Showers, Beverly (1992) **Models of Teaching.** Boston: Allyn & Bacon.

Kline, Peter. (1988) **The Everyday Genius**. Arlington, VA; Great Ocean Publishers

© 2000 by Michael Grinder & Assoc., ARR. AHC03 (360) 687-3238; FAX (360) 687-0595; http://www.michaelgrinder.com

Kohn, Alfie. (1993) **Punished by Rewards...** New York: Houghton Mufflin Company.

Kounin, Jacob S. (1977) **Discipline and Group Management in Classrooms**. Huntington, N. Y.: R. E. Krieger

Kouzes, James M. and Posner, Barry Z. (1993) **Credibility**. San Francisco: Jossey-Bass.

Kubler-Ross, Elisabeth. (1969) **On Death and Dying**. New York: Macmillan.

LaBorde, Genie Z. (1983) **Influencing with Integrity**. Palo Alto: Syntony Publishing.

Lozanov, Georgi. (1978) **Suggestology and Outlines of Suggestopedy**. New York: Gordon and Breach.

Marzano, Bob. **Dimensions of Learning.** ASCD

Merriam, Sharan B. (1993) **An Update on Adult Learning Theory**. San Francisco: Jossey-Bass.

O'Connor and Seymour. (1990) **Introducing Neuro Linguistic Programming**. England: Thorsons Publishers.

Oshry, Barry. (1995) **Seeing Systems: Unlocking the Mysteries of Organizational Life**. San Francisco: Berrett-Koehler.

Palmer, Parker. (1998) **The Courage to Teach.** San Francisco: Jossey-Bass.

Payne, Ruby F. (1995) **A Framework: Understanding and Working with Students and Adults from Poverty.** Baytown, TX: RFT Publishing.

Powell, Colin and Persico, Joseph. (1995) **My American Journey.** New York, Random House

Rose, Colin. (1992) **Accelerated Learning.** England: Topaz Publishing Limited.

Saphier, Jon and Gower, Robert. (1987) **The Skillful Teacher.** Carlisle, Mass: Research for Better Teaching.

Schulz, Charles. (1980) **Charlie Brown, Snoopy and Me.** Garden City, NY: Doubleday

Senge, Peter M. (1990) **The Fifth Discipline.** New York: Doubleday Current.

Sizer, Theodore R. (1984) **Horace's Compromise.** Boston: Houghton Mifflin Company

© 2000 by Michael Grinder & Assoc., ARR. AHC03 (360) 687-3238; FAX (360) 687-0595; http://www.michaelgrinder.com

Steverson, Herold W., and Stigler, James W. (1992) **The Learning Gap**. New York: Simon & Schuster.

Tannen, Deborah, (1990) **You Just Don't Understand.** New York: Ballantine Books, Inc.

Ury, William. (1991) **Getting Past No.** New York: Bantam Books, Inc.

Walker, Donald E. (1996) **Never Try to Teach a Pig to Sing**. San Diego: Lathrop Press

Wheatley, Margaret J. (1992) **Leadership and the New Science.** San Francicso: Barrett-Koehler Publishers.

Whitmore, John (1996) **Coaching for Performance.** London: Nickolas Breasley Publishing.

Wolfe, Patricia. (2001) **Brain Matters.** Alexandria, VA: ASCD

Wong, Harry K. and Rosemary Tripi Wong. (1991) **The First Days of School**. Sunnyvale: Harry K. Wong Publications

© 2000 by Michael Grinder & Assoc., ARR. AHC03 (360) 687-3238; FAX (360) 687-0595; http://www.michaelgrinder.com

Appendix E: Index

© 2000 by Michael Grinder & Assoc., ARR. AHC03 (360) 687-3238; FAX (360) 687-0595; http://www.michaelgrinder.com

© 2000 by Michael Grinder & Assoc., ARR. AHC03 (360) 687-3238; FAX (360) 687-0595; http://www.michaelgrinder.com

© 2000 by Michael Grinder & Assoc., ARR. AHC03 (360) 687-3238; FAX (360) 687-0595; http://www.michaelgrinder.com

© 2000 by Michael Grinder & Assoc., ARR. AHC03 (360) 687-3238; FAX (360) 687-0595; http://www.michaelgrinder.com

Y

Vignettes and Main Characters

Many readers remember concepts when they are associated with a story. The following are the titles of the vignettes and a separate listing of the main characters.

© 2000 by Michael Grinder & Assoc., ARR. AHC03 (360) 687-3238; FAX (360) 687-0595; http://www.michaelgrinder.com

© 2000 by Michael Grinder & Assoc., ARR. AHC03 (360) 687-3238; FAX (360) 687-0595; http://www.michaelgrinder.com

ENVoY: Your Personal Guide to Classroom Management

Power to Influence. *ENVoY* is a vehicle to shift educators from seeing themselves as bastions of Power to instruments of Influence. **Professional strength.** This program, when used by cadres of instructors within a school, brings out the professional strengths of all the members involved. **Wealth in our classrooms!** We need to elevate ourselves from within. . . we need systems which enable us to profit from the wealth of abilities that lie in insular classrooms. **Sharing our collective wisdom.** It is only through sharing and supporting processes that the collective wisdom of the staff emerges. **What is the *ENVoY* book? Classroom Management techniques.** This book is a collection of thirty-one techniques that every teacher uses sometimes. By becoming aware of them, the teacher can use the techniques on the days when he or she most needs them. **The Seven Gems of Classroom Management.** Chapter One is a summary of the seven best techniques of all 31. **Peer Coaching forms.** The 31 skills are presented in forms that the individual teacher can fill out on him- or herself. And these same forms are rewritten as peer observation competency sheets. This allows for **peer coaching—the single fastest way to increase professional growth. Chapters 2-5: Two dozen additional techniques.** The book also includes 24 other essential skills, many of them refinements of the Seven Gems. **Unique, nonverbal material** The techniques are mostly non verbal, and, in spite of their importance, are rarely taught in teacher preparation programs. $29.95

ENVoY II: A Cat in the Dog House

ENVoY has struck a nerve in the educational community around the world. The book has been translated into German, Russian, Spanish and Chinese, and is published in Australia. Globally teachers are discovering that while they become educators to impart knowledge, encourage self-esteem, and foster self-reliant learners, they are spending more and more time managing. *ENVoY II* is an extension of the skills that the first book introduced. The purpose of both works is to preserve relationships when managing. "Relationships" to education is what "location" is to realtors.

The demographics of the student population has changed. There is a certain segment of pupils that won't let the teachers form relationships with them. They are independent. *ENVoY II* addresses practical and specific strategies for establishing an atmosphere where the hard-to-reach students actually seek a relationship with the teacher. *ENVoY II* completes the purpose of *ENVoY* because the first book preserves the relationship with the student when managing while the second book details how to form the relationship.

The Seven Gems: Non-verbal Strategies for Classroom Management

This video is the companion to *ENVoY*. The top Seven Gems of classroom management are presented. The footage is from a training seminar so that you receive the actual sense of learning the skill. The video demonstrates the techniques used to get the compliance from the students while preserving the relationship with the pupils. Because the skills are presented live, viewing reinforces the principles taught. The tape is designed for individual viewing. $40.00 (See the 7 Gems Inservice Kit for school or district purchase.)

Michael Grinder & Associates Present

THE SEVEN GEMS

Non-verbal Strategies for Classroom Management

Michael Grinder
Founder of the ENVoY Program
(Educational Non-verbal Yardsticks)

A COMPANION TO
ENVoY Training Program for Classroom Management

AND THE BOOK
ENVoY: Your Personal Guide to Classroom Management

2nd Edition

Righting THE EDUCATIONAL CONVEYOR BELT

Michael Grinder
National Director of NLP In Education

Foreword By John Grinder

Discover powerful patterns of excellent teaching techniques
Learn effective verbal & nonverbal communication skills
Applications for all grade levels

Righting the Educational Conveyor Belt

Successful teachers have both a variety of management strategies and instructional techniques. *Righting the Educational Conveyor Belt* is the curriculum companion to *ENVoY*. *Righting...* assists the teacher in identifying and utilizing students' learning styles, establishing patterns for their long term memory and increasing the pupils' visual capacity for test taking. All concepts are explained in practical terms and easily implemented. While immediately usable for all grade levels, the book directly assists "kids at risk." $17.95

Other Works by Michael Grinder

The 7 Gems In-service Kit

(Video, 60 Transparencies, 120-page Manual)

The Kit is intended for schools, staff development and training institutes. The Kit is designed for each of the *7 Gems* to be shown from the video and then the tape is stopped and a series of transparencies allow the educators watching to practice the practical skills. The Presenter Guide indicates what to say while showing the transparencies and answers any questions that may arise. $295.00

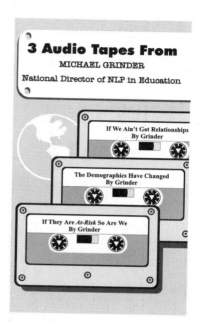

Audio Tapes

Educational tapes (3) on the At-risk, Building Relationships and Avoiding Escalations & Confrontations. $19.95

For administrators: The Fundamentals of Group Dynamics (3 tapes) on How Not to Get Shot!, Handling Attacks and Overcoming Resistance. $59.95

Pamphlets

The very best skills from *ENVoY* are known as the Seven Gems. Each pamphlet is devoted to one of the seven skills. The size allows the recipient to have a quick understanding of a practical skill. The set is ideal for giving to a colleague or using for a staff in-service. The pamphlets are a great overview and introduction. Graduates of the ENVoY programs indicated a need for something that could be handed to an educator who isn't quite ready to purchase a book. This product fills that gap perfectly. Set of 7: $5.00

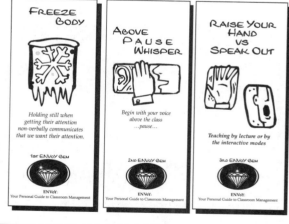

MGA PRODUCT ORDER FORM

Description	Title	Unit Price	Qty	Total
Book	ENVoY: Your Personal Guide to Classroom Management 40% discount on 10 or more	29.95		
Book & Screen Savers	A HEALTHY CLASSROOM	34.95		
Book	ENVoY II: A Cat in the Dog House	*		
DVD	The Seven Gems: Non-verbal Strategies for Classroom Management.	49.95		
Video	The Seven Gems: Non-verbal Strategies for Classroom Management. 40% Discount on orders of 10 or more	40.00		
Book & DVD	ENVoY: Your Personal Guide to Classroom Management and The Seven Gems	70.00		
Book & Video	ENVoY: Your Personal Guide to Classroom Management and The Seven Gems	60.00		
Kit	The Seven Gems In-Service Kit 20% Discount on orders of 5 or more	295.00		
Pamphlets	Seven Gems Pamphlets (set of 7)	5.00		
Book	Righting the Educational Conveyor Belt 40% discount on 10 or more	23.95		
Audio Tapes	Educational tapes (3) on the At-risk, Building Relationships, Avoiding Escalations & Confrontations	19.95		
Audio Tapes	Fundamentals of Group Dynamics (3 tapes): How Not to Get Shot!, Handling Attacks, Overcoming Resistance	59.95		
Manual & Disk	The Science of Non Verbal Communication. Vignettes of How Not to Get Shot!, a computer disk of work-sheets plus laminates. (Designed for administrators. 15% Discount on orders of 20 or more	29.95		
DVD	How Not To Get Shot	49.95		
	Subtotal			
	Washington State Residents add 7.8% Sales Tax			
	SHIPPING & HANDLING Total order $25.00 or less Total order $25.01 to $50 Total order $50.00 to $100 Total order $100 or more = cost of shipping	6.00 7.00 8.00		
	TOTAL			

Projected for 2003. Call for availability and price.
All prices subject to change.

Name _____ Phone _____

Address _____

City _____ State _____ Zip _____

Payment Method: ☐ Check Enclosed ☐PO # _____ Credit Card ☐VISA ☐MC Exp. Date _____

Card No. _____ Signature _____

Michael Grinder & Associates • 16303 N.E. 259th Street • Battle Ground, WA 98604
Phone: (360) 687-3238 • FAX (360) 687-0595
Website: http://www.michaelgrinder.com